WITHDRAWN
2 3 APR 2023

The Voluntary Sector and Criminal Justice

The Voluntary Sector and Criminal Justice

Edited by

Anthea Hucklesby
School of Law, University of Leeds, UK

Mary Corcoran
School of Social Science and Public Policy, Keele University, UK

palgrave
macmillan

First published 2016 by
PALGRAVE MACMILLAN

Palgrave Macmillan in the UK is an imprint of Macmillan Publishers Limited,
registered in England, company number 785998, of Houndmills,
Basingstoke, Hampshire RG21 6XS.

Palgrave Macmillan in the US is a division of St Martin's Press LLC,
175 Fifth Avenue, New York, NY 10010.

Palgrave Macmillan is the global academic imprint of the above companies
and has companies and representatives throughout the world.

Palgrave® and Macmillan® are registered trademarks in the United States,
the United Kingdom, Europe and other countries.

ISBN: 978–1–137–37066–2

This book is printed on paper suitable for recycling and made from fully
managed and sustained forest sources. Logging, pulping and manufacturing
processes are expected to conform to the environmental regulations of the
country of origin.

A catalogue record for this book is available from the British Library.

A catalog record for this book is available from the Library of Congress.

Contents

Acknowledgements

As with all book projects this one was influenced by the individuals and groups, too many to name, who are shaping the broader intellectual project by writing about, experiencing, working in and participating in the voluntary sector. Particular thanks go to our contributors who have produced innovative chapters despite the considerable pressures of their 'day jobs'. We also wish to acknowledge the contribution of those who participated in the ESRC-funded seminar series, The Third Sector in Criminal Justice (RES-451-26-0823), in 2010–2012, during a pivotal time of turbulence for the voluntary sector and what has transpired to be the radical restructuring of criminal justice. Dr Alice Mills, now at the University of Auckland, contributed equally to the initial proposal to the ESRC.

We are also grateful to our colleagues past and present who have supported our work in this field since the time when it was below the radar of both criminological and voluntary sector studies. These include, Susanne Karstedt, Clare Griffiths, Michelle Bellham, Anne Worrall, the Research Institute for Social Policy at Keele University and Emma Wincup. The final production of this book was greatly assisted by Rachel Evans. We would also like to thank Julia Willan and her team at Palgrave who displayed endless patience whilst waiting for the manuscript to arrive.

Notes on Contributors

Mary Corcoran is Senior Lecturer in Criminology at Keele University, UK. Her research covers two broad areas: the first comprises work on prison and custody, with a focus on women offenders. Her second area of research responds to the changing relationships between markets, states and civil society and their consequences for criminal justice. She has conducted research and evaluations on voluntary sector projects for diverting women from prison; peer mentoring; through-the-gate support programmes; and bereavement and loss in custody. She is the author of *Out of Order: The Political Imprisonment of Women in Northern Ireland* (2006) and has published extensively in major international journals and edited collections on resettlement, integrated offender management, and community based alternatives to custody. She is currently leading a major project funded by the Leverhulme Trust on voluntary sector adaptation and resilience in the mixed economy of resettlement.

Ellie Cumbo managed Clinks' policy team until February 2015, and previously worked for several years in voluntary sector organisations of various sizes, including the End Violence Against Women Coalition (EVAW), Victim Support, Object and the Fawcett Society. Her academic background includes a degree in English language and literature from Oxford University and legal qualifications from City University, London.

Rod Dacombe is Lecturer in Politics in the Department of Political Economy at King's College, London. He has studied at Oxford, Princeton and the LSE, has previously worked at Warwick University, the LSE and Oxford and held a Leverhulme Early Career Fellowship. His research focuses primarily on democratic theory and practice and on the relationship between the voluntary sector and the state. He is currently working on a project investigating empirical testing of the claims of deliberative democratic theory.

Jane Dominey worked as a probation officer in a variety of settings before moving into higher education as a senior lecturer and programme leader in probation studies. She is currently completing her PhD at the Institute of Criminology, University of Cambridge, researching the experience of community supervision in the context of the increased use of voluntary sector organisations and private companies to deliver probation services.

Lesley Frazer started her career as a probation officer in England and Wales and as a social worker with adult offenders in Scotland. In 2002 she completed an MSc in Policy Research at the University of Bristol, and published her dissertation research into older prisoners, *Ageing Inside*, in 2003. Lesley joined Clinks in 2008 and held the posts South West VSO development manager, policy manager and strategic development manager before leaving in 2013. She is now chief executive officer at Wiltshire Care Partnership.

Loraine Gelsthorpe is Professor of Criminology and Criminal Justice and Deputy Director at the Institute of Criminology, University of Cambridge. She has written widely on probation and community penalties, on the impact of late modernity on the criminal justice system, on women, crime and criminal justice, and on race and gender equality issues more generally.

Jurgen Grotz is Research Manager at the Institute for Volunteering Research and a Visiting Fellow at the School of Health Sciences, University of East Anglia. He has over 25 years' research experience in the voluntary and community sector. He has contributed to publications such as *The State of the World's Volunteerism Report* by UNV (2011) and is the managing editor for the forthcoming *Palgrave Handbook of Volunteering, Civic Participation and Non-profit Organisations*.

Kelly Hannah-Moffat is Professor of Sociology/Criminology, Vice Dean and Director of the Centre of Criminology & Socio-legal Studies at University of Toronto Mississauga. She has published several articles and books on risk, punishment, parole, gender and diversity, specialised courts, and criminal justice decision-making. Her work on risk, gender and punishment focuses on how variables such as gender and race interact with seemingly objective assessment tools, the experiences of the assessors and the institutional operationalisation of policy reforms. Her recent work studies specialised courts (domestic violence, aboriginal, community/wellness and drug courts) and how legal practices such as bail, sentencing, and case processing have collectively changed as a consequence of the hybrid approaches used in various specialised courts.

Clare Hayes worked at Clinks from July 2010 to December 2014. Following a degree at the University of Bristol in politics and philosophy, she studied for a graduate diploma in law. She recently graduated from the School of Oriental and African Studies with an LLM in Human Rights, Conflict and Justice and is now advocacy coordinator at Detention Action.

Carol Hedderman is a Visiting Scholar at the Institute of Criminology, University of Cambridge. She was Professor of Criminology, University of Leicester, from 2004 to 2014 and prior to that was Assistant Director of the Home Office Research and Statistics Directorate overseeing work on sentencing, probation, prisons and reoffending. These, along with the treatment of women in the criminal justice system, remain her main areas of research interest.

Anthea Hucklesby is Professor of Criminal Justice at the Centre for Criminal Justice Studies in the School of Law, University of Leeds. She has undertaken funded research and published in a range of areas in the criminal justice process focusing on the treatment of suspects, defendants and offenders in the criminal justice process. Her interests in the voluntary sector evolved during her research and evaluations of substantive areas of criminal justice practice including prisoner resettlement, pre-trial services and drug assessment and treatment. She led the ESRC seminar series on the Third Sector in Criminal Justice (RES-451-26-0823). She is currently leading a partnership of five European universities in a study of electronic monitoring in Europe funded by the European Commission DG Justice (JUST/2013/JPEN/AG/4510) which links with her interest in private sector involvement in criminal justice.

Mike Maguire is an Emeritus Professor at Cardiff University and a part-time Professor of Criminology at the University of South Wales. He is also Director of the inter-university Welsh Centre for Crime and Social Justice. He has researched and written widely on many crime- and justice-related topics, including policing, probation, prisons, prisoner rehabilitation and resettlement, mentoring, criminal statistics and victims of crime. He is a member of the Correctional Services Advice and Accreditation Panel, on the board of IOM Cymru, and a former member of the Parole Board. He is currently engaged with Mary Corcoran and Katherine Williams on a study of the role of the voluntary sector in criminal justice.

Paula Maurutto is an Associate Professor in Sociology/Criminology at the University of Toronto. She has published in the areas of risk, punishment, law and specialised courts and the non-profit sector. Her current project explores legal innovations in Canadian specialised courts. Her previous work has explored the increased use of risk-based technologies in the field of punishment and penal management with particular attention paid to the inequalities that are obscured and perpetuated by statistical actuarial practices and the policies they engender. She has also published on the intersections between the non-profit voluntary sector and the criminal justice system.

Clive Martin has been the Director of Clinks since its formation in 1997, having previously worked in offender education for many years. He currently chairs the Ministry of Justice's Reducing Reoffending Third Sector Advisory Group and the ACEVO Special Interest Group on crime, and also sits on the Advisory Board for Female Offenders. He is the author of various publications on the voluntary sector in criminal justice, and regularly writes and speaks on the subject in the UK and internationally.

Rosie Meek is Professor and Head of the Law School at Royal Holloway University of London, and a chartered psychologist. Together with Alice Mills, Rosie has published widely on the role of the voluntary and community sector in prison settings. Her most recent book *Sport in Prison* explores the use of sport and physical activity in prisons, particularly in promoting health and desistance from crime. Other current research activities include the development of effective measurement tools for the evaluation of mentoring and arts programmes in criminal justice settings.

Alice Mills is a Senior Lecturer in Criminology at the University of Auckland, New Zealand. Prior to this appointment, she worked at the Universities of Cardiff and Southampton in the UK. Her research interests include relationships between voluntary and community organisations and the state in criminal justice, the role of the voluntary sector in criminal justice and prisoner reintegration, problem solving courts in New Zealand, family violence, and mental health in prisons. She is currently undertaking research on the housing needs of vulnerable populations and on *ngā Kōti Rangatahi* (Māori youth courts).

Elizabeth Morrow is a PhD candidate in Politics at the Department of Political Economy at King's College, London. She has previously studied at Monash University and the University of North Carolina, Chapel Hill. Her doctoral research draws on a qualitative study of the English Defence League (EDL) and is the first detailed research on the EDL to provide an account of the experiences of front-line group members.

Katie O'Donoghue has a degree in history from Cambridge University and is currently studying for the Bar. She was policy officer at Clinks from February 2012–August 2013.

Katherine S. Williams is a Senior Lecturer in Criminology at Aberystwyth University. She is also the Deputy Director of the Welsh Centre for Crime and Social Justice, a HEFCW funded initiative which brings together researchers across eight Welsh universities and builds links with both policy and practice. Recent research has revolved around the criminal justice service in rural areas (particularly the Youth Justice Service and the Police) and the treatment of women and young people who offend (evaluation of initiatives for diverting women and young people out of the official criminal justice system). Katherine also acts as an advisor to the Youth Justice Board Cymru's Practice Development Panel, she co-chairs Domestic Homicide Reviews in two local authority areas in Wales, sits on the local Community Safety Executive, and has advised the Welsh Government on subjects such as substance misuse. Katherine is now working on a major research project funded by the Leverhulme Trust on voluntary sector adaptation and resilience in the mixed economy of resettlement.

1
Introduction

Anthea Hucklesby and *Mary Corcoran*

The voluntary sector's role in criminal justice is being transformed. Instead of supplementing the services provided by statutory criminal justice agencies it is becoming enmeshed in the day-to-day operation of the criminal justice system. Since the 1990s successive governments have actively engaged the voluntary sector in determining local crime, justice and community safety strategies. More recently, policies have aimed to increase the involvement of voluntary sector organisations (VSOs) in services which have hitherto been provided by statutory agencies. These policy developments are premised on a blend of neo-liberal political rationalities for restructuring state welfare systems into 'mixed-service markets' and communitarian aspirations to liberate the untapped social capital, expertise and consensus of the voluntary sector in securing justice at community level (Norman, 2010). Whilst voluntary sector–state partnership and contracting out are not new, a combination of funding and political reforms under successive governments has generated a profusion of new spaces for collaboration, which are unprecedented in scale. However, behind these new formations in the national and regional voluntary sector and criminal justice landscapes reside the overwhelming majority of small- and medium-sized organisations which continue to provide the backbone of volunteering, civic engagement and local service delivery.

VSOs are longstanding providers of support to suspects, defendants, offenders, victims and witnesses and their families. Historically, they have augmented state service provision. In performing this role they have relied largely on short-term, insecure funding streams which have resulted in ad hoc, patchy and short-term service provision with little strategic direction. Recently, traditional funding streams have been either replaced by competitive commissioning or squeezed as a result of

1

the financial crisis to the point where many VSOs face financial stress at a time when they are being asked to contribute significantly to criminal justice policy and practice. These conditions have resulted in turbulent times for the voluntary sector (Macmillan et al., 2013).

The radically heightened expectations of what VSOs are being expected to deliver is resulting in qualitative changes in their role. The prospect of closer partnerships with state and for-profit organisations may present advantages for VSOs in offering strategic direction, continuity of service provision and financial stability. However, it also presents challenges in terms of whether VSOs have the capacity, capability, infrastructure, expertise or willingness to deliver particular services for the criminal justice system; legal, ideological and ethical questions about taking on quasi-punitive and formal sentencing and enforcement roles; and the compatibility of service provision and advocacy and campaigning roles. The longer-term ambition of rendering VSOs fit for purpose to deliver public services necessarily incorporates them into the pervasive managerial, audit and performance management systems that operate in the statutory sector. At the same time, the onus is placed on statutory criminal justice agencies to ensure effective oversight and accountability structures are in place to support and monitor the work of VSOs as well as ensuring that high-quality services are provided and statutory duties are met in terms of equality and data protection, for example.

From one perspective, these developments herald a turning point by which the sector's historical strengths of mutuality and service are deployed to help make public services more responsive, democratically accountable and relevant to all sections of society (Putnam, 2000). From a different vantage point, the forging of partnerships by means of greater commercialisation and subordination to contract and audit cultures threatens to capture the 'soul' of the voluntary sector (Salaman, 2013). A third factor, and one which has been largely glossed over in the political rhetoric, relates to the need for a clear delineation of the voluntary sector's commitment to *social justice* in the sphere which can epitomise *legal injustice*. Viewed from within the sector, the prospect of working more closely with the state and for-profit organisations has the potential to jeopardise the very independence which ultimately underpins its claim to a distinctive social mission and function (Independence Panel, 2014). As a consequence, and with some controversy, the chameleon sector finds itself once again in the position of reinventing its relationships with markets, governments, communities and individuals as well as reasserting its independent social and civic mission (Civil Exchange, 2014). Although it may be too soon to conclusively measure the impact of economic and policy factors on the future shape and role of the voluntary sector in criminal justice, these factors are undoubtedly likely to be transformative – for better or for worse.

This volume of essays arose out of an Economic and Social Research Council (ESRC)-funded seminar series on the third sector in criminal justice (RES-451-26-0823) which ran between 2011 and 2013. It brings together critical reflections and cutting-edge research on the contemporary features of voluntary sector work by capturing the dynamic nature of the voluntary sector, its responses to the current climate, and identifying some of the conflicting positions with regard to its current and future role in criminal justice work. The volume examines the current and future potential impact of economic, political and ideological trends on the role and remit of VSOs at a time when it is perceptibly evolving from familiar models of voluntary sector service provision to one in which VSOs are potentially becoming embedded in the criminal justice administrative apparatus. In the remainder of the introduction we provide an overview of the policy context in which VSOs were operating at the time the chapters were written (2014–2015). The aim is to provide a context to debates which follow. Before doing this we define the subject of this book: the voluntary sector involved in criminal justice service provision.

Defining the voluntary sector in criminal justice

The voluntary sector has been involved in criminal justice for a long time (Carey and Walker, 2002) and in many different ways including as service providers and/or reform/campaign organisations. Yet, defining the voluntary sector which is involved in criminal justice is not an easy task. As many of the authors in this volume point out, the number of VSOs working exclusively with service users involved in criminal justice is, in some way, relatively small (Clinks, 2014). For many VSOs offenders or crime victims are just one of their service user groups. Their work focuses on an area in which many offenders and/or victims have needs and it is on this basis that they intersect with the criminal justice system. Indeed some VSOs may unknowingly be working with service users caught up in the criminal justice process whilst others may play down their work with offenders because of concerns about spoiling their reputation, therefore making those who work with offenders particularly difficult to identify. VSOs may also be involved in assisting with offenders' and victims' needs, which may or may not be linked directly to their offending or victimisation. In the main, this book is about VSOs who consider themselves as working with or alongside the criminal justice system and openly acknowledge that at least some of their service users are involved in the criminal justice system to a greater or lesser extent. Many of these VSOs have dual roles as service providers and advocacy/campaigning organisations. The tensions which this potentially creates are among the themes of this volume.

The organisations which comprise the voluntary sector involved in criminal justice are also diverse in terms of size: there are a few large national organisations, some regional organisations and many local organisations. The local organisations range in size and include very small VSOs run by one or two people and most have turnovers of less than £100,000 (Gojkovic et al., 2011). In recent years there have been mergers between some of the medium and large VSOs resulting in advantages of scale but potentially threatening some of the traditional values and working practices associated with the voluntary sector. New types of organisations have also emerged such as social enterprises which blur the already indistinct boundaries between voluntary and private sector organisations. Despite the plethora of organisational models, certain consistent features of VSOs remain (Etherington and Passey, 2002). VSOs are non-profit-making and many of them have charitable status. Consequently, they are governed by their charitable aims and are required to comply with charities law. VSOs are governed by trustees and/or directors who are volunteers and who are ultimately responsible for the management and financial affairs of the organisation whether or not they employ paid staff to run the VSO on a day-to-day basis. The diversity of the sector, however, means that policy developments and changes in the environment in which VSOs operate will impact on different parts of the sector in different ways.

Finally, we have chosen to use the terms voluntary sector and VSOs in this volume. We could have used several others, amongst them the third sector (which includes mutual and social enterprises as well as VSOs) or the voluntary and community sector. The advantage of using the term voluntary sector is that it has a long history and is understood internationally. There are drawbacks, however. The inclusion of the word 'voluntary' is a misnomer suggesting that the services provided are free and exclusively by volunteers, that is, unpaid helpers. The reality is rather different. Whilst some VSOs rely entirely on either volunteers or paid staff, most have a mixture of both.

The policy context

Recently governments have sought to increase the involvement of VSOs in core criminal justice activities. Policy is rapidly moving towards a mixed economy of service provision within criminal justice whereby core services, which have traditionally been provided only by statutory sector agencies, are supplied by a tripartite structure of statutory, private and voluntary sector organisations working singly or in partnership (MoJ, 2010, 2013; NOMS, 2014). In theory, the voluntary sector should be in a strong position to take this opportunity, having been involved in providing services in criminal justice for a considerable period of time. Nevertheless, its role is potentially being transformed from a provider of supplementary, 'nice to have' services to a provider of core criminal justice services, and in doing so arguably co-opting it, or at least parts of it, into the apparatus of the state (Maguire, 2012).

The motivations for greater involvement of VSOs have been dressed up in the cloak of greater civil society engagement in criminal justice, fostering greater public involvement in dealing with the crime problem (Morgan, 2012; Maguire, chapter three, this volume). VSOs have continued their traditional role of filling gaps left by statutory criminal justice agencies and supplementing the services they provide by becoming increasingly involved in core criminal justice activities. At the same time, government policy has colonised some areas of service delivery which have traditionally been the preserve of the voluntary sector. These include the provision of statutory support to prisoners released from prison having served sentences of less than 12 months from February 2015 and the increasing number of mentoring schemes funded by the government (MoJ, 2013). The landscape is not simply one in which more and more criminal justice services are being provided by the voluntary sector but one in which the voluntary sector is being expected to become the service deliverer of government policy. The government has asked the voluntary sector to do two things: one, to operate or at least become more involved in providing some services which have hitherto been provided by the state and, two, to maintain involvement in providing services in its traditional areas of operation but to do so from inside the criminal justice system and with government funding. It is not then a return to the 19th and early 20th centuries when VSOs operated largely outside of government control but one where the concern is that VSOs are becoming agents of the state. Such concerns are not new, as Dacombe and Morrow demonstrate in chapter four.

Government attempts to increase the involvement of VSOs in criminal justice services are motivated by a number of factors. Austerity measures have led to considerable cuts in criminal justice budgets and all agencies are being required to find new ways of doing the same (and in some cases more) for less. The voluntary sector is viewed as a resource which can provide services more cost-efficiently than the statutory sector and potentially access sources of funding not available to statutory agencies (Hucklesby and Worrall, 2007). A second related driver has been the radical transformation of public services. Diversifying the providers of public services to include private and voluntary sectors is one part of a broader reform package which includes localism – devolving responsibility, decision-making and budgets and 'improving the transparency, efficiency and accountability of public services' (HM Government, 2010; HM Treasury, 2010: 8). The third motivation is linked to a policy trend to harness the power of civil society and strengthen its involvement in the lives of citizens and residents. It is claimed that the voluntary sector has a key contribution to make in all these regards and is quantifiably 'better' at providing services than the statutory sector. It is viewed as an innovative, nimble and flexible sector which is embedded in, and reaches out to, communities and particularly hard-to-reach groups. It can therefore contribute to transforming public services by providing innovative programmes and services, which may cause a ripple effect in the public sector, at a reduced cost (Etherington, 2006; Morgan, 2012).

Whilst supporters from within and beyond the voluntary sector will extol similar virtues of the sector, they also question some of the assumptions which form the basis of government policy. Primary amongst these is that the voluntary sector should not be viewed as a cheap or in some cases free resource. A considerable infrastructure is required to ensure that the voluntary sector can provide appropriate services; moreover, 'volunteers' are not free, and they, at least, require training and expenses (Hucklesby and Worrall, 2007). Second, moves to increase its involvement in criminal justice will inevitably result in some of the voluntary sector's positive attributes being undermined (Maguire, 2012). For example, the requirements of being contracted to provide government services will increase bureaucracy and make VSOs less innovative and flexible.

Of greater concern to some commentators is that the fundamental values of the voluntary sector and its critical voice may be threatened (Corcoran, 2008; Silvestri, 2009; Mills et al., 2011). At its heart are anxieties that the voluntary sector will lose its independence and legitimacy and be co-opted into the state's apparatus (Carlen, 2002; Hannah-Moffat, 2002). Concerns have also been raised about mission drift, whereby the values and objectives of VSOs might change to align more closely to government or partners' agendas in order to receive funding to provide services alone or in partnership. Values may be further undermined via involvement in coercive aspects of the criminal justice system. Hitherto these have been almost the exclusive roles of statutory organisations (for an exception see Hucklesby, 2011). Greater involvement of VSOs in the criminal justice system, especially in its coercive elements, potentially threatens their trusted status and credibility amongst communities and hard-to-reach groups, putting at risk their work in local communities and thereby contradicting the basis of their appeal to the 'localism' agenda of the coalition and current conservative governments. Alongside the Lobbying Bill 2015, which seeks to define campaigning as 'political', it also puts at risk the dual roles many VSOs perform as service providers and advocacy/campaigning organisations, and potentially the VSOs' charitable status.

A key element of government plans under the *Transforming Rehabilitation (TR)* agenda (MoJ, 2013) is the introduction of Payment by Results whereby service providers will be paid according to reductions in reconviction rates which follow an intervention. Payment by Results is a controversial payment mechanism, particularly because it uses a binary measure of reconviction and transfers financial risks onto the service providers (Fox and Albertson, 2011, 2012). It also encourages 'cherry-picking' (working with those least likely to reoffend) and 'parking' (not working with those at high risk of reoffending). The risks to the voluntary sector are considerable, as Maguire explores in chapter three. Predominant amongst these are the withdrawal of specialist services provided to hard-to-reach groups, which have been to date an important element of VSOs' work. VSOs are also likely to have to expend considerable resources on an infrastructure to provide evidence of their work, thereby adding to their costs and making them more bureaucratic. Finally, volunteers might withdraw their services if they perceive that they are doing the government's work on the cheap.

There is much written about the distinctive contribution which the voluntary sector makes generally and within criminal justice. Yet, very little evidence is available which supports this view. Research on the voluntary sector in criminal justice remains a 'cottage industry' and there is no strong tradition of independent research within VSOs themselves. Consequently, many of the assertions about its effectiveness are not substantiated by robust or verifiable evidence, as Hedderman and Hucklesby argue in chapter six. What evidence is available varies in quality and reliability. Greater involvement in state-funded service provision brings with it requirements to measure performance and outcomes. In chapter six Hedderman and Hucklesby suggest that considerable investment will be required by the voluntary sector to meet the standards expected by the government (Harlock, 2014). Yet much of the contribution of VSOs will remain intangible and therefore immeasurable, for example their influence on community cohesion or the culture of statutory criminal justice agencies (Nutley and Rimmer, 2002).

Critical commentary on the voluntary sector has been muted not only by a lack of empirical research but also by a general agreement that the voluntary sector is something which should be valued and that its values are necessarily positive. However, as Corcoran and Grotz demonstrate in chapter five, it is important to look beyond general assertions of value and delve deeper to unearth the reality. Greater knowledge about the value and contribution of VSOs to criminal justice alongside an awareness of what works and what does not will strengthen and not diminish the voluntary sector. It will also ensure that the services it provides are necessary and appropriate whether or not they are funded by the state.

Structure of the book

The book is split into two sections. Part I examines issues facing all VSOs involved in criminal justice. In chapter two, Clinks – the umbrella organisation which represents the penal voluntary sector – explores the voluntary sector's work with offenders and its contribution to criminal justice policy. The authors consider the role of the voluntary sector in the current policy climate and conclude that VSOs face an uncertain future. In chapter three, Mike Maguire considers the implications for VSOs in the growing marketisation of criminal justice services, concluding that it will have a transformative impact on the voluntary sector. Rod Dacombe and Elizabeth Morrow's contribution in chapter four looks backwards to debates which took place in the mid-20th century about what the role of the voluntary sector should be and traces continuities with the debates taking place today. They argue that a genuine appreciation of the relationship between the voluntary sector and the state can be achieved only by taking account of historical debates. In chapter five, Mary Corcoran and Jurgen Grotz question assumptions made about the benefits of using volunteers. The final chapter in this part examines issues raised when evaluating the work of the voluntary sector drawing on the experience of the authors, Carol Hedderman and Anthea Hucklesby. In chapter six, they examine the consequences of the requirements for VSOs to 'prove' their worth under new commissioning arrangements, arguing that the very characteristics which make involving the voluntary sector in service delivery attractive to funders also make them hard to evaluate in the ways in which the government and other funders increasingly require.

Part II of the book turns its attention to the work of the voluntary sector with different groups in the criminal justice system. In chapter seven, Alice Mills and Rosie Meek explore the work of the voluntary sector in prisons. They focus on the benefits and limitations of the work undertaken by VSOs in prisons from the perspectives of those directly affected by such work. They also explore the specific features and challenges of the partnerships between VSOs and criminal justice personnel and examine how these can impact upon both VSOs and prison cultures. Chapter eight, written by Paula Maurutto and Kelly Hannah-Moffat, discusses the role played by the voluntary sector in shaping and implementing criminal justice policy relating to women offenders in Canada, focusing particularly on women's imprisonment and domestic violence courts. The authors argue that existing debates underplay the ways in which VSOs contribute to criminal justice and their capacity for innovation. In chapter nine, Loraine Gelsthorpe and Jane Dominey explore the contribution that the voluntary sector makes to the diversity agenda in criminal justice and some of the potential impacts of the *TR* on the ability of criminal justice to treat offenders from diverse communities with fairness and sensitivity. The final chapter, written by Katherine S. Williams, examines the role of VSOs in supporting and campaigning for victims of crime. In chapter ten, Williams charts the symbiotic and sometimes turbulent nature of the relationship between victims, VSOs and governments through the use of case studies.

References

Carey, M. and Walker, R. (2002) 'The penal voluntary sector', in: S. Bryans, C. Martin, and R. Walker (eds) *Prisons and the voluntary sector*, Winchester: Waterside Press: 50–62.

Carlen, P. (2002) 'New discourses of justification and reform for women's imprisonment in England', in: P. Carlen (ed.) *Women and punishment: The struggle for justice*, Cullompton: Willan Publishing: 220–236.

Civil Exchange (2014) *Making good: The future of the voluntary sector*, London: Civil Exchange.

Clinks (2014) *Guide to the sector* at http://www.clinks.org/voluntary-community-sector/guide-vcs [accessed 27.02.15].

Corcoran, M. (2008) 'What does government want from the penal voluntary sector?' *Criminal Justice Matters*, 71 (1): 36–38.

Etherington, S. (2006) 'The transformation of public services – The voluntary and community sector and the criminal justice system', in: N. Tarry (ed.) *Returning to its roots? A new role for the third sector in probation*, London: Social Market Foundation: 53–61 at http://www.smf.co.uk/wp-content/uploads/2006/09/

Publication-Returning-to-its-roots-A-new-role-for-the-Third-Sector-in-Probation.pdf

Etherington, S. and Passey, A. (2002) 'The UK Voluntary Sector', in: S. Bryans, C. Martin and R. Walker (ed.) *Prisons and the Voluntary Sector*, Winchester: Waterside Press: 17–26.

Fox, C. and Albertson, K. (2011) 'Payment by results and social impact bonds in the criminal justice sector: New challenges for the concept of evidence-based policy', *Criminology and Criminal Justice*, 11 (5): 395–413.

Fox, C. and Albertson, K. (2012) 'Is payment by results the most efficient way to address the challenge faced by the criminal justice sector?' *Probation Journal*, 59 (4): 355–373.

Gojkovic, D., Mills, A. and Meek, R. (2011) *Scoping the involvement of third sector organisations in the seven resettlement pathways for offenders*, TSRC Working Paper 57, Birmingham: TSRC at http://www.birmingham.ac.uk/generic/tsrc/documents/tsrc/working-papers/working-paper-57.pdf

Hannah-Moffat, K. (2002) 'Creating choices: Reflecting on choices', in: P. Carlen (ed.) *Women and punishment: The struggle for justice*, Cullompton: Willan Publishing: 199–219.

Harlock, J. (2014) *From outcomes-based commissioning to social value? Implications for performance managing the third sector*, TSRC Working Paper 123, Birmingham: TSRC at http://www.birmingham.ac.uk/generic/tsrc/documents/tsrc/working-papers/working-paper-123.pdf

HM Government (2010) *The coalition: Our programme for government*, London: Stationery Office.

HM Treasury (2010) *Spending review 2010*. Cm 7492, London: Stationery Office.

Hucklesby, A. (2011) *Bail support schemes for adults*, Bristol: Policy Press.

Hucklesby, A. and Worrall, J. (2007) 'The voluntary sector and prisoners' resettlement', in: A. Hucklesby and L. Hagley-Dickinson (eds) *Prisoner resettlement: Policy and practice*, Cullompton: Willan Publishing: 174–198.

Macmillan, R., Taylor, R., Arvidson, M., Soteri-Proctor, A. and Teasdale, S. (2013) *The third sector in unsettled times: A field guide*, Third Sector Research Centre Working Paper 109, Birmingham: TSRC at http://www.birmingham.ac.uk/generic/tsrc/documents/tsrc/working-papers/working-paper-109.pdf

Maguire, M. (2012) 'Big society, the voluntary sector and the marketization of criminal justice', *Criminology and Criminal Justice*, 12 (5): 483–505.

Mills, A., Meek, R. and Gojkovic, D. (2011) 'Exploring the relationship between the voluntary sector and the state in criminal justice', *Voluntary Sector Review*, 2 (2): 193–211.

Ministry of Justice (MoJ) (2010) *Breaking the cycle: Effective punishment, rehabilitation and sentencing of offenders*, London: MoJ at http://webarchive.nationalarchives.gov.uk/20120119200607/http:/www.justice.gov.uk/consultations/docs/breaking-the-cycle.pdf

Ministry of Justice (MoJ) (2013) *Transforming rehabilitation: A strategy for reform*, London: MoJ at https://consult.justice.gov.uk/digital-communications/transforming-rehabilitation

Morgan, R. (2012) 'Crime and justice in the "Big Society"', *Criminology and Criminal Justice*, 12 (5): 463–481.

National Offender Management Service (NOMS) (2014) *An introduction to NOMS offender services co-commissioning*, London: MoJ at http://www.justice.gov.uk/

downloads/about/noms/Introduction-to-NOMS-offender-services-co-commissioning.pdf

Norman, J. (2010) *The Big Society: The anatomy of the new politics*, Buckingham: University of Buckingham Press.

Nutley, K. and Rimmer, S. (2002) 'A governor's perspective', in: S. Bryans, C. Martin, and R. Walker (eds) *Prisons and the voluntary sector*, Winchester: Waterside Press: 121–129.

Panel on the Independence of the Voluntary Sector (2014) *An independent mission: The voluntary sector in 2015*, London: The Independence Panel & Baring Foundation.

Putnam, R. D. (2000) *Bowling alone, the collapse and revival of American Community*, New York: Simon and Schuster.

Salaman, L. (2013) *The resilient sector: The state of nonprofit America*, Washington: The Brookings Institution.

Silvestri, A. (2009) *Partners or prisoners? Voluntary sector independence in the world of commissioning and contestability*, London: Centre for Crime and Justice Studies.

Part I

Part One

2
Paved with Good Intentions: The Way Ahead for Voluntary, Community and Social Enterprise Sector Organisations

Clive Martin, Lesley Frazer, Ellie Cumbo,
Clare Hayes and *Katie O'Donoghue*

Clinks is a membership or umbrella organisation that exists to support voluntary sector organisations (VSOs) that work with offenders and their families in England and Wales. Drawing on our extensive knowledge of VSOs working in criminal justice, this chapter explores the sector's past, current and future role in criminal justice, and the barriers and opportunities that organisations face in the current political and economic climate. It provides a background and historical context to the role of the criminal justice VSOs in England and Wales, noting that, despite the stated intention of successive governments, and numerous policy and structural changes, the full potential of the sector has never been realised owing to patchy and unstable support. It then gives an account of how Clinks was formed in response to these challenges, how infrastructure organisations have helped to shape the sector's independent voice and what the current threats are to this crucial aspect of the sector's role.

The varied nature of the present-day sector is depicted alongside an account of the most pressing challenges it faces in a turbulent policy environment, from commissioning and funding changes to fundamental debates about how to measure the impact and value of the interventions it provides. The chapter then explores the sector's distinctive contribution, demonstrating what may be lost if the sector is not supported, including its holistic, person-centred services that work with people's strengths, foster social capital and link to desistance from crime. It outlines the particular achievements of the sector in working with 'hard-to-reach' offenders, raising the profile of minority groups and promoting enabling practices, such as service user involvement. Overall, the authors conclude that, despite some progress from successive administrations, criminal justice VSOs and the service users they support continue to confront an insecure and unpredictable future.

Background: the voluntary sector in criminal justice

VSOs have a long history of complementing the work of statutory agencies in criminal justice, both in prisons and in the community. This has not, however, been without difficulties, particularly in the level of formal commitment to partnership working from statutory services, which has not been consistent or stable. This constitutes a double jeopardy for the sector: firstly, the sector is prevented from reaching its full potential, and secondly, its existing work is disrupted by changes in criminal justice policy which may exacerbate the problem.

In prisons, the sector's work dates back at least to the philanthropic activities of 18th- and 19th-century reformers such as John Howard and Elizabeth Fry, who worked to achieve more humane and rehabilitative regimes. Most early voluntary activity was faith-based and channelled through the prison chaplains, and much of it focused on promoting temperance and abstinence from alcohol. Many locally based Discharged Prisoners' Aid Societies and other charities sought to work positively with offenders not only inside the prison but 'through the gate', following their release.

The sector has continued to play a recognised role in service provision both inside the prison and on release despite the formal handing over of the 'throughcare and aftercare' role to the Probation Service in 1963. As Carey and Walker (2002: 59) describe, the 1970s witnessed a proliferation of professionally run, secular VSOs operating in and beyond the prison, many established by those with first-hand experience of the penal system. Working alongside the more traditional church-based organisations, their development reflected wider societal shifts and changing needs in relation to substance misuse, cultural diversity, and recognised economic, health and gender inequalities. The Wolfenden Committee report (1978) paid tribute to their work and acknowledged its significant role in complementing, supporting and extending the statutory system.

Yet there were difficulties in gaining acceptance within individual prison establishments and also in remaining financially viable (Hobhouse and Brockway, 1922 cited in Carey and Walker, 2002: 55). Over the subsequent decades, the coordination of the sector's work in the prison setting continued to fluctuate, and some earlier gains, for example the appointment of a member of prison staff in each establishment to act as voluntary sector coordinator, have receded. The funding of VSOs working in prisons has also continued to be fragmented, with some services being centrally specified and procured by the National Offender Management Service (NOMS); some smaller-scale services being locally commissioned at the discretion of prison governors; and much work being delivered free of charge to the establishment through the support of charitable trusts and foundations (Hucklesby and Hagley-Dickinson, 2007). This is problematic in that it not only results in geographic variations in the provision of services, but also means the sector is less able to engage strategically and cohesively with the direction of criminal justice policy and practice.

Beyond prison, work with ex-offenders in the community has a similar history of waxing and waning strategic and financial support. This is despite the fact that the Probation Service itself has its own roots in voluntary work, specifically that of 19th-century voluntary court missionaries. Over the succeeding hundred years, the Probation Service continued to work closely with VSOs, at one time even actively recruiting and involving its own groups of volunteers. This was, however, informal and not linked to funding streams.

This situation began to change in the 1980s when responsibility for offender accommodation was devolved from central government to local probation areas, and probation for the first time entered into a more explicit commissioning relationship with voluntary providers. Even then there were significant fluctuations in that commitment (Clinks, 2012a, 2012b). By the mid-1990s local probation areas were expected to spend at least 7 per cent of their budgets on 'partnership' arrangements, including offender accommodation, but when the National Probation Service was formed in 2001, this requirement was removed. As other local commissioners took over responsibility for some key services to offenders, probation expenditure on services provided by VSOs dwindled to as little as 2 per cent in some areas.

In 2004 the creation of NOMS, to oversee both probation and prisons, saw a second wave of enthusiasm for diversifying providers and including the voluntary and community sector. When the current Probation Trusts were established in 2007, the Ministry of Justice and NOMS renewed their pledge to open up the market and enable VSOs to play a more active role in local service delivery (MoJ, 2008). At this time, many probation trusts began to commission a wider range of services from VSOs and other partners to meet specific needs, and also to engage with the sector collectively over their plans and possible partnership opportunities.

This, then, is indicative of the climate in which the voluntary sector working with offenders operates today. Although there is significant support available from some statutory services, it is not a long-established feature of the system, and remains patchy and unstable. The consequence of this is that, despite the plethora of activity still being carried out by VSOs concerned with supporting rehabilitation, the scope for the sector to play a more significant strategic role in delivering rehabilitation and resettlement support in prison and beyond the prison gate has remained fairly limited. Moreover, as this chapter explores further, even these fragile foundations are once again being disturbed, as the coalition government implements its *Transforming Rehabilitation* (*TR*) proposals (MoJ, 2013a) to outsource the bulk of the work hitherto undertaken by the probation service. Whether this will strengthen the voluntary sector or force it to go through the lengthy process of securing engagement once again will be a key question for criminal justice decision-makers for at least the next 10 years.

Clinks and the role of infrastructure organisations

These challenges facing the sector over the last few decades led directly to the formation of Clinks in 1998, its aim being to support voluntary and community-based organisations working in prisons and with ex-prisoners in the community (Martin, 2002: 68). There had been a much earlier incarnation of an umbrella body for the sector, in the form of the Central Discharged Prisoners' Aid Society – later the National Association of Discharged Prisoners' Aid Societies (NADPAS) – which was formed in 1935 to coordinate local VSOs and act as a link between them and the Prison Commission. NADPAS itself became a service delivery organisation, Nacro, during the 1960s expansion of the sector.

Clinks came into being in the immediate aftermath of the 1997 election. The New Labour government seemed to herald a resurgence of political interest in the concept of active citizenship, and in the role of the voluntary sector working with the state to build social capital and effect positive change, at both the individual and societal levels. This new spirit of recognition and partnership was most notably reflected in the signing of a *Compact on Relations between Government and the Voluntary and Community sector in England* (HM Government, 1998). This document, refreshed in 2010 by the new coalition government, continues to be in wide use as the foundation text for best practice in delivering services that include voluntary sector involvement (Cabinet Office, 2010b).

As an infrastructure organisation, Clinks' founding purpose is not to deliver directly to service users but to support and represent VSOs that do. As such, it has had a unique role to play in channelling their voices and raising awareness of the opportunities and challenges that they have faced over a number of years. An initial study of the work of VSOs in four prisons (Clinks, 1999) showed at that time that the relationship between prisons and the voluntary sector lacked both a philosophical and practical framework, which left staff and volunteers in both sectors operating on the basis of personal conviction without any coherent policy to guide them. Where there was a positive relationship it was a nervous one and much depended on the extent to which individual prison governors were willing to take action without direction from Prison Service HQ. It was also unclear which VSOs were active inside each prison, resulting in a lack of coordination and awareness of their work, which was consequently underutilised.

A number of positive gains flowed from the Clinks study and related work. Clinks' *Good Practice Guide* (2000) was adopted by the Prison Service in 2001, at the same time as a new national post of Voluntary Sector Coordinator was created at Prison Service HQ (Sanderson and Gordon, 2002: 76). A significant constituency of locally based VSOs with a long history of working in prisons was able to develop its collective voice through Clinks for the first time with the aim of influencing government policy and practice.

This advocacy role is in fact an essential correlative to the sector's involvement in service delivery, since both are equally informed by its distinctive ethos. Set up and run by private individuals, the voluntary sector is defined by its legal, economic and ideological independence from the public and private sectors. Organisations can focus exclusively on the needs of the specific users or communities for whom they were created, and who are enshrined in their founding documents as their beneficiaries. Not only are they free of the profit motive that drives the private sector, but they are also exempt from the need to balance these alongside competing interests, as statutory services must. For this reason, the voluntary sector's role is often to act as a safety net where statutory services either fail or do not exist. It follows from this that the voluntary sector also has an ethical duty to scrutinise policy decisions on behalf of their service users, who are already marginalised, and to some extent disenfranchised, from mainstream public services. In many cases, such as where policy changes might reduce the need for a voluntary organisation's services, it might in fact be more advantageous for the sector *not* to speak out. For example, criminal justice VSOs are known for their long record of supporting alternatives to custody to reduce the number of people in prison, even where they themselves are funded to work with prisons and might otherwise be seen to have a financial interest in a growing number of prisoners. This commitment to amplify the voices of its users is indicative of the sector's foundational values, and of the contribution it is able to make beyond its role as an alternative service provider to the public or private sectors. So important is this aspect of the sector's work that it was enshrined as the first principle of the Compact, in which the government commits to doing the following (Cabinet Office, 2010b: 8):

> 1.1. Respect and uphold the independence of CSOs [Civil Society Organisations] to deliver their mission, including their right to campaign, regardless of any relationship, financial or otherwise, which may exist.

In recent years, however, there have been signs of increasing pressure upon the sector not to speak out. The Panel on the Independence of the Voluntary Sector, founded by the Baring Foundation in 2011, warned in its most recent annual report that the overall independence of the sector is 'undervalued and under serious threat', and that there had been a particular deterioration in respect of its ability to use its voice (Baring Foundation et al., 2014: 6). Perhaps the most notable instance of this was the passing of the Transparency of Lobbying, Non-Party Campaigning and Trade Union Administration Act, otherwise known as the Lobbying Bill, in January 2014. A highly vocal campaign was run by many organisations, including Commission on Civil Society and Democratic Engagement, of which Clinks is a member, arguing that the provisions of the Act risked limiting the ability of VSOs to engage in legitimate campaigning activity because it might inadvertently influence the outcome of elections (Commission on Civil Society and Democratic Engagement, 2013). The outspoken hostility of some politicians and sections of the media who labelled voluntary sector campaigning as 'political', and therefore illegitimate (sometimes because campaigns were seen as critical of government policy), however, predates the Lobbying Act (Baring Foundation et al., 2014: 33).

In this climate, there is a particular need for infrastructure organisations such as Clinks to articulate the value of the sector's independent voice to effective and democratic policy-making. Since their role is not to promote the interests of any individual organisation but to support and represent the sector as a whole, and its marginalised users, such organisations have a strong platform from which to speak about its constituency's purpose and achievements. The scale and magnitude of forthcoming changes to criminal justice policy make such an undertaking both more urgent and more challenging.

In order to draw out the full potential of current policy proposals, however, it is first necessary to present both a snapshot of the sector's current make-up and an outline of the overarching policy context in which it finds itself.

The profile of the sector working with offenders and their families

The criminal justice voluntary sector includes a rich variety of organisations and there are multiple ways in which it might be organised and understood. Perhaps most obviously, organisations can be categorised in terms of their size or the specific constituency of service users that they support. However, decision-makers should also be aware of the wide variety of organisational structures, approaches to delivering services, business models and political or faith orientations within the sector.

Given its history, with its roots mainly in small-scale voluntary services delivered by volunteers and small numbers of paid staff in particular prisons or local communities, the voluntary sector can be seen as being polarised between a sizeable majority of small, local voluntary groups and a minority of larger national or regional organisations (Gojkovic, 2012). This is reflected in Clinks' own membership of around 600 VSOs: at least three quarters of these have 20 or fewer paid staff members. A recent Centre for Social Justice (CSJ, 2013: 7) study, drawing on the 2010 National Survey of Charities and Social Enterprises (Cabinet Office, 2011), estimated that, although as many as 13,596 VSOs in England may work in some way with offenders as part of their wider remit, only 1475 organisations have offenders, ex-offenders and their families as their primary beneficiaries. Of these, 51 per cent have an annual income of less than £150,000, and 5 per cent have no income at all. Most reported having few employees, with 24 per cent having no full-time equivalent staff and 58 per cent having five or fewer staff. The predominant focus was also very local, with 61 per cent carrying out their activities at county council level or at a smaller scale. At the other end of the scale, the CSJ study revealed 23 per cent of organisations with an annual income of more than £500,000, and just a handful with very substantial incomes of £50 million or more. Only 4 per cent of VSOs have more than 100 staff, with 21 per cent operating nationally and 33 per cent operating regionally. These findings clearly have significant implications for the ability of the sector to participate in larger-scale contracted activity, with relatively few VSOs having the income, staffing or geographical reach to operate at more than local level. In addition, the current economic climate has brought multiple challenges to the sector in relation to both its own funding and the level of need faced by its service users; it is in short being asked to do more with less. This has two obvious consequences: on the one hand, it may be seen to increase the level of urgency with which organisations feel they must work to amplify the voices of their service users and, where necessary, criticise government policy. On the other hand, however, it impacts on the level of choice they have about engaging with commissioning processes where opportunities to do so arise, even where it is on terms that they may find financially, or even ethically, problematic.

Impact of the economic downturn

Although the precarious economic situation of many VSOs is not a new phenomenon, the work of Clinks and others in mapping the impact of the economic downturn has highlighted some stark trends. VSOs working with offenders have in the past been strongly reliant on grants from a limited number of charitable trusts. Raising funds through public donations has historically been difficult given the lack of public traction for the plight of offenders and former offenders as a worthy cause. Fundraising from the public constitutes just 3 per cent of total income for those organisations who responded to our most recent survey (Daly, 2013: 3).

The economic downturn has had a detrimental impact on the financial situation of VSOs. Biannual surveys conducted by Clinks since 2010 have indicated that as many as 50 per cent of responding organisations are not recovering their core costs, and 65 per cent are using their reserves to cover these. The level of income that responding organisations have secured over the last three years particularly varies by size; our most recent survey found that medium-sized organisations were more likely to have seen a drop in turnover than either larger organisations (with over 50 staff) or smaller ones (with fewer than 10 staff) (Daly, 2013: 9). VSOs have also reported that reduced income and the need for staff to dedicate more time and energy to fundraising are interfering with the quality and flexibility of service provision for service users. Clinks' previous monitoring has also revealed reports from organisations that service user demand is escalating in parallel with the bite on their resources. Daly (2012: 31) notes that

> national and local government cuts over the last twelve months have resulted in a decrease in the quantity and quality of the services on which the most vulnerable depend. In the past, the charities and not-for-profit organisations have provided a safety net for those whose needs are not met by the public sector. But with large cuts to the public sector services coinciding with cuts to the not-for-profit sector, some of the most disadvantaged and vulnerable are falling through the gaps.

The obvious result of this is that providers report that they are stretching their resources even further to cover the rising level of need, without additional funding. Organisations have also expressed concern not only about their own financial position but also about the tapering number of services to which to signpost and refer clients onwards (Daly, 2013: 4).

These factors give an insight into some of the reasons why contracts with statutory authorities to provide services have become such an important option for the sector (Meek et al., 2010: 10). Contracts bring with them both the promise of stable income and a more formalised strategic relationship with the authority contracting out the service. Yet, even financially, these are no panacea: for a start, they overwhelmingly favour larger organisations with 50 or more staff (Daly, 2013: 3). Moreover, these organisations are particularly exposed to the shifts in commissioning landscape and overall reductions in public spending. This presents a number of sobering questions about the future of wider voluntary provision in the criminal justice system, given the clear political preference for contractual relationships exemplified by *TR*. It also has obvious consequences for the sector's independent identity and voice if it becomes ever more dependent on statutory sources of funding.

Current policy climate and challenges for the voluntary sector

Reference has already been made above to the endemic strategic and economic uncertainties that have characterised the sector's relationship with the state throughout its history, and how they may have undermined the independence and versatility of the sector. These are largely to do with how the delivery of services is envisioned at the local and national political levels, which has led to a constantly shifting commissioning and procurement landscape. It is important, set against these longer-term factors, not to overstate the implications of the current turbulent policy environment. Many organisations will attest that the peaks and troughs of each new policy cycle are a familiar and accepted characteristic of this sector. Nevertheless, the forthcoming changes to how rehabilitation services are delivered are among the most significant in their history. These changes, like any overhaul of a major public service, carry risks alongside opportunities. We now explore some of these through the lens of a sector which, as the previous sections have sought to demonstrate, has a sizeable stake in whether or not they achieve their stated aims.

Transforming rehabilitation

It has been noted already that the late 2000s heralded the introduction of more significant outsourcing of criminal justice services. The further expansion of competition has also been an acknowledged priority of the current government from the outset. In the 2010 Coalition Agreement, the very first of the nine commitments given on justice was as follows:

> We will introduce a 'rehabilitation revolution' that will pay independent providers to reduce reoffending, paid for by the savings this new approach will generate within the criminal justice system. (Cabinet Office, 2010a: 26)

Following a reshuffle in which Chris Grayling replaced Ken Clarke as Secretary of State for Justice, the final *TR* agenda was launched in the *Strategy for Reform* white paper in 2013 (MoJ, 2013a). This announced the government's intention to contract out the management of low and medium risk adult offenders in the community, and those leaving custody, to new providers – Community Rehabilitation Companies – who would be incentivised to drive down reoffending rates by a Payment by Results (PbR) scheme. As part of the new regime, a number of prisons would be redesignated as 'resettlement prisons', where prisoners from the area would start working with the new providers during the last three months of their sentence, to ensure continuity through the gate and in the community after release. For the first time, supervision would also be applied to those completing sentences of less than 12 months, who would serve all or most of their sentence within their local resettlement prison. The cost of extending rehabilitation in this way would be met by efficiencies driven by the new providers, and longer-term savings would be delivered by the projected reduction in reoffending. Meanwhile, high-risk offenders would be the responsibility of a newly constituted National Probation Service (NPS), which would also undertake risk assessment, advise courts and the Parole Board and work closely in partnership with the new providers to ensure public protection.

A further, important aspect of the new regime was the commitment given in *A Strategy for Reform* to including the voluntary sector in the new arrangements:

> There are organisations across all sectors which have value to add in reforming offenders. A large number of consultation respondents agreed that voluntary and community sector organisations could have a strong impact on reducing reoffending. We know that there are challenges for smaller organisations in all sectors in participating in delivery under 'payment by results' contracts and across large areas. We are determined to design a system which brings together the best of the public, private and voluntary and community sectors and we asked questions on how we could achieve this in the Transforming Rehabilitation consultation. (MoJ, 2013a: 16)

This was a welcome statement of intent, appearing to promise an approach to the sector that is both assured and flexible, particularly for smaller organisations. However, the challenges posed by certain aspects of the proposals are indeed significant; whether or not they will in fact translate into more comprehensive support for the sector remains to be seen.

The problem of scale

One of the key uncertainties that remain concerns the extent to which the small localised nature of much of the sector can be accommodated in the new structures. The question for VSOs is whether and how meeting local need can be reconciled with an attempt to create economies of scale through large-scale procurements. In its report on the future of the Probation Service in England and Wales prior to the launch of *Transforming Rehabilitation; A Strategy for Reform* (MoJ, 2013a), the Justice Committee advised that such large contracts were a false economy and an inappropriate vehicle for commissioning probation services (Justice Committee, 2011). An even wider concern than the practicability of the new arrangements is that competition itself is problematic for a sector which has traditionally thrived on partnership and complementary working. Competing with other providers poses both practical and existential anxieties for organisations, not least about the ultimate effect on their service users.

One issue of particular concern is the impact of large-scale commissioning of specialised services currently carried out by local, community-based organisations, particularly where these are targeted at minority groups, such as women or Black, Asian and Minority Ethnic (BAME) offenders. The future of local partnership working also remains uncertain, with Contract Package Areas cutting across a wide range of local authorities and statutory bodies, and little indication as to how collaborations between voluntary, statutory and commissioners will actually transpire. On non-statutory partnerships, VSOs are explicitly given 'the flexibility to decide how they engage in such arrangements and with whom' (MoJ, 2014: 47). This raises clear questions about the future of, for example, Integrated Offender Management (IOM), the well-established scheme in which all local agencies and organisations working with the most high-risk offenders in a community, whether statutory or voluntary, are brought together to ensure a coordinated approach (MoJ, 2010).

In this way, the *TR* proposals do not necessarily sit comfortably alongside the drive towards localism in other areas of government policy, not least that of its sister department, the Home Office. In 2011, the Home Office created a new level of directly elected local decision-makers, Police and Crime Commissioners, to set the strategic priorities and budget for each police force in England and Wales. The aim of this was precisely to devolve governance of policing and community safety services to local areas, and hence to secure more locally tailored provision. The extent to which Police and Crime Commissioners might be involved in commissioning offender management services in the future is unknown. However, the new local landscape of contracting, with its plethora of commissioners who must be approached for funding, risks creating confusion and threatens to overload smaller local VSOs that might want to work with them all.

Even for the small number of large national VSOs, there are significant barriers to leading one or more of the new contracts, even though the government has stressed its desire not to have the sector limited to being subcontractors in supply chains led by others (MoJ, 2013a). In reality, however, organisations that compete for large contracts must have substantial capital and resources. Taking on large contracts would also have major legal implications, such as the requirement to take on employees transferring to the new providers from existing services, whose job terms and conditions are protected by the Transfer of Undertaking (Protection of Employment) (TUPE) regulations. Although one option would be developing a consortium to bid for contracts, doing so successfully is usually a lengthy and complex process, requiring trustee approval, due diligence checks and a good cultural 'fit' between organisations. A useful case study is provided in Hucklesby and Wincup's (2007) evaluation of the Pyramid partnership project between Depaul Trust and Nacro, piloted by Northern Rock foundation between 2004 and 2007 which highlights some of the benefits and pitfalls of VSOs working in partnership with each other.

Despite the mutual interest from government and the sector in seeing VSOs and consortia as lead providers, it may still be the private sector that dominates the list of successful bidders, because they have the resources to absorb all the various risks. The majority of voluntary providers will enter the market as subcontracted partners to a private sector lead provider. This once again highlights the importance of all parties committing fully to the sector's ability to maintain an independent voice even when it is part of a commercial supply chain, upholding the values of the *Compact* (Cabinet Office, 2010b). It is too early to say whether this level of commitment exists, given that negotiations are under way at the time of writing between lead providers and VSOs, but considering the situation captured by the Panel on the Independence of the Voluntary Sector (Baring Foundation et al., 2014), it seems reasonable to assume that scrutiny will be necessary.

Payment by Results

An important element of the *TR* proposals is the introduction of PbR into the new contracts, whereby full payment will only be paid to service providers if reconviction rates of offenders under their supervision are reduced, compared with a given baseline. It will be a mandatory part of the contracts for the main providers, who will include the level of PbR they propose to take on as part of their bid for the new services. The extent to which PbR will be passed down to subcontractors providing specific rehabilitation services is a live question; there is no prescribed maximum amount of risk they are allowed to pass on, though the Ministry of Justice has committed to ensure that this is not done 'disproportionately' (MoJ, 2013c: 7).

Although this is notably not the most controversial aspect of the changes at a political level, where most of the opposition has been to privatisation as a principle in itself, it has provoked serious debate within the voluntary sector. Some voices have welcomed PbR as an important way to hold services to account (Pollard, 2013). Others have pointed to the difficulties likely to be faced by small to medium-sized organisations in joining the supply chain under conditions where payment is conditional, particularly given the typical size and capacity of such organisations (CSJ, 2013: 7). Even for larger organisations, the risks of PbR are not insignificant, especially given the experiences of some VSOs involved in PbR contracts as part of the Department for Work and Pensions (DWP) flagship Work Programme (Rees et al., 2013). In an attempt to militate some of the concerns about PbR and as a result of its earlier use in other areas such as health, there has been investment in new ideas to ensure that the sector is enabled to be part of such commissioning arrangements. One example is the use of social finance such as the Social Impact Bond (SIB). In this model, social investment funds are pooled into a Special Purpose Vehicle (partnership or limited company), which then contracts with VSOs to provide innovative resettlement support to short-term prisoners. These providers are paid 100 per cent of their delivery costs upfront and all of the risk is carried by the investors, who also receive a return on investment from government proportionate to the outcomes achieved, that is, the reductions in reoffending achieved (Social Finance, 2011). However, the complexity of assessing outcomes and the levels of start-up capital required appear to make it unlikely at the time of writing that the SIB model will be rolled out extensively. Even though the Social Investment market is more generally expanding, it is impossible to predict how fast or how far it will develop over the next few years. Therefore, while there are reasons to be optimistic regarding the future role of social finance in funding interventions run by VSOs, it must be viewed as one among several options for the next few years.

Evidencing outcomes

Closely related to the challenges of PbR is the question of how best to measure the impact of interventions. Evaluating very diverse, often small-scale interventions is not a straightforward undertaking, and the sector has been grappling for some time with demanding expectations from national and local commissioners. Although it is not contested that public money should not be spent without paying regard to whether the interventions it funds are successful, there is less of a consensus over how VSOs can reasonably be expected to demonstrate that they are successful. Moreover, there is an ongoing debate over what success actually means, even within the stated aim of reducing reoffending. This has been brought into sharp relief by PbR, under which reoffending rates of service users over the 12 months from the start of the intervention will be measured and compared to a historic baseline. There will be two different calculations as part of this: the number in a cohort who go on to commit any further offences (known as the binary metric), and the number of further offences per individual service user (the frequency metric). Providers will be able to receive payments if both metrics reduced. However, they will only be rewarded for reductions on the frequency metric if the binary metric at least stays constant, that is, there is no increase in the number of individuals committing further offences.

This method of measurement immediately prompts questions about the extent to which interventions working with those who are harder to reach will find a home within the new system. The academic literature on desistance from crime has continually stressed that it is a process rather than an event, and that it is marked by a number of largely subjective, rather than overt, changes, such as developing social capital and building a non-criminal identity (Maruna and Farrall, 2004; McNeill and Weaver, 2010). While NOMS (2012) has recently acknowledged the importance of measuring intermediate outcomes, such as improved family relationships, progress towards employment and stable accommodation, these understandings have yet to penetrate the binary orthodoxy of the *TR* programme. So where an intervention achieves success over a longer period by reducing reoffending in the longer term, despite reconviction levels remaining constant or getting worse in the first 12 months, this will not be recognised by current PbR proposals.

A further example of the restricted way in which government currently approaches evaluation of the work of the sector is the new Justice Data Lab, through which organisations can gain access to official data on the reconviction rates of their service users, and how this compares to similar service users in a matched control group (MoJ, 2013b). In other words, the Data Lab aims to analyse whether or not specific interventions are succeeding in reducing reoffending. This represents a valuable opportunity for the sector within the context of the changes to probation, but does not yet go beyond this fairly restricted view of success. The Data Lab is currently confined to measuring changes in reconvictions, with no measures as yet for intermediate outcomes; in this sense, some successes may be missed simply because the data are extracted too early in individuals' desistance process. In addition, there is the perennial problem of attributing change in an individual to one particular intervention or organisation, where a number of services have been working in combination.

These issues speak to wider tensions over whether the expectations commissioners have of the sector's ability to demonstrate its impact are proportionate. Policy makers prefer high-quality, quantitative evidence, but relatively few voluntary sector evaluations are currently thought to meet the methodological standards required (Hucklesby and Worrall, 2007, see Hedderman and Hucklesby, chapter six, this volume). Obstacles include small cohorts, lack of capital to fund evaluations and difficulties in accessing official data relating to service users beyond the specific provisions of the Data Lab. In relation to intermediate outcomes, these can be difficult to assess and measure, particularly when they are largely subjective in nature, for example with building personal relationships. Furthermore, the specific intermediate factors most strongly associated with desistance will differ between different individuals and groups, for example women and BAME offenders.

This may seem like a very technical and rarefied debate, but it is a crucial one given the very close link that exists in principle between evaluation and funding. Although *TR* may have an impact on wider commissioning practice, it is not an overstatement to say that, at present, inappropriate evaluation can be the difference between which parts of the sector survive and which do not. There are, of course, other local commissioners of services related to criminal justice that are becoming important to VSOs working in this field, including Police and Crime Commissioners and local and regional Health commissioners, which may offer the sector a chance to build new relationships and diversify funding sources. In all these commissioning contexts, however, evidencing impact and value is becoming increasingly important. The conversation about the most appropriate and viable methods of evaluation will have to continue if the contribution of VSOs is to be sustained.

How is the voluntary sector distinctive?

Although the sector and its work are far from homogeneous, an insight into these overlapping networks of organisations can find many common themes and consistencies. We now turn our attention to what distinguishes the ethos, activities and interventions of criminal justice VSOs from those of statutory agencies and private companies, in order to capture the full range of activity that is at stake if the voluntary sector's work alongside the criminal justice system is not secured.

The commitment by the voluntary sector to 'enable' and 'empower' the marginalised is widely understood by the public to be its primary purpose. This has specific connotations in criminal justice, however, given that the user group is effectively 'disempowered' by virtue of the fact that they are subject to the mandatory, rather than the voluntary, intervention of the state. The voluntary sector's claim to distinctiveness is that, despite operating within these confines, it prioritises the needs of offenders as independently as it can from the formal machinery of justice, although that is often difficult and contentious. VSOs have traditionally stressed this independent stance and their roots in the local community as the basis for reciprocal, trusting relationships with service users and communities.

For many individuals, there is also a very important social dynamic to their journey away from crime. The ability to enhance social capital and to assist a person to forge new or renewed connections in their community is possibly the voluntary sector's most significant claim to distinctiveness in working with offenders. Offenders and ex-offenders generally face structural stigmatisation in employment, housing and social relations which perpetuates punishment and hinders complete rehabilitation. VSOs, as value-driven bodies, have an inherent interest in tackling this kind of structural disadvantage. Much of the contribution of the voluntary sector in criminal justice is therefore related to the challenge of accessing and mobilising social capital (Farrall and Calverley, 2005). This work takes many different guises. The sector has, for example, a long and distinguished history of working to create strong, reciprocal ties among those who have offended and their families. Restorative Justice programmes have been shown, in certain circumstances, to be deeply beneficial for both victims and offenders (Shapland et al., 2011). However, a unique goal of the sector is to help the service user move beyond their immediate circle, into the society from which they are disengaged and stigmatised. A meta-analysis of numerous North American criminal justice interventions found, for example, that communities were much more likely to accept the presence of a high-need sex offender in their midst if they were a member of a Circles of Support and Accountability group (Wilson et al., 2007). This last point has recently been developed by McNeill (2012), who suggests that VSOs that support reintegration into the community are contributing more than just practical support for individual offenders. Such organisations are in fact contributing to a fair and just system by assuming responsibility for ending state-sponsored punishment at the appropriate time, so that former offenders can move back into active citizenship. The contribution of the voluntary sector therefore goes beyond crime reduction solutions to creating a more credible and efficient criminal justice system.

Desistance and the voluntary sector

A particular recent boon to the sector's work has been the burgeoning academic literature on desistance theory, which has become a subject of interest amongst policy makers and practitioners alike (McNeill and Weaver, 2010; NOMS, 2012). Desistance refers to the process – as opposed to the event – of ceasing and refraining from offending, and the individual's eventual reintegration back into the community (McNeill and Weaver, 2010). It distinguishes between primary desistance (any lull or gap in offending) and secondary desistance (the complete cessation of offending, accompanied by the development of an altered identity as a non-offender, and the person's full reintegration into the family, community and society) (McNeill and Weaver, 2010). Critically, the process of desistance is attributed to a combination of subjective and objective factors. While practical support such as finding accommodation, steady employment and addressing substance misuse issues are all acknowledged as important, researchers have also devoted considerable attention to the importance of the individual's own social context, priorities and motivations in the desistance process (Ward and Maruna, 2007). This reflects the pre-existing narrative that has informed voluntary sector services in criminal justice for decades, which emphasises that offenders are individual agents, and that a 'one size fits all' approach to rehabilitative interventions is unlikely to be effective.

The sector's distinctive contribution to the criminal justice system, then, can be summarised as offering holistic, person-centred interventions, deeply embedded in the appropriate social and local context, with significant points of synthesis with desistance theory. As noted above, this does not have to be carried out in isolation from, or in opposition to, statutory or other interventions. Indeed, partnership arrangements such as IOM have been shown to be particularly successful when they include a variety of partners from different sectors (Wong et al., 2012). In a Home Office–commissioned evaluation of a series of IOM pilots, the positive contributions of VSOs were attributed to their flexibility, their ability to respond quickly and the fact that they are embedded in the community and can provide a source of 'informal intelligence' on unique features of the local area (Wong et al., 2012).

Working with complex needs, hard-to-reach offenders and minority groups

In addition to its general ethos, VSOs have made particular and acknowledged strides in providing for individuals who present with particularly complex needs. In their review of the Circles of Support and Accountability programme, O'Connor and Bogue (2010: 317) point to the unique role of the volunteer, arguing that finding the right volunteer and community support could be critical in supporting individuals' desistance, and noting that people are more responsive to interventions where they find a 'match with their own way of being in the world'. Where VSOs find a way of facilitating this, they may be uniquely well equipped to assist statutory partners to meet the challenges of particularly disempowered or disenfranchised individuals. An evaluation of the 2nd Chance Sports Academies Project at HMYOI Portland found delivering specialist help and mentoring relationships, tailored to individual complex needs, yielded significant improvements in the reconviction rates of a cohort of young service users who had committed violent offences, when compared to the national average (Meek, 2012). Significantly, despite initial fears that the programme would merely duplicate existing resettlement provision, members of the prison staff reported that 2nd Chance had become an indispensable aspect of their work.

Flowing directly from its independence and ethos, the sector has also played a vital role in raising the profile and meeting the needs of marginalised groups of people within the criminal justice system. One of the terms often used by the sector itself to capture its unique value is the commitment of organisations to working with the 'hard-to-reach' populations (Nacro, 2011: 3; Clinks, 2013: 3). Far from being a derogatory label to the individual service user, this term recognises that many people caught up in the criminal justice system find themselves persistently alienated from mainstream services, from an early stage in life and in relation to the full spectrum of social welfare, health and education provision. The role of the voluntary sector in advocating for particular models of working and for service change is perhaps best illustrated by its recent achievements in regard to women and BAME service users.

Women offenders

Women constitute a numerically small proportion of those subject to criminal justice disposals, accounting for just 5 per cent of the prison population (MoJ, 2013a). The relatively low number of women perhaps partially accounts for a historical tendency at both a strategic and operational level to overlook the very high levels of multiple and complex needs typically experienced by women in the criminal justice system. In most recent estimates, 46 per cent of women in prison have suffered a history of domestic abuse and 53 per cent report having experienced emotional, physical or sexual harm as children, compared with 27 per cent of men (Prison Reform Trust, 2013a). In 2007, the Independent Review on women in the criminal justice system led by Baroness Corston (2007: 3) presented a piercing critique of provision for women, on the basis that prisons and practices within them have 'for the most part been designed for men'. In the course of her review, Corston (2007: 61) visited three voluntary sector women's community centres, Calderdale in Halifax, Asha in Worcester and 218 in Glasgow and described their services as follows:

> What unites these three centres is their broad approach which is to treat each woman as an individual with her own set of needs and problems. They recognise the impact that victimisation and isolation by disadvantage can have on a woman's circumstances and behaviour; the shame and stigma that many women feel by a number of life experiences, not just being convicted of an offence but also mental illness or being a single parent. [They] seek to provide constructive and humane responses to many women who need a whole range of support from community-based services including both psychological therapy to aid personal development and practical assistance to help them develop economic prospects. They are primarily 'women' not 'offenders'.

The evolution of a one-stop-shop to women service users is just one example of a voluntary sector initiative that provides a practical answer to entrenched social neglect.

While government policy responses to the Corston recommendations have been frustratingly slow, alliances across the voluntary sector and interested funders, most notably the collaboration by the Corston Independent Funders Coalition, have been evermore active in their development and advocacy efforts (Kaufmann, 2011). Since 2007, novel solutions for assisting women have continued to proliferate in the voluntary sector. For example, the SWAN project in Northumberland developed a virtual one-stop approach to address rural isolation and associated service inequality (Barefoot Research and Evaluation, 2010). Experienced VSOs have also pioneered new resources to help others better understand how to respond to the distinct profile of women service users. For example, the Together Women Project (2013) has developed an online gender-specific mentoring toolkit, which provides detailed but accessible guidance on approach, design and practice. The toolkit emphasises the importance of a user-led approach to designing effective services, informed by the three questions: 'Who are these women? What are the women's needs? What do the women say?'

The voluntary sector has also played an important scrutiny and campaign function. For example, Women in Prison (2013) recently published a report *State of the Estate*, which includes a fact file of every women's prison and contextualises this with the testimonies of women prisoners. In their strategic work, the voluntary sector providing gender-specific services to women and the Corston Independent Funders Coalition have been advocates of a new language introduced by the Corston Report (2007). For example, it promotes an approach that refocuses attention upstream to women and girls 'at risk', rather than solely upon 'women offenders'. Strong voices in the sector have also urged a new discourse about gender-specific understanding of equal treatment (Prison Reform Trust, 2014). A consistent theme of strategic and local activism from criminal justice VSOs is to challenge fixed categories of 'victim' and 'offender'. Unpicking this dichotomy, and pointing out the harm and neglect that many women who enter the criminal justice have experienced, and the failure of a network of services to intervene, has been at the heart of the sector's strategy for effecting alternative service response (Hayes and Frazer, 2012).

Black, Asian and Minority Ethnic (BAME) offenders

Particular BAME groups are notoriously over-represented in the criminal justice system. In March 2013, 26 per cent of the prison population was from a minority ethnic group, compared with one in ten of the national population (Prison Reform Trust, 2013a: 5). Clinks commissioned a study entitled *Double Trouble* to explore the specific resettlement needs of BAME groups, in recognition of continuing direct and indirect racism across the criminal justice system as a whole (Jacobson et al., 2010). The researchers found that, in addition to the generic practical barriers that face all prisoners, there are often added challenges and nuances in meeting the needs of those from minority ethnic backgrounds. It was recognised that VSOs can have a critical 'bridging' role to play in engendering trust with service users whose experiences may have led them to be mistrustful of statutory services (Jacobson et al., 2010: 5). They do this by delivering culturally sensitive provision and 'personalised services tailored to the needs and circumstances of offenders as individuals as well as members of minority ethnic groups' (Jacobson et al., 2010: 4). For example, the Nilaari Agency, a community-based drug treatment provider that supports primarily BAME adults and young people in Bristol, was created as a result of consultations with service users who did not feel that existing mainstream provision was meeting their needs (Jarman, 2012: 7).

In a recent small-scale study of BAME VSOs more generally, Ware (2013: 1) noted that while most organisations are facing funding challenges, both the service provision of BAME organisations and their capacity to influence strategic decision-making are threatened. There is no consensus in the literature about whether there is a 'distinct and definable' BAME VSO but Ware's (2013: 2) study revealed a view that there is a 'sector', albeit diverse and fragmented. Exacerbated by the economic downturn, Runnymede Trust argues that the work of BAME VSOs working in criminal justice has been reduced to 'fire-fighting and crisis management' (Sviensson, 2012: 7). In a sense, one could think of the plight of VSOs that deliver specialised services to BAME communities as 'triple trouble'. The experience of BAME organisations in criminal justice illustrates not only how a vibrant voluntary sector has evolved to fill gaps at a local level and address entrenched institutional discrimination, but also how a lack of political traction for addressing racism has led to marginalisation of the organisations themselves.

Filling the gaps

Beyond this, there is work by VSOs to address other protected characteristics such as age and disability. Clinks has been increasingly alert to the need to emphasise to policy makers that even a cursory appraisal of the statistical profile of service users within the criminal justice system reveals that an overwhelming proportion of this population has vulnerabilities associated with protected characteristics under the Equalities Act 2010. The sector has also played a pivotal role in highlighting flashpoints and articulating solutions in relation to young people, for example as captured by the work of the Transitions to Adulthood Alliance (Transitions to Adulthood, 2010). An example of a frontline organisation filling an emerging gap within mainstream provision is RECOOP (RECOOP, 2014), which works to address the needs of older offenders at a time when the fastest-growing age group in the prison estate is the over-sixties (HMI Prisons, 2014). It would be fair to say that one of the most distinctive contributions of the sector has been relentlessly to champion the rights and needs of those service users who might otherwise remain invisible to policy makers and commissioners.

Promoting and enabling user involvement

Related to its record on advocacy on behalf of service users is the sector's development of vehicles by which service users themselves can be empowered to have a voice in how the criminal justice system operates. In recent years, there has been an increasing amount of activity both at statutory level and in the sector to promote 'service user involvement' in the criminal justice system. Service user involvement connotes processes by which the people using services participate in their design and delivery to make them more effective, which has historically been less developed in the criminal justice system, as compared with health and social care fields. A Clinks (2008) Taskforce identified a culture and mentality of 'ingrained resistance to the concept of offenders, former offenders and their families as experts' as perhaps the greatest barrier to their involvement in service design and review.

There are many examples, however, of VSOs pioneering projects to include service users in consultative and preventative work, such as prison councils, peer-led housing schemes, listener schemes, prisoner-led education schemes and peer-mentoring and through-the-gate support. An example of this is the SOS Gangs Project, run by the St Giles Trust, which offers intensive support and mentoring to young offenders in London, particularly around gang-related crime, usually provided by former service users themselves. Peer-mentoring projects are designed to be mutually beneficial: the caseworkers bring with them 'first-hand experience of the issues their clients are working through', and, following a six-month intensive training course, they also gain an accredited qualification in Information, Advice and Guidance (St Giles Trust, 2012: para. 3).

Clinks was commissioned by NOMS in 2011 to undertake a review of service user involvement in prisons and probation trusts across England and Wales. The research found many examples of VSOs assisting with and promoting service user consultative groups, particularly in prisons. For example, Age Concern Older Offenders Project was facilitating monthly forums for older prisoners to bring their specific concerns to the attention of senior prison staff (Hayes, 2011: 21). Women in Prison have taken steps to enable service users to contribute to national policy by conducting policy consultations with women while they are held in prison. The nature and extent of this activity were relatively unknown in 2010 and much voluntary involvement seemed to be operating 'under the radar'. However, there are promising indications of greater buy-in from statutory partners and service user involvement seems a growth area in the criminal justice system. User Voice, a national charity led and staffed by ex-offenders, was one of the pioneers of the 'Prison Council' model for including prisoners in democratic participation within prisons. At the time of writing, User Voice has also been commissioned by the London Probation Trust to develop Community Councils, in which users of probation services are elected to engage with staff over improvements, in every London borough (User Voice, 2014).

Conclusions

The voluntary sector in criminal justice is a formidable presence in providing services to offenders that would not otherwise exist. It goes well beyond the minority of larger charities that are perhaps best known to the public, providing a vast range of localised and individualised interventions that, in line with desistance theory, are likely to play a significant role in making communities safer.

The history of the sector's relationship with the state is characterised by a series of false dawns in terms of genuine recognition of its value. Even where new opportunities arise, such as through the *TR* changes to probation services, these are characterised by inadequate opportunities for small and localised organisations, and a very restrictive set of criteria for success. The increasing use of contracts to fund the sector is also having a clear effect on the sector's ability to have an independent voice on policy and practice, at a time when the effects of austerity mean that it is perhaps more important than ever.

Despite the stated good intentions of government, the future role of the sector in delivering this work continues to look far from secure, caught as it is between the various, insufficiently mitigated risks of contracts, and a small and shrinking set of alternative funding sources. Organisations require more flexible support if they are to preserve their defining, holistic focus on supporting offenders as individuals and fostering community reintegration, to the benefit of society as a whole.

The likelihood that tightly defined contracts might miss some of the most significant needs and aspirations of the most marginalised people, along with the sector's roots in communities, probably means that in the longer term the sector will survive these changes as it has others. What is more difficult to predict is whether a sector that divides itself between small isolated community groups and large quasi-corporate structures can provide adequate voice and leadership for the growing numbers of marginalised and alienated citizens. Who will be left to speak for them and offer a vision that builds on their strengths and assets?

References

Barefoot Research and Evaluation (2010) *Support for Women around Northumberland: Project Evaluation*, http://www.barefootresearch.org.uk/wp-content/uploads/SWAN-Report-Single-Pages.pdf [accessed 21/10/13].

Baring Foundation, Civil Exchange and DHA (2014) *Independence Undervalued: The Voluntary Sector in 2014*, http://www.independencepanel.org.uk/wp-content/uploads/2014/01/Independence-undervaluedfinalPDF-copy.pdf [accessed 11/04/14].

Cabinet Office (2010a) *The Coalition: Our Programme for Government*, https://www.gov.uk/government/uploads/system/uploads/attachment_data/file/78977/coalition_programme_for_government.pdf

Cabinet Office (2010b) *The Compact*, https://www.gov.uk/government/uploads/system/uploads/attachment_data/file/61169/The_20Compact.pdf [accessed 23/10/13].

Cabinet Office (2011) *2010 National Survey of Charities and Social Enterprises*, https://www.gov.uk/government/news/2010-national-survey-of-charities-and-social-enterprises [accessed 15/10/13].

Carey, M. and Walker, R. (2002) The Penal Voluntary Sector, in: Bryans, S., Martin, C. and Walker, R. (eds) *Prisons and the Voluntary Sector: A Bridge into the Community*, Winchester: Waterside Press: 50–62.

Centre for Social Justice (CSJ) (2013) *The New Probation Landscape: Why the Voluntary Sector Matters If We are Going to Reduce Reoffending*, London: Centre for Social Justice.

Clinks (1999) *Community-based Organisations and Four Prisons in England*, York: Prisons-Community Links.

Clinks (2000) *Good Practice Guide*, York: Prisons-Community Links.

Clinks (2008) *Unlocking Potential: How Offenders, Former Offenders and Families can Contribute to a More Effective Criminal Justice System*, http://www.clinks.org/sites/default/files/Unlocking%20Potential%202008.pdf [accessed 29/10/13].

Clinks (2012a) *Clinks Briefing on 'Punishment and Reform: Effective Probation Services'*, http://www.clinks.org/sites/default/files/Member%20Briefing%20-%20Probation%20review%20briefing%2010%20April.pdf [accessed 23/10/13].

Clinks (2012b) *Clinks Response to 'Punishment and Reform: Effective Probation Services'*, http://www.clinks.org/sites/default/files/Clinks%20Response%20-%20Probation%20review.pdf [accessed 23/10/13].

Clinks (2013) *Clinks' Response to Ministry of Justice Consultation: Transforming Rehabilitation: A Revolution in the Way We Manage Offenders'*, http://www.clinks.org/sites/default/files/Transforming%20rehabilitation%20consultation%20response%20Feb%202013.pdf [accessed 28/10/13].

Commission on Civil Society and Democratic Engagement (2013) *Non Party Campaigning Ahead of Elections, Consultation and Recommendations Relating to Part 2 of the Transparency in Lobbying, Non-Party Campaigning, and Trade Union Administration Bill*, http://civilsocietycommission.info/wp-content/uploads/2013/10/civil-society-commission-report-WEB.pdf [accessed 11/04/14].

Corston, J. (2007) *A Review of Women with Particular Vulnerabilities in the Criminal Justice System*, http://www.justice.gov.uk/publications/docs/corston-report-march-2007.pdf [accessed 13/08/13].

Daly, P. (2012) *When the Dust settles: An Update*, http://www.clinks.org/eco-downturn [accessed 30/09/13].

Daly, P. (2013) *Economic Downturn: State of the Sector 2013 (October 2013)*, http://www.clinks.org/eco-downturn [accessed 17/12/13].

Farrall, S. and Calverley, A. (2005) *Understanding Desistance from Crime: Theoretical Directions in Rehabilitation and Resettlement*, Maidenhead: Open University Press.

Gojkovic, D. (2012) *Results from a National Survey of Offenders – Why is Awareness and Use of Third Sector Services So Low?*, http://www.slideshare.net/3sectorrc/national-survey-of-offenders-dina-gojkovic-offenders-and-the-third-sector-may-2012 [accessed 15/10/13].

Hayes, C. (2011) *A Review of Service User Involvement in Prisons and Probation Trusts*, http://www.clinks.org/criminal-justice/service-user-involvement [accessed 29/10/13].

Hayes, C. and Frazer, L. (2012) *RR3: A Report of the Task and Finish Group – Breaking the Cycle of Women's Offending: As System Redesign*, http://www.clinks.org/sites/default/files/basic/files-downloads/RR3%20Breaking%20the%20Cycle.pdf [accessed 21/10/13].

Her Majesty's Inspector of Prisons (2014) *Justice Committee Inquiry into Older Prisoners, Submission by HM Chief Inspector of Prisons*, http://www.justiceinspectorates.gov.uk/prisons/wp-content/uploads/sites/4/2014/02/justice-commitee-older-prisoners-inquiry-submission-HMCIP.pdf

HM Government (1998) Compact on Relations between Government and the Voluntary and Community sector in England, London: Home Office.

Hucklesby, A. and Hagley-Dickinson, L. (eds) (2007) *Prisoner Resettlement: Policy and Practice*, Cullompton: Willan Publishing.

Hucklesby, A. and Wincup, E. (2007) Models of Resettlement Work with Prisoners, in: A. Hucklesby and L. Hagley-Dickinson (eds) *Prisoner Resettlement: Policy and Practice*, Cullompton: Willan Publishing: 43–66.

Hucklesby, A. and Worrall, J. (2007) The Voluntary Sector and Prisoners' Resettlement, in A. Hucklesby and L. Hagley-Dickinson (eds) *Prisoner Resettlement: Policy and Practice*, Cullompton: Willan Publishing: 174–198.

Jacobson, J., Phillips, C. and Edgar, K. (2010) *'Double Trouble'? Black, Asian and Minority Ethnic Offenders' Experiences of Resettlement*, http://www.clinks.org/double-trouble [accessed 29/10/13].

Jarman, B. (2012) *Volunteering Case Studies: Highlighting Good Practice in the Recruitment, Engagement and Retention of Volunteers*, http://www.clinks.org/sites/default/files/basic/files-downloads/clinks_volunteering-case-studies_2012.pdf [accessed 02/10/13].

Justice Committee (2011) *The Role of the Probation Service*, http://www.publications.parliament.uk/pa/cm201012/cmselect/cmjust/519/51902.htm [accessed 28/10/13].

Kaufmann, J. (2011) *Funders in Collaboration: A Review of the Corston Independent Funders Coalition*, http://www.citybridgetrust.org.uk/NR/rdonlyres/E32D2A83-79E7-42CB-BFCF-6E5AFF50B86F/0/CorstonReport.pdf [accessed 25/09/13].

Martin, C. (2002) Recent Progress in Community-based Voluntary Sector Work with the Prison Service, in: Bryans, S., Martin, C. and Walker, R. (eds) *Prisons and the Voluntary Sector: A Bridge into the Community*, Winchester: Waterside Press: 63–73.

Maruna, S. and Farrall, S. (2004) Desistance from Crime: A Theoretical Reformulation, *Kölner Zeitschrift für Soziologie und Sozialpsychologie*, 43: 171–194.

McNeill, F. (2012) *Blog: Whose Responsibility is Successful Re-entry?*, http://blogs.iriss.org.uk/discoveringdesistance/2012/11/21/whose-responsibilities-are-rehabilitation-and-reentry [accessed 28/10/13].

McNeill, F. and Weaver, B. (2010) Changing Lives? Desistance Research and Offender Management, *SCCJR Project Report No. 03/2010*, http://www.sccjr.ac.uk/publications/changing-lives-desistance-research-and-offender-management [accessed 02/10/13].

Meek, R. (2012) *The Role of Sport in Promoting Desistance from Crime: An Evaluation of the 2nd Chance Project Rugby and Football Academies at Portland Young Offender Institution*, http://eprints.soton.ac.uk/210815/1/Meek_2nd_Chance_Portland_Evaluation_Final_Report.pdf [accessed 21/10/13].

Meek, R., Gojkovic, D. and Mills, A. (2010) *The Role of the Third Sector in Work with Offenders: The Perceptions of Criminal Justice and Third Sector Stakeholders. Third Sector Research Centre Paper 34*, http://www.birmingham.ac.uk/generic/tsrc/documents/tsrc/working-papers/working-paper-34.pdf [accessed 28/10/13].

Ministry of Justice (2008) *Working with the Third Sector to Reduce Re-offending: Securing Effective Partnerships 2008–2011*, London: Ministry of Justice.

Ministry of Justice (2010) *Integrated Offender Management, Key Principals*, London: Ministry of Justice.

Ministry of Justice (2013a) *Transforming Rehabilitation; A Strategy for Reform*, https://consult.justice.gov.uk/digital-communications/transforming-rehabilitation [accessed 29/10/13].

Ministry of Justice (2013b) *Justice Data Lab*, http://www.justice.gov.uk/justice-data-lab [accessed 21/10/13].

Ministry of Justice (2013c) *Principles of Competition*, http://www.justice.gov.uk/downloads/rehab-prog/competition/moj-principles-of-competition.pdf

Ministry of Justice (2014) *Target Operating Model 3*, http://www.justice.gov.uk/downloads/rehab-prog/competition/target-operating-model-3.pdf, [accessed 21/07/14].

Nacro (2011) *Response to Punishment and Reform: Effective Probation Services*, http://www.nacro.org.uk/data/files/nacros-response-to-the-consultation-on-effective-probation-services-971.pdf [accessed 25/09/13].

NOMS (2012) *NOMS Commissioning Intentions for 2013–14: Negotiation Document*, http://www.justice.gov.uk/downloads/about/noms/commissioning-intentions-2013-14-oct12.pdf [accessed 21/10/13].

O'Connor, T. and Bogue, B. (2010) Collaborating with the Community, Trained Volunteers and Faith Traditions; Building Social Capacity and Making Meaning to Support Desistence, in: McNeill, F., Rayner, P. and Trotter, C. (eds) *Offender Supervision: New Directions in Theory, Research and Practice*, Collumpton: Willan Publishing: 301–322.

Pollard, Fran (2013) *How has Entering Payment by Results Made Catch 22 Better Able to Understand and Respond to 'Risk' in the Public Service Market?*, NCVO blog: http://blogs.ncvo.org.uk/2013/03/11/how-has-entering-payment-by-results-made-catch22-better-able-to-understand-and-respond-to-risk-in-the-public-service-market/ [accessed 08/05/14].

Prison Reform Trust (2013a) *Prison: The Facts – Bromley Briefings Summer 2013*, http://www.prisonreformtrust.org.uk/Portals/0/Documents/Prisonthefacts.pdf [accessed 25/09/13].

Prison Reform Trust (2014) *Why Focus on Reducing Women's Imprisonment*, London: PRT, available at: http://www.prisonreformtrust.org.uk/ProjectsResearch/Women

RECOOP (2014) *RECOOP: Home*, http://www.recoop.org.uk/ [accessed 25/07/14].

Rees, R., Taylor, R. and Damm, C. (2013) *Does Sector Matter? Understanding the Experiences of Providers in the Work Programme, Third Sector Research Centre Working Paper 92*, http://www.birmingham.ac.uk/generic/tsrc/documents/tsrc/working-papers/working-paper-92.pdf [accessed 29/10/13].

Sanderson, N. and Gordon, J. (2002) Prison Service Policy on Voluntary and Community Sector Partnerships, in: Bryans, S., Martin, C. and Walker, R. (eds) *Prisons and the Voluntary Sector: A Bridge into the Community*, Winchester: Waterside Press: 74–81.

Shapland, J., Robinson, G. and Sorsby, A. (2011) *Restorative Justice in Practice*, London: Routledge.

Social Finance (2011) *Social Impact Bonds: The One Service. One Year on*, http://www.socialfinance.org.uk/sites/default/files/sf_peterborough_one_year_on.pdf [accessed 23/10/13].

St Giles Trust (2012) *The SOS Project*, http://www.stgilestrust.org.uk/what-we-do/p491-the%20sos%20project.html [accessed 25/07/14].

Sviensson, K. P. (2012) *Runnymede Perspectives: Criminal Justice v Racial Justice. Minority Ethnic Overrepresentation in the Criminal Justice System*, http://www.runnymedetrust.org/uploads/publications/pdfs/CriminalJusticeVRacialJustice-2012.pdf [accessed 25/03/13].

Together Women Project (2013) *The TWP Gender-Specific Mentoring Toolkit*, http://www.togetherwomen.org/mentoring [accessed 25/09/13].

Transitions to Adulthood (2010) http://www.t2a.org.uk/ [accessed 25/07/14].

User Voice (2014) *London Probation Community Council*, http://www.uservoice.org/our-work/our-services/councils/lpt-council-pilot/ [accessed 25/07/14].

Ward, T. and Maruna, S. (2007) *Rehabilitation*, Oxon: Routledge.

Ware, P. (2013) *Very Small, Very Quiet, a Whisper – Black and Minority Ethnic Groups: Voice and Influence. Third Sector Research Centre Briefing Paper 103*, http://www.birmingham.ac.uk/generic/tsrc/documents/tsrc/working-papers/briefing-paper-103.pdf [accessed 13/08/13].

Wilson, R. J., McWhinnie, A., Picheca, K., Prinzo, M. and Cortoni, F. (2007) Circles of Support and Accountability: Engaging Community Volunteers in the Management of High-Risk Sexual Offenders, *The Howard Journal of Criminal Justice*, 46 (1): 1–15.

Wolfenden, Lord (1978) *The Future of Voluntary Organisations*, Report of the Wolfendon Committee, London: Croom Helm.

Women in Prison (2013) *State of the Estate: Women in Prison's Report on the Women's Custodial Estate 2011–12*, http://www.womeninprison.org.uk/userfiles/file/StateoftheEstateReport.pdf [accessed 25/09/13].

Wong, K., O'Keeffe, C., Meadows, L., Davidson, J., Bird, H., Wilkinson, K. and Senior, P. (2012) *Increasing the Voluntary and Community Sector's Involvement in Integrated Offender Management*, https://www.gov.uk/government/uploads/system/uploads/attachment_data/file/116528/horr59-report.pdf [accessed 28/10/13].

3
Third Tier in the Supply Chain? Voluntary Agencies and the Commissioning of Offender Rehabilitation Services

Mike Maguire

In this chapter I consider the implications of the growing marketisation of criminal justice services for voluntary sector organisations, looking in particular at the expansion of competitive commissioning as a means of delivering offender management and rehabilitation. Until recently, the pace of change in this direction has been slower in the penal field than in many other areas of public services, and most voluntary agencies that work with offenders appear so far to have adapted fairly comfortably to new developments. However, it will be argued that the advent of the *'Transforming Rehabilitation'* (*TR*) initiative (MoJ, 2013), whereby the majority of work previously undertaken by the probation service was outsourced on a 'payment by results' (PbR) basis to 21 'community rehabilitation companies' (CRCs) in February 2015, represents a likely tipping point or step change. While opening up new opportunities for some individual agencies, this will create major risks and challenges for a substantial segment of the voluntary sector.[1] Most CRCs are headed by a large private company (or a partnership which includes a large private company) which manages a 'supply chain' comprising a combination of other private companies, voluntary agencies, social enterprises, cooperatives and/or mutual funds. In such a structure, whose aims and outcome targets are set by public sector commissioners, and whose modes of operation are controlled (in most cases) by private sector organisations, subcontracted voluntary agencies may find it difficult to maintain their traditional values, working practices and independence. Moreover, those left outside the supply chain may find it harder to obtain funding and access.

The chapter is structured as follows. To locate the discussion in a wider context, I begin by noting the frequently articulated wish of

UK governments since the 1980s to involve the voluntary sector more centrally in the delivery of public services, ostensibly as a catalyst both for improvements in the quality of provision and for a broader agenda of 'civil renewal'. I also point out that moves to bring this about have generally taken place within a market framework, where charities are expected to compete for contracts on an equal footing with bidders from other sectors, and to deliver the outputs and outcomes specified by commissioners: many commentators agree that, although this system offers benefits and opportunities, it can create over-reliance on government funding and threats to the character and independence of the voluntary sector. I then look specifically at voluntary agencies working in the criminal justice field, arguing that they face a set of additional challenges which arise from the statutory status of many penal interventions. Charities have a long history of working with offenders on a consensual basis, but have increasingly been asked to deliver interventions (including those specified by the courts) which contain coercive elements – a situation with which some are uncomfortable. They have also faced growing pressure to focus on activities directly related to criminal justice priorities and outcomes, sometimes at the expense of the wider welfare or social justice goals typically expressed in their charitable aims – arguably a reflection of broader social trends encapsulated in concepts such as Garland's (2001) 'culture of control', Wacquant's (2009) 'penal drift', or Simon's (2007) notion of 'governing through crime'. The limited evidence available suggests that most voluntary agencies working in this field have so far been able to cope with such pressure – as well as with the general challenges posed by competitive commissioning – without seriously compromising their principles or values. However, in the final section I argue that the introduction of *TR* will create a new situation which is likely to present far greater threats and challenges.

It should be noted at the outset that the term 'voluntary sector' is used here in its broadest sense. Recent years have seen increases in both the numbers and types of organisations that are neither state agencies nor private companies; indeed, it has been argued that distinctions between them are becoming blurred and we are seeing the emergence of some new 'hybrid' organisational forms (Corcoran and Fox, 2013). This complexity is also reflected in changing labels. The term 'voluntary, community and social enterprise' (VCSE) sector is now often preferred in government literature to either 'voluntary' or 'third' sector. This is the latest in a line of attempts to capture under one heading a highly diverse set of bodies which range from local community groups to national organisations with turnovers of millions; from charities to quasi-businesses; from those run totally by volunteers to those whose executives and staff are all paid; from campaigning organisations to service providers; from those with highly specialised charitable aims (often underpinned by particular ideological positions and strongly articulated values) to those prepared to take on a wide range of commissioned activities; and from those which raise their funds from donations or grants to those which depend almost entirely on competitive bidding for government contracts.

Policy background: the voluntary sector and public services

Over the last 25 years or so, there has been a persistent and intensifying drive by successive governments to create opportunities for non-state organisations to expand their involvement in the delivery of services previously regarded as primarily or solely the preserve of the public sector. The main mechanism for outsourcing such work – common across virtually the whole gamut of public services – has been competitive commissioning, whereby potential providers bid for contracts to deliver a specified set of services and, in growing numbers of cases, a set of target outcomes to which rewards or penalties may be attached. The development of policies to widen and facilitate voluntary sector participation in these processes can be traced through a series of key reports and initiatives that have been launched at frequent intervals since the mid-1990s. These include the *Independent Commission on the Future of the Voluntary Sector in England* (the Deakin Report) in 1996, which set a clear direction for change; the *Compact on Relationships between Government and the Voluntary and Community Sector* in 1998, which set out ground rules and principles; the *Cross-Cutting Review on The Role of the Voluntary and Community Sector in Public Service Delivery* in 2002, which proposed concrete reforms to strengthen the sector, including capacity-building initiatives and the direct involvement of sector representatives in the planning of public service delivery; the creation of the Office of the Third Sector in 2006; the establishment of Futurebuilders (the first of a number of significant capacity-building funds) in 2007; the revised Compact in 2010; and the current Open Public Services agenda, which encourages bids from a wide variety of providers to run mainstream public services (including setting up Free Schools and Academies).[2]

The persistence of such policies can be linked to two recurrent preoccupations of recent governments. The first is a perceived need for public sector reform. From the 1980s onwards, economic policy has been dominated by neo-liberal thinking, with an emphasis on reducing taxation and government spending. It has become a common refrain that the rising costs of welfare are an unsustainable burden on the economy and seriously hamper growth. At the same time, the state agencies delivering public services have been regularly painted as wasteful and inefficient in their use of resources, bureaucratic, inflexible, impersonal and unresponsive, producing poor outcomes for service users. Concrete policy initiatives associated with these arguments have included attempts to make public sector agencies more efficient and effective through various forms of 'managerialism' or 'performance management' (prominent in the Thatcher government's 'Three Es' initiative and in New Labour's 'modernisation' agenda[3]) and, to an increasing degree, the 'contracting out' of services to alternative providers who are expected to deliver them more cheaply and in new ways.

The second recurrent preoccupation involves concerns about an increasing detachment of individuals from community life, including reduced participation in local political processes and the various institutions of civil society. Since the 1990s, there has been a frequently expressed aim of promoting 'civil renewal', 'community engagement' or the 'empowerment' of citizens, underlined by the Blair government's references to Etzioni's philosophy of 'communitarianism', and encapsulated more recently in the coalition government's 'Big Society' slogan (see, for example, Hale, 2006; HM Government, 2010b; Maguire, 2012; Morgan, 2012).

In the light of both sets of concerns, it is easy to see why successive governments have found the idea of a more prominent role for VSOs in public service delivery attractive. Not only are they ostensibly cheaper than agencies staffed by professionals, but they have a reputation for innovation, flexibility and the ability to engage socially excluded clients; many have close links with local communities; and they promote and facilitate the community-spirited act of volunteering to help others. Indeed, a recurrent claim has been that the voluntary sector offers a special set of qualities which, if effectively 'harnessed', can potentially have a 'transformative' effect on the delivery of public services (Etherington, 2006; House of Commons, 2008).

Key debates and concerns

The developments outlined above raise some controversial issues and have provoked a wide range of views both within the voluntary sector and among external commentators. At one extreme, the Association of Chief Executives of Voluntary Organisations (ACEVO), which tends to reflect the views of the larger charities and social enterprises, vigorously supports the opening up of public service delivery to competition and has for many years argued that the voluntary sector should aim to increase significantly its share of the cake (see, for example, ACEVO, 2003). In doing so it has lobbied the government for the creation of a 'level playing field' in competitions for funding, at the same time urging voluntary agencies to become more businesslike in terms of organisation and management: the stark choice being to 'professionalise or perish'. Its consistent message – supported to varying degrees and with varying caveats by other third sector representative bodies such as the National Council for Voluntary Organisations (NCVO) and Social Enterprise UK – has been that a greater voluntary sector presence can both improve public service delivery and offer a healthier financial future for the sector.

At the other extreme, those with serious doubts about the wisdom of going further down this road have repeatedly warned of the dangers of voluntary agencies becoming over-dependent on government funding. It is often pointed out that there has been a significant fall in the amount of funding available through traditional grants (which allow charities to design their own ways of working and have few 'strings attached') and a concomitant increase in competitive commissioning and procurement, whereby the services to be delivered are (often narrowly) defined in advance and put out to tender.[4] Winning such contracts is thus becoming increasingly important to the survival of many voluntary agencies, and they can suffer catastrophic losses of income if a major contract is not renewed. This creates the risk that fear of displeasing commissioners becomes a central factor in determining their organisational behaviour and working practices. Such fear, it is argued, can undermine their independence and their readiness to point out the negative effects of government policies or to speak out as advocates of vulnerable groups. Concerns have also been expressed that if voluntary organisations come to see themselves primarily as contracted delivery agents providing tightly prescribed services, they will lose much of their distinctive culture and value-driven approach, focus too much on targets at the expense of individual client need and ultimately become simply a pale reflection of the public sector – part of what Wolch (1990) presciently called a 'shadow state'. Ironically, too, moves in this direction are likely to stifle innovative practice – one of the core strengths of the voluntary sector which attracted the government to it in the first place.[5]

In recent years, concerns about charities' co-option as agents of the state have been supplemented by new concerns about their growing subservience to private companies. This stems largely from the coalition government's rapid acceleration of policy in several fields from limited outsourcing exercises into the development of large-scale competitive markets in public service provision, in which the private sector is generally seen as taking the lead role, with voluntary agencies as subcontractors. In the words of Benson (2014: 3) in a recent report for the National Coalition for Independent Action:

> (T)he move from grants to commissioned contracts is the single most important factor in the progressive co-option of VSGs ['voluntary service groups'] as servants of state plans and policy and, increasingly, as subservient to the profit-making activities of private companies.

Hemmings (2013: 346) goes further, arguing that the third sector has been deliberately used over a long period as a kind of decoy or Trojan horse, to prepare the way for the eventual wide-scale privatisation of public services:

> The nature of the relationship of voluntary organisations, between the public and private sector, enabled voluntary organisations to act as a staging post in the incremental move of public services from the public to the private sector. While in the public sector managerial initiatives on public service reform continued to be contested, the voluntary sector provided an alternative and a compliant route to break down resistance to privatisation, marketisation and the spread of private sector managerial values and practices.

Finally, Milbourne and Murray (2014: 3) argue that parts of the voluntary sector itself have begun to embrace marketisation too enthusiastically and to behave in predatory ways that further exacerbate the threats to those small and medium-sized local organisations which are striving to sustain traditional values and working practices:

> Disquiet is also evident among many longer-standing, small and medium-sized voluntary organisations that have a history of localised service provision, who perceive a triple threat. Corporations with little experience of, or interest in, specific service users are gaining an increasing share of the scaled-up service contracts, extracting profit from welfare funding and often excluding them from the supply chain. Secondly, new, entrepreneurial, purportedly non-profit, entrants to an area are successfully competing for scarce funding, often with low-priced bids, based on casualised labour and minimal

overheads. Thirdly, there is a growing mistrust of very large charities, for appropriating funding and services, with little regard for the casualties left behind, whether through the loss of local expertise and specialist services as small centres close or the loss of local jobs and volunteer experience.

The criminal justice arena

These kinds of debates have been prevalent in the criminal justice arena as in most other areas of public policy, and I shall return to them in more detail later. First, however, I shall consider some rather different issues which are peculiar to the outsourcing of work with convicted offenders. Most obviously, court sentences and their implementation involve elements of punishment, coercion and control which do not sit easily with the welfare-oriented ethos of many voluntary agencies and staff. There are also issues around risk management and the protection of the public which do not arise with most other kinds of service users. Importantly, too, in both awarding and monitoring contracts, commissioners of offender-related services tend to focus on criminal justice goals – especially that of 'reducing reoffending' – rather than the broader outcomes (such as promoting clients' well-being, empowering the disadvantaged or combating social exclusion), which many in the voluntary sector regard as the primary purpose of their work. In terms of practice, this can put pressure on providers to place less emphasis on welfare services and personal support and to introduce more interventions which accentuate clients' criminal status and are perceived to be more directly aimed at changing their offending behaviour or managing their 'risk'.

It is important to recognise that these issues are not new. Voluntary agencies have worked with convicted offenders for many years, often funded directly or indirectly by the Home Office or Ministry of Justice and in some form of partnership with criminal justice agencies. This has sometimes created tensions and dilemmas, but generally speaking the roles of each partner have been relatively distinct and the differences in aims, values and working practices have been understood and respected by funders. As illustrated below, the situation has become more blurred in recent years as voluntary agencies have become more directly involved in the delivery of court-ordered interventions, creating new challenges for some. However, it will subsequently be argued that such challenges have been minor in comparison to those which will arise as a result of *TR*.

Charities, offender work and the coercion issue

As has often been pointed out, the direct involvement of charities and volunteers in rehabilitative work with convicted offenders has a very long history. Indeed, the probation service grew out of pioneering work by 19th-century 'court missionaries', and until the 1960s most post-release work with ex-prisoners was undertaken by volunteer-based Discharged Prisoners' Aid Societies, whose National Association later evolved into the national charity Nacro[6] – still a major player in the provision of resettlement services. Numerous charities still send workers and volunteers into prisons to offer prisoners help and advice, in some cases funded by individual establishments, in others by government, charitable foundations or sources such as the Big Lottery. Until recently, probation trusts regularly commissioned services such as drug counselling, housing advice, or training and employment services, from a variety of local voluntary agencies.[7] However, it is important to put all this into perspective. In the context of the voluntary sector as a whole, it is only a small minority of agencies that specialise in or have substantial experience of offender-related work (although, as will be discussed later, these are now being joined by growing numbers of 'newcomers'). This includes, on the one hand, those whose services are aimed principally or exclusively at offenders (estimated at less than 1 per cent of all voluntary sector agencies) and, on the other, a larger number whose expertise lies in a specific area such as substance misuse or housing services, which they offer to a range of clients but also attract criminal justice funding by tailoring them for delivery to offender groups.[8] Furthermore, the majority in both the above categories are small, locally based organisations which employ relatively few staff.[9]

Voluntary and coerced participation from the perspective of 'old hands'

Probably the most common form of voluntary sector work with offenders is variants of 'mentoring' or support by volunteers (offered in prison, 'through the gate' or post release) to assist prisoners' resettlement. Agencies with long experience in this include large charities such as Nacro, SOVA and St. Giles Trust (which particularly promotes peer support) and smaller organisations which work in limited geographical areas or with particular groups of offenders, such as women or minority ethnic prisoners. To date (though this changed in 2015 – see below), the bulk of such work has been undertaken on a purely voluntary basis with short-term prisoners, who have not been subject to probation supervision or licence conditions on release. This means that, while collaboration with prisons or probation is often necessary for the purposes of obtaining information about prisoners and contacting and recruiting them as participants, once people leave prison they are no longer under any form of coercion or control from the criminal justice system, and the voluntary agency concerned is relatively unconstrained in how it works with them.

Similarly, participation in rehabilitative interventions (such as group-work, arts projects or drug counselling) offered by voluntary agencies inside prison has always been uncoerced from the offender's point of view (although there may be some pressure to participate in cases where the possibility of early release is at stake).

However, there are also many long-standing examples of community-based interventions delivered by charities which include statutory elements and hence involve them, indirectly at least, in a degree of coercion. For example, the Stonham Housing Trust has long experience of running hostels for ex-prisoners, some of whom are compelled to reside there for a period as a post-release licence condition. For many years, too, voluntary agencies have been commissioned by local probation services to deliver interventions such as drug or alcohol treatment to convicted offenders in fulfilment of requirements specified by the courts when passing community sentences. Participation in such activities is compulsory (albeit in the case of Drug Rehabilitation Requirements or Alcohol Treatment needing the offender's consent before the original order is made) and non-attendance can result in breach proceedings.

Important as they are, such arrangements have traditionally left control and decision-making firmly in the hands of criminal justice agencies, voluntary organisations always being regarded as junior partners. The underlying threat of breach for failure to comply with conditions has therefore remained to some extent distanced from the day-to-day dealings that offenders have with project workers, making it easier for the latter to maintain open and trusting relationships. Certainly, experienced 'offender specialist' organisations such as Stonham appear to be broadly comfortable with the responsibility of monitoring compliance and reporting breaches where necessary to the probation service. There is little evidence that this causes resentment or undermines trust, or that offenders confuse their role with that of probation officers (see, for example, Maguire et al., 2007: 78).

The picture is a little less clear regarding voluntary agencies delivering court-ordered interventions to offenders on community sentences, especially those agencies which also work with a variety of other client groups. This kind of work has both increased in volume and been subject to considerable change since the 1990s. The proportion of probation orders augmented by 'additional requirements' grew from a quarter to a third between 1992 and 2002 (Morgan, 2003), while the introduction under the Criminal Justice Act 2003 of a generic community sentence to which one or more of a menu of requirements could be added by sentencers led to a further steep increase, to the extent that a majority of community sentences now include at least one such requirement. Around 15,000 offenders a year receive sentences including Drug Rehabilitation Requirements or Alcohol Treatment, the delivery of most of which is contracted out to third sector agencies.[10] Anecdotal evidence from informal discussions with current and former probation officers and drugs agency managers and staff suggests that, for many years, it was quite common for such agencies to fail to report missed appointments by offenders who were generally compliant, partly because they saw this as counterproductive to efforts to help them address their substance misuse problems, and partly in order to avoid being seen by service users as too close to the criminal justice system.[11] However, it was generally agreed that such practices became far less common during the 2000s as a result of efforts by probation boards (with NOMS encouragement) to tighten up the wording and monitoring of contracts and to promote more transparent record-keeping systems. This was said to have caused some concerns among drugs agency staff who work with their other (non-offender) clients on an entirely voluntary basis, but the general view appeared to be that, over time, most 'old hands' (in terms of working with offenders) have adapted to the new situation without feeling that they are seriously compromising their principles or alienating clients. Similar views were expressed by experienced voluntary sector staff attached to an Integrated Offender Management (IOM) scheme, where some offenders were likewise compelled to attend their interventions.[12]

Newcomers to the field

In addition to agencies with substantial experience or expertise in working with offenders, there are numerous others which have newly entered the criminal justice field in recent years or are currently attempting to do so. The *TR* initiative has undoubtedly been the major factor in the ignition of what has recently become an explosion of third sector interest, but the sector's desire to work with offenders had already been building up gradually since the passing of the Offender Management Act in 2007, which opened the door to the 'contestability' of core probation services (as recommended by the Carter Report of 2003), thereby laying the foundations for the later emergence of a substantial new 'penal market' (Corcoran, 2008, 2011).[13] During this pre-*TR* period, some important probation services (notably Unpaid Work) were contracted out to private companies, but outsourcing to voluntary agencies progressed more slowly. Nevertheless, a number of relative newcomers to offender-related work began to enter the market by competing for smaller projects funded by NOMS or probation trusts, in some cases clearly hoping to establish a foothold in anticipation of greater funding opportunities to come.

These 'newcomers' range right across the board in terms of size, aims and ethos. At one end of the spectrum are small and medium-sized charities, typically those which already work with a variety of vulnerable or disadvantaged clients. A good example known to the author is a local agency which has for many years offered mentoring and support services to vulnerable women and disadvantaged young people, receiving most of its funding from a combination of charitable foundations and local authority grants. It came more into the orbit of the criminal justice system by being commissioned (partly by NOMS) to provide similar services for female offenders leaving prison, and is at the time of writing bidding to become a lower-tier partner in a *TR* bid. At the other end of the spectrum are a growing number of large charities, as well as 'social businesses' or not-for-profit 'social enterprises', some of which have been recently set up or have been created through mergers between existing voluntary sector organisations. These tend to be more diverse in their activities than local charities, and to see their role primarily as one of 'service delivery' in accordance with commissioners' wishes, in many cases obtaining a large proportion of their funds through competitive bids for government contracts. While pursuing (in name at least) some form of social mission, social enterprises tend to be closer in ethos to private companies than to traditional charities, in that most engage in business-type activities and aim to generate surplus income to reinvest in the organisation.[14] Some of the larger charities and social enterprises (both old hands and newcomers to criminal justice work) have also gained a reputation for aggressive bidding and 'hoovering up' funds previously given to smaller local or specialist charities – in some cases without possessing much expertise or previous experience in the particular type of work concerned (Centre for Social Justice, 2013b; Baring Foundation, 2014; Milbourne and Murray, 2014).

Among the 'newcomers', it is the smaller charities which tend to have the most qualms and doubts about the potentially coercive aspects of working with offenders, some of which have become more overt as the contracting out of services by NOMS and other criminal justice commissioners has progressed. To continue with the example outlined above, whereas the organisation's first forays into working with offenders involved entirely voluntary attendance and engagement, it was later funded to offer services to female offenders as an alternative to sentencing, in which a minimum level of attendance was a condition of diversion from the courts. Although set at a very undemanding level, even this modest degree of 'coercion' caused concerns for an agency whose management team held strong views about the importance of voluntary engagement and 'client-led' services. Moreover, even when the notion of compulsory participation is accepted, lack of awareness of the importance that is attached by the criminal justice system to consistent enforcement practice can also result in broad differences among voluntary agencies in how they respond to non-compliance. For example, in a diversion scheme in which offenders were given community sentences with the requirement to attend a skills course as an alternative to custody, significant variations were found between local voluntary organisations involved in delivering the course, in terms of the reporting of non-attendance to offender managers: in one area, indeed, staff asked each offender group to design its own 'rules' as to what was to count as an unacceptable absence.[15] As will be discussed in the next section, if and when such organisations expand their services under *TR* to work in a statutory capacity with offenders on community sentences and/or post-custody licence, compliance and enforcement issues are likely to loom very much larger.

By contrast, some of the larger voluntary sector organisations (VSOs) (again, including old hands as well as newcomers) appear to be fully prepared to take on responsibility for the 'management' of offenders on a non-voluntary basis. Prior to the advent of *TR*, perhaps the best-known examples were Nacro's (eventually unrealised) partnership bid with a private company to run a new prison, which drew stinging criticism from the Assistant Director of the Howard League, Andrew Neilson, in a widely quoted journal article (Neilson, 2009), and the successful partnership bid between Serco and two large charities (Catch 22 and Turning Point) to manage Thameside prison, which opened in 2012. Neilson commented on the latter:

> If charities are equal partners in decisions on prison boards, they could be implicated in decisions on restraints, segregation or suicide. This could have a reputational risk for the whole sector. The *Daily Mail* would have a field day.[16]

The 'prime and supply chain' model: a step change?

While much of what has been described so far might be seen as illustrating a process of 'creep' towards new roles and new challenges for the voluntary sector in relation to criminal justice, it can be argued that the *TR* initiative represents something of a step change or tipping point. *TR* will almost certainly have a major impact both on individual organisations and on the sector as a whole.

The basic delivery model on which *TR* is based is one in which, in each of 21 'contract package areas', a 'prime' provider is commissioned by the NOMS to deliver a number of specified services and outcomes. In doing so, the prime is expected to put together a 'supply chain' made up of a variety of 'second and third tier' providers, to which it subcontracts aspects of the work. In the case of *TR*, the prime manages the work through a Community Rehabilitation Company (CRC), which is responsible for the management of all medium- and low-risk adult offenders on community sentences, in custody or on post-release licence in the relevant area (those assessed as high risk becoming the responsibility of the new National Probation Service, which remains in the public sector). As noted earlier, most primes are either large private companies or partnerships including large private companies, and the supply chain will be made up predominantly of voluntary agencies. A very similar model was adopted in the Work Programme, which was overseen by the same government minister in a previous post (DPP, 2012).

Another important feature of *TR*, also used in the Work Programme, is the application of PbR principles, whereby the amount ultimately paid to providers is dependent on the achievement of specified targets: in the case of *TR*, reductions in 12-month reoffending rates. Although it has been applied in several other public policy areas, there is as yet very little experience of PbR in the criminal justice field (Fox and Albertson, 2011).

For voluntary agencies, the above changes are likely to accentuate or bring to a head many of the issues already referred to, as well as giving rise to some new problems and dilemmas. While they will also bring benefits for some individual organisations, most published commentary has focused on the potential risks they create for the sector more widely, both in the short and long terms. These include particular concerns about their immediate impact on small and locally based charities, as well as more general worries about longer-term effects on organisational culture and working practices. Some of the main concerns raised are summarised below. As in the rest of the chapter, I am approaching the topic here from the point of view of the voluntary sector: there is much more that could be said about the impact of *TR* from the point of view of other stakeholders, not least the probation service (as was), other criminal justice agencies and indeed the private sector.

Coercion, enforcement and breach: threats to trust and legitimacy?

TR will entail for the first time the transfer of statutory case management responsibilities (albeit excluding final decisions on whether to breach[17]) to private and in some cases voluntary sector providers. While some voluntary agencies may remain at arm's length from case management, providing only brief specialist interventions, others will take on roles involving substantial levels of supervisory contact. For the latter, this raises important questions about the nature of their relationships with service users – or 'offenders', as they will probably come to call them more often – and about possible longer-term effects on legitimacy.

Where relationships with offenders are concerned, the *TR* arrangements will place many voluntary sector workers in a position much closer to that occupied by probation officers, in which – reflecting a long period of 'penal drift' – enforcement and risk management have become central ingredients of the work, and the coercive nature of relationships with offenders is often overt.[18] While it appears (from admittedly limited evidence) that VSO staff who are 'old hands' in work with offenders are often able to maintain their trust even when there is an underlying threat of breach for non-compliance, the general view within the sector is that voluntary participation is a critical factor in successful client engagement and that to achieve it without this requires exceptional skill and experience (Centre for Social Justice, 2013a).[19] By no means all voluntary sector staff who take on work under *TR* will possess these qualities and, particularly if (as seems likely) they are pressed for time due to large caseloads, the compliance issue may undermine attempts to build trusting relationships. Such problems are likely to be particularly prominent in the case of prisoners released from sentences of under 12 months, who will for the first time be subject to statutory supervision (for a period of 12 months) after release. It is well known that such offenders often have complex problems, lead 'chaotic' lives and are notoriously difficult to engage or maintain contact with: indeed, many have received a short prison sentence for the very reason that they have been assessed as unlikely to respond to probation supervision (Social Exclusion Unit, 2002; Maguire, 2007). CRC managers and staff will have to find a balance somewhere between the extremes of strict adherence to guidelines on attendance (which would almost certainly result in large-scale breaching, with an adverse effect on relationships with clients) and 'turning a blind eye' to numerous missed appointments (which, although possibly more conducive to winning client trust, is unlikely to meet with approval from primes, commissioners or sentencers).

The greater involvement of some VSOs in statutory activities involving a degree of coercion may also have a long-term effect on their image – and hence their legitimacy – in the eyes of the public, as well as of other members of the voluntary sector. Many people hold the view that punishment should be both allocated and delivered by the state, and that implementing court requirements and managing offenders sits uneasily with what is perceived to be charities' primary role of helping people. Threats to legitimacy may be further exacerbated by voluntary organisations' close association under *TR* with private companies: again, despite the existence of several private prisons in England, there is still a widespread view that punishment should not be used as a vehicle for the generation of private profit. (For further discussion of such issues, see Benson and Hedge, 2009; Corcoran, 2011; Mills et al., 2011; Maguire, 2012.)

Working practices and organisational culture

Although by no means always clear-cut, there are undoubtedly some basic differences in working practices and organisational culture between the public, private and voluntary sectors. In very broad terms, the public sector model of service delivery is based on principles of universalism, whereby all clients are entitled to a minimum (and are sometimes restricted to a maximum) level of service which should apply regardless of geography or individual circumstance. In addition, it often includes rules stipulating different levels or kinds of intervention for different categories of clients. For example, probation services have for several years followed the principle of 'resources follow risk', which underpins the tier system in the NOMS Offender Management Model (NOMS, 2006). Such principles are commonly translated into standardised work practices (such as formal assessments, written plans of action, regular appointments and comprehensive case notes). On the other hand, the voluntary sector tends to individualise its services to a much greater degree, depending upon perceptions of need, clients' wishes, client–worker relationships, volunteer availability and so on, leading in many cases to irregular patterns of client contact (much of which may take place in community settings rather than in offices) ranging from highly intensive to sporadic, and sometimes reflected in wide variability in the depth and quality of action plans and case notes.[20] As a result, it can be difficult to describe a 'standard' way of working even within a single voluntary organisation. In the words of a witness to the House of Commons Public Administration Select Committee (House of Commons, 2008: 19):

We do discretion. The voluntary sector is not about equity.

Finally, although many other factors are taken into account, working practices in private companies tend to be driven to a large extent by rational calculations about the most cost-effective ways of producing specified results. The work of front-line staff, too, tends to be fairly tightly managed to ensure that they have a clear understanding of the prescribed goals and keep a firm focus on them as they carry out their duties.

In situations which will arise frequently under *TR*, where work with offenders is commissioned by the public sector, managed by a private company and delivered by a voluntary agency, it will be interesting to see how these different approaches interact.[21] One of the issues that has caused considerable debate is that of 'creaming and parking': concern that private companies will decide that, in order to maximise their chances of meeting reoffending reduction targets, they will invest little time and resources (i.e. will 'park') in the most unpromising cases – typically, recidivist offenders with major social and personal problems – and will focus instead on those they judge to need relatively little input to significantly increase their chances of avoiding criminal behaviour (Marples, 2013). Voluntary agencies tend to take the opposite view, that they should concentrate mainly on working with the most vulnerable and needy, recognising that this can be highly resource-intensive and will often produce poor results in the short term, but at the same time knowing from experience that perseverance can ultimately lead to total transformations in the lives of some individuals.[22] Indeed, there is some evidence that, even when they know that their 'performance' will suffer as a result, voluntary agencies will continue to work intensively with those in most need (Maguire et al., 2014).

Clearly, there is potential for considerable friction arising from these differences of views and approach, as many workers in voluntary agencies would be reluctant to reduce the attention they give to those most in need (McGarry, 2013). However, the application of a PbR system in which payment is triggered by a narrowly defined and short-term binary target[23] is likely to encourage primes to engage in some form of creaming and parking, leading to pressure on voluntary agencies to change their working practices significantly. This was certainly the experience of many voluntary agencies taking part in the Work Programme, which applied a similar PbR-based model (Maddock, 2012; Rees et al., 2012, 2013a; Sheil and Breidenbach-Roe, 2014). The Ministry of Justice has insisted that steps are being taken to prevent similar problems occurring in *TR* (for example, by stipulating certain minimum levels of intervention with all offenders), but doubts remain about how effective this will be, as it is difficult to enforce and monitor in practice.

Further potential conflict or disagreement over working practices could arise in relation to the types of intervention offered to offenders. Both public and private sector providers tend to favour 'off the peg' or 'one size fits all' programmes, which staff can be trained to deliver in a systematic fashion to groups of participants. Voluntary agencies, on the other hand, often prefer more individualised, tailored and 'client-led' approaches, based mainly around one-to-one work (Corcoran, 2008; Holloway and Brookman, 2010; Macmillan, 2010; McGarry, 2013). Some primes may ask second and third tier providers to implement, for example, manualised offending behaviour programmes, which research evidence suggests can be effective – and, importantly, *cost*-effective – in reducing criminal behaviour in the short term. These may be alien to voluntary sector workers who are used to adopting more holistic, personalised approaches which are aimed primarily at helping service users achieve greater self-confidence and lead more fulfilled lives, rather than directly at offending behaviour. Just as many probation officers initially opposed the introduction of accredited offending behaviour programmes in the early 2000s, employees of VSOs may be reluctant to go down this new route, especially if – as is likely, given the large caseloads expected as a result of the inclusion of short-term prisoners in CRCs' caseloads – they have considerably less time available for developing trusting personal relationships with their clients. Similar staff resistance has been reported in evaluations of other commissioned services which have introduced standardised packages of interventions (see, for example, Vennard and Hedderman, 2009).

Vulnerability to exploitation by primes

Evidence from the Work Programme, which adopted a similar delivery model, suggests that there are risks that some second and third tier providers will gain little from their participation in supply chains and may be exploited in various ways by their primes, on whom they are reliant for funding. For example, some participating charities did not receive sufficient referrals to trigger expected payments; others were told to act in ways they did not consider were in clients' interests; some, too, had their subcontracts terminated at an early stage for not meeting the challenging targets quickly enough (see, for example, Maddock, 2012; NCVO, 2012; Stuffins, 2012; Centre for Social Justice, 2013a; Rees et al., 2013a, 2013b). These kinds of experiences have given currency to the phrase 'bid candy' as a description of how some voluntary agencies have been used by some of the big private companies: that is, they have been included in tender bids to impress commissioners, but largely sidelined once the contract is won.

Exclusion of those outside the supply chain

It is likely that many voluntary agencies which currently work with offenders, but for whatever reason do not become members of *TR* supply chains, will find it difficult to obtain further funding (either from NOMS or elsewhere) to continue this work, as funders will tend to assume that the *TR* initiative will supply sufficient resources to cover rehabilitative work as a whole (Marples, 2013). Moreover, some of those who currently provide services in prisons may find themselves excluded from access, either because governors decide that the *TR* providers alone are responsible for supplying all the necessary resettlement and 'through the gate' work, or – particularly in overcrowded resettlement prisons – simply in order to reduce the pressures on meeting rooms, escort duties and so on, which will be created when *TR* arrangements are in full swing and CRC staff are dealing with large numbers of short-term prisoners. Both the above situations would have negative consequences not just for the voluntary agencies that were excluded, but for the overall welfare of prisoners. At present, a great deal of 'unsung' resettlement work is undertaken by numerous small charities, funded from a wide variety of sources; it is unlikely that this can be replaced by the *TR* supply chains alone, which are anyway operating on a budget lower than that previously available to the probation service.

Mergers, consortia and shrinking localism

In order to make themselves attractive to primes as potential subcontractors, many VSOs have increased their capacity and geographical coverage by entering into mergers or consortia. This was a trend already occurring throughout the voluntary sector as a result of financial austerity and shrinking grants, as well as the rising costs of bidding for contracts (Rees et al., 2012), but has been given further impetus by *TR*. Such mergers clearly have their advantages, but they can also adversely affect the character and culture of local charities. Many of the smaller charities have strong roots in local communities, as well as close personalised and cooperative links with other local agencies, which can be lost as organisations grow in size, become more competitive and are managed at a distance (Corcoran, 2011; Mills et al., 2011; Benson, 2014). Equally, larger organisations are often more impersonal and managerialist, which may alienate employees used to the 'democratic' staffing traditions of small charities, as well as reducing their attractiveness to volunteers (Rochester, 2014).

Over-dependence on one source of funding

As the competition areas are large, funds acquired by VSOs through *TR* will in many cases form a major proportion of their annual income. Many will also need to take on extra staff to cover the increased workload. This, of course, brings with it extra management responsibilities, perhaps necessitating new specialist posts in human resources, finance, record keeping, and so on. While such rapid expansion may be welcome, it also carries a risk that if the contract is lost after two or three years, the organisation may be faced with an urgent need to cut its spending by more than half and make staff redundant: sudden retrenchment can be highly expensive and may result in some cases in bankruptcy.

Loss of independence, critical voice

In addition to the financial risks, over-dependence on *TR* funds could lead to the undermining of voluntary agencies' traditional independence and the muffling of critical voices, manifested in reduced willingness to speak out on behalf of clients about poor services or adverse effects of government policy. It has often been pointed out that over-reliance on state funding can produce excessive self-censorship, in which charities remain silent out of fear of losing crucial funding (see, for example, Wolch, 1990; Benson, 2014). *TR* potentially adds to this a further disincentive to voicing criticism or concerns in public: the risk of exclusion from supply chains as a consequence of displeasing private sector primes. Indeed, this may not be only a matter of self-censorship. In the Work Programme, a number of charities were persuaded to sign 'gagging clauses' which restricted their freedom to criticise either the prime or the Work Programme more generally (Marples, 2013; Rees et al., 2013a). It is possible that similar clauses will be inserted into *TR* subcontracts by some of the successful primes. The silencing of criticism would be particularly important in the case of the big national charities, whose voice can be relatively influential in policy circles.

Undermining of traditional voluntary ethos

More generally, there is a risk that the sector becomes increasingly driven by the need to win contracts, with less and less attention to how closely what voluntary agencies are asked to deliver fits with their charitable aims and guiding principles – a process sometimes referred to as 'mission drift' (Corcoran, 2011; Benson, 2014). Winning contracts also requires a good track record in terms of performance indicators, which means that managers may become focused on these to the exclusion of broader aims and outcomes, further undermining traditional practices and values. This in turn could result in fewer people being willing to volunteer, as opposed to working for money, in an environment no longer perceived to be primarily value-driven.

Threats to innovation

Finally, it will be remembered that one of the main arguments for greater involvement of the third sector in statutory service delivery has been that this will produce innovative ways of working. However, while voluntary agencies often work in imaginative ways if left to their own devices (as under traditional grant-based funding systems), there are many examples of commissioners over-prescribing how services should be delivered, thereby actively *discouraging* innovation. This is encapsulated in a comment by the manager of a charity contracted to deliver a skills programme:

> Don't prescribe exactly how it has to be done. It's not necessary to micromanage everything because otherwise then they might as well do it themselves. If you want to bring in the way that the voluntary sector do things then allow us to do it. (Pierpoint and Maguire, 2010: 22)

Generally speaking, the coalition government has made efforts to reduce the extent to which ways of working are prescribed by commissioners, replacing process and output targets by outcome targets and giving more freedom to providers to decide how these can best be achieved. This thinking is clearly evident in the plans for *TR*, with the added incentive of PbR. However, it is by no means certain that this will generate the innovation they are seeking either. On the contrary, it has been argued by Maddock (2012), using evidence from the Work Programme, that the supply chain model can actually *discourage* innovation. Sheil and Breidenbach-Roe (2014) further argue that, if applied under conditions where intermediate outcomes are not rewarded, where the price of failure is high, where little research investment is made to test new approaches and where learning is not shared, PbR is likely to deter rather than promote innovation:

> PbR is in part intended to give providers flexibility; by purely specifying outcomes, not the way a service should be delivered, providers are able to try new ways of delivering. Yet the PbR financial model demands certainty of results which runs counter to the scope for failure and learning which is required for innovation. . . .
>
> Without the evidence of what is working, providers are taking unknown risks by trialling new approaches. Given that PbR already transfers risks to providers, adopting unproven 'innovations' would not only fail to manage this original risk, but would also enhance it. In response, voluntary sector providers are less likely to make changes to their ways of working. Instead, providers will manage the PbR risk by maintaining services as they are, seeking efficiencies, or even disinvesting. . . .
>
> PbR does not automatically provide the necessary systems to support ongoing improvement and innovation, from conception and trial, to adoption. The transactional approach it takes is not sufficient to enable new models and new entrants to develop: there is still a very real need for holistic commissioning and for markets to be as collaborative as they are competitive. (Sheil and Breidenbach-Roe, 2014: 22–25)

Concluding comments

Despite the rhetoric of 'contestability' following the Carter report, and the enabling legislation of 2007, the outsourcing and marketisation of offender management and rehabilitation services progressed quite slowly for some time. For the most part, it involved a gradual increase in competitive commissioning (by a variety of local and regional commissioning bodies) of interventions such as training and employment services, mentoring and substance misuse, many of which had anyway been provided to probation boards for many years by local voluntary agencies. Moreover, most of those bidding were still from the voluntary sector, although it was noticeable that these included some large new organisations and some established charities that were keen to expand into offender-related work and new areas of the country, perhaps in anticipation of future opportunities – in some cases displacing experienced specialist local providers. The overall impact of these developments on the voluntary sector was quite limited in comparison with that of the more radical outsourcing policies being pursued in some other areas of public services.

They probably contributed to wider trends such as professionalization, the growth of mergers and consortia, and greater acceptance of the role of voluntary agencies as 'delivery agents' of public services. In addition, a more direct focus by commissioners on criminal justice goals and targets (such as reduced reoffending) and on coerced compliance rather than voluntary engagement may also have contributed a little to general concerns in the sector about 'mission drift' and threats to collaborative working styles and client trust. Nevertheless, the (admittedly limited) evidence available suggests that most agencies experienced in working with offenders were able to adapt to such changes without seriously compromising their principles or undermining relationships with clients.

However, the emergence of *TR* has changed the picture entirely. Many voluntary organisations will now become second and third tier providers in large service supply chains led mainly by private companies. Others who are left out may find it difficult to find alternative sources of funding for offender work, or to obtain access to prisons. Such changes are likely to create major financial, managerial and organisational challenges, particularly for small and medium-sized local charities, which tend to be less well equipped than larger organisations to survive in large competitive markets. As outlined above, they also contain potentially significant risks to the independence, reputation, traditional values, community links, innovative working practices and client relations of a substantial section of the voluntary sector, as it struggles to meet the demands of both public sector commissioners and private sector directors. Ironically, indeed, there is a risk that, rather like the couple in the Aesop fable who killed the goose that laid the golden eggs, there is a risk that a journey that began (rhetorically, at least) with the ambition of 'harnessing' the elusive and fragile qualities of the voluntary sector could ultimately have the perverse effect of stifling them.

Of course, much of what I have said about the likely impact of *TR* – which has been predominantly, though not entirely, pessimistic in tone – inevitably falls into the category of, at best, informed speculation': nothing similar to *TR* has previously been attempted in the criminal justice field. Nevertheless, evidence from marketisation initiatives in other areas (especially the Work Programme, in which a similar model was applied) flags up serious risks to voluntary agencies that could well materialise if little is done to counteract them. To end on a more optimistic note, it is clear that these issues are well understood by many within the sector, which has a reputation for resilience as well as adaptability in the face of change, and there is potentially much that can be done to mitigate their impact. This includes determination on the part of voluntary sector managers to maintain a cooperative rather than excessively competitive or predatory approach to relations with other voluntary agencies; refusal to compromise core values in pursuit of winning or keeping contracts; resistance to pressures to exploit the goodwill of staff and volunteers and ratchet up workloads; continuing efforts to maintain close local community links, even as organisations grow; and courage to 'speak out' when this is felt necessary, even at the risk of displeasing primes or commissioners. The leadership and tone-setting role of representative bodies such as NCVO and Clinks will also be crucial. Finally in the longer term, while it is perhaps inevitable that as the new penal landscape develops, some VSOs will eventually 'morph' into entities which behave little differently than public or private sector agencies, it is also likely that others will find effective new ways of working with offenders outside the 'supply chains' and of continuing the more radical and independent traditions of the voluntary sector.

Notes

1   In this chapter, my primary focus is on the implications and challenges for the voluntary sector. *TR* also has major implications for agencies in other sectors, most obviously the probation service (as was) and other criminal justice institutions, as well as raising broader questions about the privatisation of criminal justice, which I do not discuss here. The most comprehensive academic discussion of *TR* to date can be found in a wide-ranging collection of papers published in a Special Issue of the *British Journal of Community Justice*, vols 2–3, 2013.
2   See, *inter alia*, NCVO (1996), Home Office (1998), Cabinet Office (2007, 2010, 2012), House of Commons (2008), Futurebuilders (2008), HM Government (2010a, 2011).
3   Thatcher's '3 Es' were Economy, Efficiency, and Effectiveness: for a discussion in the context of criminal justice, see Jones (1993). For a broad analysis of Blair's modernisation agenda, again in the context of criminal justice, see Senior et al. (2007).
4   Between 2003/04 and 2010/11, government spending on grants decreased from £5.6 billion to £3 billion, while spending on contracts increased from £10.9 billion to £14.2 billion (NCVO, 2013).
5   Many of the points made in this paragraph have been rehearsed many times in the considerable literature on the topic that has built up over the last decade. See, for example, Harris and Rochester (2001), Paxton et al. (2005), Corner (2006), Seddon (2007), Silvestri (2009), Macmillan (2010), Mills et al. (2011), Benson (2014).
6   National Association for the Care and Resettlement of Offenders. For a brief history, see Goodman (2012).

7   Indeed, until quite recently it was a government requirement for probation areas to allocate a minimum percentage (normally 7 per cent) of their budget to 'partnerships' of this kind. As will be explained later, under *TR* such work will in future largely be undertaken by agencies in the 'supply chains' of CRCs.

8   Based on returns from the 2010 National Survey of Charities and Social Enterprises, the Centre for Social Justice (2013a) estimates the number of voluntary organisations with offenders as their primary beneficiaries at 1475 and the number which work with offenders as part of a wider remit at 13,596.

9   In the above-mentioned survey, 61 per cent reported working at county level or lower, and only 4 per cent reported employing more than 100 staff (Centre for Social Justice, 2013a; for further statistics on this branch of the voluntary sector, see Gojkovic et al., 2011).

10   This represents about 9 per cent of all community orders (Ministry of Justice, 2014, Table 4.4). The management of considerably larger numbers of offenders with a requirement to undertake Unpaid Work is outsourced to private companies.

11   Some even claimed that, despite the existence of a court requirement, the principle of 'client confidentiality' justified refusal to keep probation officers fully informed about offenders' progress.

12   IOM, which in some areas involves the co-location of voluntary sector and criminal justice staff (Senior et al., 2011), provides a good example of the gradual increase in voluntary sector involvement in compulsory interventions which has preceded the introduction of *TR*. Under the Offender Rehabilitation Act 2014, offenders given the new Rehabilitation Activity Requirement can now be required by their offender manager to engage in a range of activities not specified by the courts – a device used frequently by IOM teams to compel participation.

13   The 2007 Act was later used by the coalition government as the main legal vehicle to underpin the introduction of *TR*, despite opposition claims that the new proposals went far beyond the intention of that act.

14   See, for example, http://www.socialenterprise.org.uk/.

15   For example, one group decided that the doors would be shut after 15 minutes and anyone arriving after this point would be reported to Probation for non-attendance (Pierpoint and Maguire, unpublished 2010). This example also provides an illustration of the traditional 'democratic' approach to staff management associated with the voluntary sector (see also Hemmings, 2013).

16   http://www.civilsociety.co.uk/finance/news/content/5180/howard_league_to_tackle_catch_22_over_prison_concerns?Para. 6.

17   Final decisions on breach will remain with the National Probation Service, the remaining public sector part of the old probation service. However, it is not unlikely that such decisions will become akin to 'rubber stamping' for many offenders supervised by the CRCs, as it is CRC staff who control the information about their behaviour.

18   This trend was encapsulated many years ago by Nash (1999) in his account of the decline of the concept of probation as a branch of social work and the entry of the 'polibation officer'.

19   Of course, despite concerns about a general decline in probation officers' engagement skills, despite more rigid enforcement of sentence requirements

and despite their unambiguous position of authority, many experienced offender managers have also continued for years to balance empathy and authority to earn the trust of a large proportion of those they supervise.

20 Maguire et al.'s (2010) evaluation of an all-Wales mentoring scheme provides an example of major cultural differences between partners from different sectors who were ostensibly delivering the same intervention in different regions of the country. One region was managed by staff with a public sector criminal justice background (albeit seconded for the duration of the project to the private company which won the contract) and the other by a voluntary agency. The numbers and patterns of referrals, contacts and activities were strikingly different in each.

21 An interesting additional complication involving intersecting cultures will be that ex-probation officers will be transferred (under 'TUPE' rules) into the workforces of private companies and in some cases of VSOs, where their line managers may have very different ideas about how they should work.

22 In fact, it can be argued that to 'turn round' the life of one individual of this kind has a higher cost/benefit ratio over the long term than to prevent several 'occasional' offenders from reoffending in the short term.

23 The primary target under *TR* is a specified percentage reduction in the 'proven reoffending rate' (i.e. the proportion of offenders in the relevant cohort who are convicted or cautioned at least once over a one-year follow-up period). Further payments may be triggered by a secondary target, a reduction in the number of proven reoffences committed by the whole cohort.

References

ACEVO (2003) *Replacing the State: The Case for Third Sector Public Service Delivery*. London: Association of Chief Executives of Voluntary Organisations.

Baring Foundation (2014) *Independence Undervalued: The Voluntary Sector in 2014*. London: Baring Foundation.

Benson, A. (2014) *"The Devil that has come amongst us": The Impact of Commissioning and Procurement Practices*. Working Paper 6, Independent Inquiry into the Future of Voluntary Services. London: National Coalition for Independent Action.

Benson, A. and Hedge, J. (2009) Criminal justice and the voluntary sector: a policy that does not compute, *Criminal Justice Matters*, 77: 34–6.

Cabinet Office (2007) *The Future Role of the Third Sector in Social and Economic Regeneration: Final Report*. London: Cabinet Office.

Cabinet Office (2010) *The Green Paper, Modernising Commissioning: Increasing the Role of Charities, Social Enterprises and Cooperatives in Public Service Delivery*. London: Cabinet Office.

Cabinet Office (2012) *Open Public Services*. London: Cabinet Office.

Carter, P. (2003) *Managing Offenders, Reducing Crime – A New Approach*. London: Strategy Unit of the Cabinet Office.

Centre for Social Justice (2013a) *The New Probation Landscape: Why the Voluntary Sector Matters If We are Going to Reduce Reoffending*. London: Centre for Social Justice.

Centre for Social Justice (2013b) *Something's Got to Give: The State of Britain's Voluntary Sector.* London: Centre for Social Justice.

Corcoran, M. (2008) What does government want from the penal voluntary sector? *Criminal Justice Matters*, 71 (1): 36–8.

Corcoran, M. (2011) Dilemmas of institutionalisation of the penal voluntary sector in England and Wales, *Critical Social Policy*, 31 (1): 30–52.

Corcoran M. and Fox, C. (2013) A seamless partnership? Developing mixed economy interventions in a non-custodial project for women, *Criminology and Criminal Justice*, 13 (3): 336–53.

Corner, J. (2006) Just another service provider? The voluntary sector's place in the National Offender Management Service, in: Tarry, N. (ed.) *Returning to Its Roots? A New Role for the Third Sector in Probation*. London: Social Market Foundation: 53–61.

DPP (2012) *The Work Programme.* London: Department for Work and Pensions.

Etherington, S. (2006) The transformation of public services – The voluntary and community sector and the criminal justice system, in: Tarry, N. (ed.) *Returning to Its Roots? A New Role for the Third Sector in Probation.* London: Social Market Foundation: 36–43.

Fox, C., and Albertson, K. (2011) Payment by results and social impact bonds in the criminal justice sector: New challenges for the concept of evidence-based policy? *Criminology and Criminal Justice*, 11 (5): 395–413.

Futurebuilders (2008) *Investment Plan 2008–2011.* London: Futurebuilders England.

Garland, D. (2001) *The Culture of Control.* Oxford: Oxford University Press.

Gojkovic, D., Meek, R. and Mills, A. (2011) *Offender Engagement with Third Sector Organisations: A National Prison-based Survey.* Working Paper 61. Birmingham University, Third Sector Research Centre.

Goodman, A. (2012) *Rehabilitating and Resettling Offenders in the Community.* Chichester: Wiley-Blackwell.

Hale, S. (2006) *Blair's Community: Communitarian Thought and New Labour.* Manchester: University of Manchester Press.

Harris, M. and Rochester, C. (eds) (2001) *Voluntary Organisations and Social Policy in Britain: Perspectives on Change and Choice.* Basingstoke: Palgrave.

Hemmings, M. (2013) *Public Service Reform, the Labour Process and Changes in Labour Management in the Voluntary Sector*, Unpublished PhD thesis, Keele University.

HM Government (2010a) *The Compact.* London: HM Government.

HM Government (2010b) *Building a Stronger Civil Society.* London: Cabinet Office.

HM Government (2011) *Open Public Services.* White Paper, Cmnd. 8145. London: Stationery Office.

Holloway, K. and Brookman, F. (2010) *An Evaluation of the Women's Turnaround Project.* Pontypridd: University of Glamorgan Centre for Criminology.

Home Office (1998) *Compact on Relations between the Government and the Voluntary and Community Sector.* London: Home Office.

House of Commons (2008) *Public Services and the Third Sector: Rhetoric and Reality.* Public Administration Select Committee, Eleventh Report of Session 2007–08, Volume I. London: House of Commons.

Jones, C. (1993) Auditing criminal justice, *British Journal of Criminology*, 33 (2): 187–202.

Macmillan, R. (2010) *The Third Sector Delivering Public Services: An Evidence Review.* Working Paper 20. Birmingham University, Third Sector Research Centre.

Maddock, S. (2012) *The DWP Work Programme–The Impact of the DWP Procurement Model on Personal Service Innovation.* Manchester Institute of Innovation Research, Working Paper Series, No. 72. Manchester: Manchester Business School.

Maguire, M. (2007) The resettlement of ex-prisoners, in: Gelsthorpe, L. and Morgan, R. (eds) *Handbook of Probation Studies.* Devon: Willan: 398–424.

Maguire, M. (2012) Big Society, the voluntary sector and the marketization of criminal justice, *Criminology and Criminal Justice,* 12 (5): 483–94.

Maguire, M., Holloway K. and Bennett, T. (2014) *Evaluation of ESF Peer Mentoring Wales.* Social Research 14/2014. Cardiff: Welsh Government.

Maguire, M., Holloway, K., Liddle, M., Gordon, F., Gray, P., Smith, A. and Wright, S. (2010) *Evaluation of the Transitional Support Scheme.* Cardiff: Welsh Assembly Government.

Maguire, M., Hutson, S. and Nolan, J. (2007) *Accommodation for Ex-Prisoners in the South West Region.* Pontypridd: University of Glamorgan and Government Office of the South West.

Marples, R. (2013) Transforming rehabilitation: The risks for the voluntary, community and social enterprise sector in engaging in commercial contracts with Tier 1 providers, *British Journal of Community Justice,* 11 (2–3): 21–32.

McGarry, S. (2013) Why cultural differences between sectors mean probation won't work as a commodity, *British Journal of Community Justice,* 11 (2–3): 103–6.

Milbourne, L. and Murray, U. (2014) *The State of the Voluntary Sector: Does Size Matter?* Working Paper 9, Independent Inquiry into the Future of Voluntary Services. London: National Coalition for Independent Action.

Mills, A., Meek, R. and Gojkovic, D. (2011) Exploring the relationship between the voluntary sector and the state in criminal justice, *Voluntary Sector Review,* 2 (2): 193–211.

Ministry of Justice (2013) *Transforming Rehabilitation: A Strategy for Reform.* London: Ministry of Justice.

Ministry of Justice (2014) *Probation Tables, Q1 2014.* London: Ministry of Justice.

Morgan, R. (2003) Thinking about demand in probation services, *Probation Journal,* 50 (1): 7–19.

Morgan, R. (2012) Crime and justice in the Big Society, *Criminology and Criminal Justice,* 12 (5): 463–81.

Nash, M. (1999) Enter the polibation officer, *International Journal of Police Science and Management,* 1 (4): 360–8.

NCVO (1996) *Meeting the Challenge of Change: Voluntary Action into the 21st Century: The Report of the Commission on the Future of the Voluntary Sector* (the Deakin Report). London: National Council of Voluntary Organisations.

NCVO (2012) *The Work Programme. Perceptions and Experiences of the Voluntary Sector.* London: National Council for Voluntary Organisations.

NCVO (2013) *UK Civil Society Almanac.* London: National Council for Voluntary Organisations.

Neilson, A. (2009) A crisis of identity: Nacro's bid to run a prison and what it means for the voluntary sector, *Howard Journal,* 48 (4): 401–10.

NOMS (2006) *The NOMS Offender Management Model.* London: Ministry of Justice.

Paxton, W., Pearce, N., Unwin, J. and Molyneux, P. (eds) (2005) *The Voluntary Sector Delivering Public Services*. York: Joseph Rowntree Foundation.

Pierpoint, H. with Maguire, M. (2010) *Third Sector (Future Skills) Demonstrator Project Evaluation*. Final Report to National Offender Management Service Cymru, Unpublished. Pontypridd: University of Glamorgan.

Rees, J., Mullins, D. and Bovaird, T. (2012) *Third Sector Partnerships for Public Service Delivery: An Evidence Review*. Working Paper 60. Birmingham University, Third Sector Research Centre.

Rees, J., Taylor, R. and Damm, C. (2013a) *Does Sector Matter? Understanding the Experience of Providers in the Work Programme*. Working Paper 92. Birmingham University, Third Sector Research Centre.

Rees, J., Whitworth, A. and Carter, E. (2013b) *Support for All in the UK Work Programme? Differential Payments, Same Old Problem*. Working Paper 115. Birmingham University, Third Sector Research Centre.

Rochester, C. (2014) *The Impact of Commissioning and Contracting on Volunteers and Volunteering in Voluntary Services Groups*. London: National Coalition for Independent Action.

Seddon, N. (2007) *Who Cares? How State Funding and Political Activism Change Charity*. London: Civitas.

Senior, P., Crowther-Dowey, C. and Long, M. (2007) *Understanding the Modernisation of Criminal Justice*. Milton Keynes: Open University Press.

Senior, P., Wong, K., Culshaw, A., Ellingworth, D., O'Keefe, C. and Meadows, L. (2011) *Process Evaluation of Five Integrated Offender Management Pioneer Areas*. Project Report. London: Ministry of Justice and Home Office.

Sheil, F. and Breidenbach-Roe, R. (2014) *Payment by Results and the Voluntary Sector*. Future of Public Services Series. London: National Council of Voluntary Organisations.

Silvestri, A. (2009) *Partners or Prisoners? Voluntary Sector Independence in the World of Commissioning and Contestability*. London: Centre for Crime and Justice Studies.

Simon, J. (2007) *Governing Through Crime: How the War on Crime Transformed American Democracy and Created a Culture of Fear*. Oxford: Oxford University Press.

Social Exclusion Unit (2002) *Reducing Re-offending by Ex-prisoners*. London: Office of the Deputy Prime Minister.

Stuffins, C. (ed.) (2012) *Open Public Services: Experiences from the Work Programme*. London: NCVO.

Vennard, J. and Hedderman, C. (2009) Helping offenders into employment: How far is voluntary sector expertise valued in a contracting-out environment? *Criminology and Criminal Justice*, 9 (2): 225–45.

Wacquant, L. (2009) *Punishing the Poor: The Neoliberal Government of Social Insecurity*. Durham, NC: Duke University Press.

Wolch, J. (1990) *The Shadow State: Government and Voluntary Sector in Transition*. New York: The Foundation Center.

4
The Voluntary Sector and Public Services: Context, Continuity and Change

Rod Dacombe and *Elizabeth Morrow*

In this chapter we examine the context to some of the current debates over the respective roles of the state and voluntary sector in public service provision. Our aim is to provide an account of recent policy trends in this area, and in doing so to highlight some of the continuities in the history of the relationship between the voluntary sector and the state which might seem, at first glance, to be rather distinct. Throughout, we discuss recent developments in the voluntary sector's public service role in the context of what came before, outlining some of the literature dealing with the contribution of voluntary action to public services before sketching two significant stages in the relationship between the voluntary sector and the state: the influence of the New Public Management on public services, and in particular on the 'mainstreaming' of the voluntary sector into government policy since 1997. Our account is then brought up to date with an analysis of some of the implications of these shifts. Our argument is that there are common threads running through each of these periods which remain influential today, and despite some of the significant changes which have accompanied recent government policy, a genuine appreciation of the relationship between the voluntary sector and the state needs to take these into account.

Our analysis begins with an account of the development of the voluntary sector's public service role, which takes as its starting point the work of Elizabeth Macadam, whose seminal *The New Philanthropy* (1934) provided the template for much of the subsequent discussion of the role of voluntary agencies in public service reform during the middle of the 20th century. Perhaps the most prominent voice arguing for greater state management of voluntary effort in the interwar period, she articulated a vision of the relationship between the voluntary sector and the state which involved public funding of voluntary agencies, whose primary function was to act through coordination by the state in the provision of public services. We suggest that this perspective has resonance with more recent policy towards the voluntary sector, and that an analysis of recent literature in this context reveals some of the continuities in relations which would otherwise not be apparent.

In making this argument, we add to an already rich literature. The last decade has seen a boom in scholarship focused on the voluntary sector's contribution to public services, and a distinct field of research has taken shape. Within this body of work, there is a consistent theme which places discussion of the voluntary sector in the UK in relation to the state, conceptualising the development of the relationship as part of an interplay between the two. This now represents something of an orthodox position in the literature (see Finlayson, 1994; Lewis, 1995, 1999; Alcock, 2010b). As we shall see, there are good reasons for this approach and our analysis broadly focuses on the role played by recent government policy in shaping the voluntary sector's role, and the implications for both voluntary sector organisations (VSOs) and public managers.

The chapter begins with a brief introduction to state–voluntary relations in the UK, focusing on *The New Philanthropy*, its antecedents and its critics, to provide a contextual foundation for the discussion that follows. We then sketch the development of state–voluntary relations, focusing on the effect of recent policy themes on the voluntary sector's role as a provider of public services. The chapter goes on to provide an account of some of the cumulative effects of these developments through a focus on one area of policy, the emergence of the commissioning agenda, before considering the continuities between the New Philanthropic ideas deriving from Macadam's work and current debates over the efficacy of the relationship between the voluntary sector and the state.

Understanding state–voluntary relations

The turn of the 21st century has seen the voluntary sector enjoy high policy visibility in the UK. Despite the voluntary sector's long-established role in the provision of welfare and public services, commentators interested in this area have wasted little time in proclaiming a 'rediscovery' of voluntary action, signalled by a range of policy measures and institutional reforms which positioned VSOs firmly in the public policy 'mainstream' (Kendall, 2003). Typically, this trend has highlighted the role of the state in providing incentives and institutional structures which facilitate the voluntary sector's entry into the public services market.

Clearly, this is not the only perspective on this issue, and some of the impetus for reform has come from the voluntary sector itself – indeed, Pete Alcock has written of a 'strategic unity' within the voluntary sector, based on a concerted engagement with service provision which can be of benefit to both sectors (Alcock, 2010a). However, the most recent changes in the relationship between the voluntary sector and the state have been prompted by government policy to encourage closer relations, and consequently this approach provides the foundation for much of the literature in the area (Lewis, 2005).

This rediscovery has also been driven, to some extent, by an approach to understanding the voluntary sector's role, which rests on the exceptionalism of the UK case. Numerous commentators point to unique features which are contextually important in understanding recent policy in the UK despite the international reach of the phenomenon and the recent growth in the importance of VSOs in public services in several countries (see Evers and Laville, 2004; Bode, 2006). Jane Lewis (1995) notes the extensive literature on state contracting of voluntary agencies in the US, but describes a policy context which is rather different from that in Britain, whereby contracts were developed to reduce state provision rather than expand the reach of welfare services. Kendall and Knapp (1996) also emphasise this idea of a unique relationship in the UK, suggesting that, historically, the voluntary sector has had far closer links to the apparatus of the state than is the case in other countries, raising distinct challenges as the relationship has been formalised. More recently, commentators have noticed the distinctive policy attention on the voluntary sector which has been pursued by successive governments in the UK which has not been replicated elsewhere (Anheier and Kendall, 2001; Kendall, 2003). The challenges this brings for the voluntary sector in the UK are unlike those experienced elsewhere. The sector's central place in government policy, coupled with a funding environment which emphasises purchaser control over finances, has meant that a distinctive tone has developed in relations between the two sectors in recent years.

The origins of this approach have their roots in the development of a subsidiary role in welfare provision for the voluntary sector during the interwar period. Of the numerous commentaries on the dynamics of voluntary action at the time, Macadam's (1934) influential *The New Philanthropy* provides the clearest articulation of the rationale behind these developments. She argues that by the interwar period Britain had developed 'a close interrelation between private philanthropic effort and State control' (p. 17) which was distinct from relations elsewhere. Indeed, the development of this system of cooperation[1] between state and voluntary agencies could be thought of as emphatically British. As Macadam states, 'in no other country in the world can anything on similar lines be found' (p. 17). This very specific phenomenon brought with it particular problems which were to be addressed by a reconfiguration of the way in which the state engages with VSOs.

Macadam was a social worker and academic, and both these roles proved important in shaping her understanding of the working relations between the public and voluntary sectors. Her aim in writing *The New Philanthropy* was ambitious: to provide an account of public and voluntary services which was at once practically focused and would contribute to the literature on voluntary work and philanthropy. In her words, such a task required 'at once a historian, a philosopher, and an experienced administrator' (Macadam, 1934: i). Consequently, she cast a wide net in her analysis, describing the contribution of VSOs in a wide range of different fields, and considering the scope, funding and social value of voluntary work.

Fundamental to her argument was the idea that the voluntary sector's role in service provision is best understood as something akin to that of a subordinate actor, subject to coordination by the state. As Macadam (1934: 27) neatly put it, in an environment of increased cooperation and state funding of service provision, VSOs had 'harnessed themselves to the coach of the State and must obey the reins', seeking guidance from the state over the direction of voluntary effort. From this perspective, there are clear benefits to the incursion of the state into the activities of the voluntary sector, with more direct control over the actions of VSOs necessary in order to eliminate 'muddle and waste' (p. 53). Macadam lauded the work carried out by VSOs, but was concerned that effort might be duplicated, and that the focus of voluntary action might not be in the areas where there was greatest social need. In the second (and probably most significant) chapter of *The New Philanthropy*, she outlines her diagnosis, in essence a problem of coordination. Macadam (1934: 49–50) suggests that the voluntary sector

> resembles rather a tractless jungle. Societies for this or for that take root, flourish or die unchecked according to the caprice of their founders or dictators. [. . .] [A]gainst wastefulness, incompetency, autocratic control, the perpetuation of institutions which have outgrown their usefulness or, on the other hand, the premature winding up of useful bodies for lack of support, there is little redress.

The solution, according to the principles of her *New Philanthropy*, was a centralised and rationalised form of state regulation which would serve to instil 'institutional discipline' amongst all parties. The development of bureaucratic structures for coordinating voluntary sector activities and rationalising funding for services would help to ensure that the energies of voluntary action were focused in the right direction and, crucially, that the partnership (Macadam's term) between the voluntary sector and the state might be organised to ensure that the respective strengths of each sector were harnessed. This is not to say, however, that the voluntary sector was simply to act as a meek arm of the state, silently taking direction from a central bureau. Significantly, Macadam's vision included roles for the sector as a democratic buffer against state domination of the social sphere, as well as a lobbying function, directing the attention of the state towards areas of the most pressing need (Whelan, 1999).

Dissent to the perspectives provided by *The New Philanthropy* followed almost immediately. Previously, writing on the role of voluntary action in welfare had relied upon a principle of complementary (but institutionally separate) action between the state and the VSOs. Sidney and Beatrice Webb (2010[1912]), for example, imagined this relationship as an 'extension ladder', and the arena of voluntary action, while sharing similar social aims to the state, was thought to be institutionally separate, acting in areas where the state could not meet demand or where new areas of need were identified. Voices within the sector signalled dismay at the challenge to this tradition from Macadam and raised concerns over the inability of VSOs to compete with state provision and, particularly, the danger of a loss of independence which accompanied increasing direction by the state (Kendall and Knapp, 1996; Whelan, 1999).

The genie was out of the bottle, however, and it is clear that the environment described by Macadam became more prominent in the years that followed. Jose Harris (1993) notes that during the early part of the 20th century, VSOs operated largely independently of state interference. There was little by way of regulation and few VSOs received funding from the public sector. However, the economic, social and political pressures that followed the 1914–18 war began to set the scene for significantly closer relations between the state and the voluntary sector. The interwar period saw an increase in funding of voluntary services by local authorities in particular, and the period was characterised by a growth in cooperation between the sectors in service provision (Thane, 1982). It was this shift which Macadam recognised and described in her work – she was at pains to emphasise that the analysis in *The New Philanthropy* was based on the reality of changes which were already taking place. This insurgence of the state into welfare probably reached its zenith with the great swathe of reforms that followed the election of the Attlee Government in 1945. These reforms effectively relegated the voluntary sector to that of a 'junior partner' where they were of secondary importance in public service provision (Kendall and Knapp, 1996). The most zealous proponents of the reform programme were confident that the result would be a withdrawal of voluntary action from the welfare sphere leaving the voluntary sector to a marginal role (Deakin, 2001). By contrast, there were others who argued that an independent, active voluntary sector was essential not only to a properly functioning system of welfare, but to citizenship and social life (Ware, 1989; Whelan, 1999).

This expansion of state provision vexed even one of the architects of post-war state expansion, William Beveridge, who voiced concerns in his publication *Voluntary Action* (1948), echoing the arguments made by the Webbs decades before. Beveridge was interested in identifying a role for VSOs which allowed them to remain distinct from the state. He also highlighted areas where needs were not being met by public agencies – gaps he acknowledged could be filled by voluntary action. Like many other commentators of the time, Beveridge's concern was that the speed and scope of the changes in the state's role in areas such as education and social insurance were, while often appropriate, fundamentally altering the nature of voluntary action. Accordingly, increasing state control challenged the voluntary sector's conventional roles, and this had wider social implications which reached beyond the scope of service provision (Kendall and Knapp, 1996). As he put it, 'ceaselessly the state has extended its activity in fields in which voluntary action has pioneered' (Beveridge, 1948: 301). The uncertainty caused by the increasingly visible hand of the state is, as we shall see, something that concerns even contemporary commentators.

These debates inform us about the development of the dynamics of state–voluntary relations in the UK, and their relevance to the discussion of contemporary relations between the sectors will be clear to observers of contemporary policy. The principal elements of Macadam's work – the exceptionality of the British case which required an institutional environment which is unique; the notion of a distinct value brought by VSOs; the perceived need for state-coordinated voluntary action, particularly when funded by the state; and the centralisation of institutional structures governing state–voluntary relations – reverberate through subsequent analyses of the voluntary sector's public service role.

This brief sketch of debates held in the mid-20th century about relations between the state and the voluntary sector demonstrates the importance of contextualising the recent trajectory of government policy on the voluntary sector. For example, the emergence of philanthropic action, and the attempts made to coordinate the activities of charitable organisations as a result, laid the foundations for the modern welfare state. Furthermore, as Billis and Glennerster (1998: 80) suggest, the recent scholarly preoccupation with the emergence of a 'mixed economy of welfare' has a deep-rooted history in the UK that is often overlooked, pointing out that 'the state in Britain came relatively late to the provision of human services, and only since 1945 to a dominant role'.

These historical debates can be useful in helping us to understand contemporary concerns over the direction of state–voluntary relations. It is not hard to see continuities between Macadam's desire for coordination and the more recent attempts to account for the activities of VSOs through contracting and to coordinate work through service planning. Her critics are echoed too; the emergence of a complex process of commissioning the voluntary sector for contractual work has, for some, resulted in an unstable funding environment for VSOs (Kramer, 1994; Lewis, 2005). Further, the increased bureaucracy which has come with monitoring contract compliance has raised concerns about the impact of VSOs to focus on their core mission (Deakin, 1996; Milbourne, 2009; Dacombe, 2011). However, at the same time, there can be no doubt that the increased role of VSOs in public service provision has driven the rapid growth in the number of VSOs active in the public service arena and opened up new areas of activity because of the ability of VSOs to quickly meet demand (Alcock, 2010b), a point which echoes the increased resources made available through subcontracting from the state in the post-war era (Whelan, 1999).

Clearly then, the turbulent period in the relationship between the voluntary sector and the state, which has accompanied more recent policy changes, has not happened in a vacuum and should not be analysed in isolation from its history. In particular, the state's position in the welfare mix, although relatively constant in the period following the post-war reforms, has not always been one of dominance. Rather, the tale here is one of interdependence. It is the interplay between different actors – a notable feature of recent policy developments – that marks out the longer-term development of voluntary action in Britain. From here, the chapter examines these debates in the context of more recent policy towards the voluntary sector.

Welfare reform, New Public Management and the voluntary sector

The putative consensus that had prevailed in the post-war welfare state in the UK came to an end with the election of the first of a series of

Conservative Governments in 1979. The new administration embarked on a campaign of restriction and redefinition of the state's role, a move which gathered pace in subsequent years, particularly after the 1987 general election. In some ways, the reform programme which followed represented a glance back to an earlier era of atomised service provision by a variety of providers which had existed before the Second World War, as well as a (partial) embracing of neo-liberal critiques of the state's role in public services. Fundamentally, the aim was to inject an element of marketisation into the welfare state. Strongly influenced by the New Public Management agenda (Hood, 1995) the structural changes in public services during this period represented the most sustained period of welfare reform since Beveridge's time. Some of the most significant changes that occurred during this period had far-reaching implications for relations between the voluntary sector and the state. The social programme implemented by successive governments from the 1980s to the present opened up new opportunities for VSOs to become involved in service provision, albeit on vastly different terms than those previously in place.

Numerous commentators have noted that the breadth and scale of reform during this time were astonishing, with the shifts taking place to service delivery in (to name a few) education, personal social care and primary healthcare, forming part of a radical agenda for change (Osborne and Gaebler, 1993; Ferlie et al., 1996; Newman, 2001). The mechanisms of reform were closely modelled on principles deriving from New Public Managerialism:

(i) A separation of the roles of purchaser and provider;
(ii) The introduction of choice in the operation of welfare markets;
(iii) The importance of the contract in framing relations between actors.

These principles have remained the basis of the orthodoxy surrounding public service reform. For instance, the use of contracts has continued to grow and spread raising concerns about their impact on the voluntary sector. The focus of these concerns has been about the increasing formalisation of relations between VSOs and the state and the potential loss of independence for VSOs (Lewis, 1999, 2005).

Despite the radical and far-reaching agenda pursued during this period, it would be wrong to characterise this agenda as working to break down monolithic state provision into something entirely new. Despite the formalisation of the state's role in providing services in the post-war period, VSOs have played an important role in public service provision, and there is ample evidence to suggest that the close relationship between the voluntary sector and public agencies in service delivery identified by Macadam and others persisted during this period (Kendall and Knapp, 1996). The significance of the reforms of the late 1980s, instead, rests in part on the challenges presented to the established relations between VSOs and the state. These challenges focused on the reform of both the logic of relations (with the voluntary sector increasingly viewed as part of a range of market alternatives to state provision of services) and the emerging forms of accountability that the voluntary sector was expected to satisfy – (with the emphasis on contracts resulting in increasingly formal relations developing across a wide range of public service areas).

Beyond this, it is significant that the changes to the public service environment enacted during the late 1980s and early 1990s were in no way uniform. That is to say, the development of marketisation in public services has been inconsistent across the spectrum of different service areas (Deakin, 1996). For example, one of the basic tenets of public service reform – the separation of purchasers and providers of services – has taken on a variety of forms in different sectors. In personal social care, the development of quasi-markets based on the public sector contracting organisations (usually from the private or voluntary sectors) to provide care services is characteristic of the reform programme. Elsewhere, in healthcare, the split between purchaser and provider took the form of GP fundholding, where responsibility for spending was devolved to the level of local doctors. As a result of initiatives like these, the relationship between the state and the voluntary sector has been affected by reform in different ways depending on the sector.

Public service reform during this period also required significant changes in the roles played by public managers. From the mid-1990s, there was a growing realisation that in order for the government's programme of marketisation to function correctly, some degree of public management or oversight of the structure and functioning of markets was necessary (Ferlie et al., 2011). This implied new roles for public agencies, with public managers becoming increasingly responsible for the management of markets in the public service arena, taking on a range of new tasks including identifying potential providers, building market infrastructure, establishing service need, collaborative planning with other purchasers as well as contract specifications and monitoring (Bovaird, 2006).

Considering these developments, we can sum up the period from 1979 to 1997 as one of dramatic change to the public services environment.

In many ways, a necessary function of many of these changes was the formalisation of relations between the voluntary sector and the state. This occurred in a number of areas but is particularly associated with shift in the form of funding, with a growth in purchase of service contracts (and the formalisation of accountability inherent in this process), and the conceptualisation of the role of VSOs as market-like providers that needed to demonstrate their ability to compete alongside other organisations (in effect, to develop a competitive advantage).

Despite the apparently radical departures that were implied by this era of reform, it is possible to detect continuities with previous thinking about the voluntary sector's role. Macadam would have recognised aspects of voluntary–state relations that emerged during this period. Indeed, she predicted the rise of state funding and the subsequent control it exerts over voluntary action, while suggesting that it could bring benefits to VSOs as 'the receipt of public funds is regarded as an outward and visible sign of a certain standard of efficiency' (1934: 38–39). While the mechanisms of state control over the activities of the voluntary sector had changed somewhat – Macadam prescribed centralised institutions, rather than locally based contractual controls – similar concerns about the capture of the voluntary sector by the state which initially greeted Macadam's work in the 1930s were also observable half a century later (Kramer, 1994).

New Labour and the partnership agenda

Soon after New Labour's 1997 election victory, it became clear that the public services environment established by its Conservative predecessors was not going to change dramatically (Knapp et al., 2001; Newman, 2001). Contracts remained the principal arbiter of relations in service provision and, indeed, most of the elements of marketisation were retained (Ferlie et al., 1996). However, some differences in approach did emerge. These included a wider range of market relations being embraced as a basis for service provision, particularly (in an echo of the language of *The New Philanthropy*) the revived language of 'partnership' and collaborative working between agencies (Lewis, 2005; Bovaird, 2006). Significantly, the voluntary sector was to become a central focus of New Labour's public service agenda, providing a convenient means of signalling a break with the 'old Labour' statism whilst also claiming to avoid worst excesses of the market (Kendall, 2003).

The development of partnership as a policy theme had far-reaching implications for the voluntary sector's role as a service provider.

A particular focus has been on the idea of partnerships as collaborative service provision (Huxham, 1996), reflecting the decentralising tendencies of that period (Wilson and Game, 2002) and, significantly, as indicating a predilection for networks, rather than hierarchies, as the preferred mode of governance in public services (Ferlie et al., 2011). Jane Lewis (2005) notes that as a mode of governance, 'partnership' has a particular resonance for the voluntary sector because it seeks to engage VSOs directly in activities that until recently have been undertaken by the state, such as service planning and the identification of need. However, as she suggests, the sector's role in these activities is far from certain – as Dahrendorf (2001) points out, there is a persistent danger of co-opting VSOs into the agenda of the state, pulling them into closer institutional proximity than was previously the case.

It is important to note that the emergence of 'partnership' as one of the dominant narratives of New Labour's social programme occurred within a context of broader attempts by the government to reform its relations with the voluntary sector. A significant aspect of this included moves to enhance the voluntary sector's capacity to engage in public service provision. This focused on changes in policy but also took in moves towards investment in the voluntary sector's infrastructure, with significant funding invested in the sector at the local, regional and national level through initiatives such as the CapacityBuilders programme (initially ChangeUp) (Macmillan, 2011). Similarly, the (now defunct) FutureBuilders programme, set up in 2004, provided grants and loans to VSOs to build up their skills and expertise to bid for, and deliver, public service contracts (Macmillan, 2011).

Beyond this, a number of high-profile policy reviews placed the voluntary sector near the top of the government's agenda (HM Treasury, 2002, 2005). At the same time, references to the voluntary sector begun to appear alongside the government's wider policy agenda. Take, for example, the official guidance accompanying the Local Government Act 2000, which specifically encouraged the co-option of representatives from VSOs into local authority committees (DETR, 2001). Elsewhere, the voluntary sector was seen as essential to determining the shape of service provision in areas as diverse as crime and disorder, education and healthcare (Kendall, 2003). Arguably, the most significant signal of a shift in relations between the state and the voluntary sector was the development of the Compact (Kendall, 2000) or formal agreement, governing working relations between the state and the voluntary sector. Adopted by central government early in New Labour's first term, and widely replicated locally, the Compact was heralded as a significant breakthrough in relations and the most obvious indicator that the voluntary sector enjoyed a more prominent place in the government's thinking (Osborne and McLaughlin, 2002).

The Compact contained 'Codes of Good Practice' which dealt with specific (usually contentious) areas of relations between the voluntary sector and the state partly in order to ease its passage into the everyday working practices of the organisations which choose to sign up. For example, one of these dealt with funding and procurement, ensuring that participating organisations enshrined principles such as transparency, the recovery of full costs in contracting, good governance and adequate notice of the termination of funding, into their financial relations. The effectiveness of the Compact has been the subject of much debate in the literature, with particular discussion over the document's lack of legal 'teeth' (Osborne and McLaughlin, 2002). The implementation of the Code of Practice dealing with funding and procurement practice has provided a particularly interesting window into the ways in which relations between VSOs and the state work in practice. As Murray (2008) indicates, it is this code of practice which is significantly more likely to be breached than any other elements of the Compact package.

Taken together, these developments both cemented and altered the changes in state–voluntary sector relations that occurred under the preceding Conservative governments. The importance of state contracts as a source of funding to the voluntary sector, as well as the role of VSOs in public service delivery, increased. However, a number of distinctive developments also arose. The emergence of the partnership agenda meant that the myriad relations between public officials and VSOs added, and have continued to inject, a different tone to service delivery, with a particular emphasis on the rhetoric of 'joint working' and 'needs assessment' rather than instrumental service delivery.

It is clear that the changes sketched out above had significant implications for state–voluntary sector relations in service provision. It has also been suggested that these changes have brought about fundamental challenges to the 'purchaser–provider' dichotomy previously used as the basis for discussion of public service provision (Lewis, 2005). In essence, the idea of a 'principal–agent' relationship, with a single purchaser contracting services from providers drawn from a range of market actors, does not always seem appropriate in the context of the kinds of social reform pursued by the government over recent years. It is possible to identify four distinct challenges to these respective roles that resulted from the trends in public service reform outlined above.

First, alongside the many opportunities for engagement in service provision that have opened up in recent years, the place of VSOs in public services during this period has grown increasingly prominent in policy terms. Consequently, the shifting expectations of varying governments has meant that public officials have needed to balance sometimes long-standing relations with VSOs with the need to develop a competitive market, and adapt to new narratives emerging in government policy. Second, the variation in the development of marketisation in public services has meant that this growth in the voluntary sector's role in provision was focused on only a few areas. As Kendall (2000) notes from the mid-1990s, the growth in the voluntary sector's welfare role primarily occurred in a distinct number of service areas (such as day care, housing and education). The implication of this is clear; the voluntary sector's growth has been largely driven by the needs of the state. Therefore, the timbre of relations between officials and the voluntary sector has varied, depending on the service area concerned. Third, accompanying these developments was an increase in the costs to the voluntary sector of its relations with the state. These costs included the growth in uncertainty throughout the sector, particularly with the risk of loss of funding that comes with an increasing reliance on competitive tendering for contracts (often, until relatively recently, on an annual basis). At the same time, the new funding environment resulted in greater monitoring costs and bureaucracy and direct costs incurred in preparing contract tender submissions (Lewis, 1999). Finally, the implementation of the public service reform agenda did not run as smoothly as expected. In many areas, the generation of competitive markets proved difficult, with the diversity of providers essential to competition proving hard to achieve (Deakin, 1996). As a result, the job of public officials has broadened from simply one that focused on making decisions about which providers to choose for a particular service towards a more complex role involving knowledge of the local market, needs assessment, connection with potential local providers and capacity building.

The commissioning agenda and its implications

The pressures on VSOs and on the public sector have ensured that altering public management practice in managing markets for public services has been a high priority in recent policy. With this in mind, it is perhaps unsurprising that a particular feature of recent trends in public service reform has been a consolidated attempt to refine the public manager's role in this new environment, while at the same time curbing some of the unintended consequences of marketisation for the voluntary sector. Primarily, this has been associated with the various attempts to reframe public sector procurement and marketisation as 'commissioning' and it is to this topic that this section now turns.

The idea of commissioning is broad-reaching and ill-defined. Although commissioning is a prominent theme in government policy, there is no overarching, cross-governmental approach to its definition or implementation. Alongside this, there is a conspicuous absence of scholarly attention to its concepts and practice, and especially with its application/applicability to the voluntary sector. Instead, there is a tendency for the term 'commissioning' to be used in a poorly defined manner, often conflating the idea with 'procurement', and rarely spelling out the breadth of use of the term elsewhere. Most fundamentally, across central government there is a clear and consistent separation of the ideas of procurement and commissioning. For the Cabinet Office (2006: 4) procurement is one element of a broader commissioning process, which focuses 'on the process of buying services, from initial advertising through to appropriate contract arrangement'. Commissioning, conversely, is far wider in its scope, and involves 'assessing the needs of people in an area, designing and then securing appropriate service'. Elsewhere, the Department of Health followed a similar approach, describing commissioning as 'a complex process with responsibilities ranging from assessing population needs and prioritising health outcomes, to procuring products and services, and managing service providers' (Glasby, 2012: 5).

To an extent, the lack of clarity reflects the fact that, despite its high profile, the commissioning agenda has not been defined or supported by legislation or coherent, wide-reaching policy narratives. Instead, its development has been rather piecemeal. The emergence of 'commissioning' can be traced through a variety of initiatives, announcements and discussion documents, often articulated through a dominant reformist discourse. By and large, the aim has been to influence practice across central and local government by outlining policy, providing good practice guidance, or through training provision. Commentators have noted the lack of clarity. For example, Knapp et al. (2001) consider commissioning to mean the range of interactions in public service markets, including, but not limited to, procurement, and varying depending on the tone of relations. Murray (2008) suggests that distinguishing between 'commissioning' and 'procurement' is at the heart of government policy, but has not been wholly accepted in practice, noting several examples where these two activities are considered synonymous. Unwin (2004) also notes that the two ideas may be quite separate in practice, as commissioning does not necessarily result in 'procurement' in the form of contracts, but perhaps a grant, investment or donation. Clearly then, an understanding of this distinction is fundamental to discussion of commissioning in policy and practice.

A second strong element of the commissioning agenda is the promotion of networks as essential to the effective management of public service markets. For example, the Department of Health (2009) – where commissioning has perhaps the highest profile of all central government departments – has adopted a programme aimed at developing its staff into 'World Class' commissioners. Directly influenced by the White Paper, *Commissioning a Patient-Led NHS* (DoH, 2005), there are four key elements to this programme – a 'vision' outlining its aspirations for commissioning, a number of commissioning competencies, an assurance system, and a support and development framework for commissioners. The competency framework included in the World Class Commissioning programme reveals much about the importance of networks to the commissioning agenda. This includes: specific requirements for commissioning organisations to work with other actors in the community; engage the public and patients in the commissioning process; collaborate with clinicians; stimulate the market to promote a diversity of providers; and maintain appropriate relationships and contracts with providers. The underlying theme of much of this is that commissioners are being asked to carry out their work in close proximity to a range of other actors. The importance of networks is stressed by other commissioning initiatives. The Department of Communities and Local Government (DCLG), in their Eight Principles of Good Commissioning, highlight the importance of a partnership approach, with specific reference to the involvement of the voluntary sector in providing specialist knowledge and information on local needs (DCLG, 2006). In essence, the importance of open dialogue between all interested parties in service provision, not simply between 'purchasers' and 'providers', is clearly apparent.

A third aspect of the agenda is the centrality of needs assessment in the commissioning process. Almost every example of recent central government policy dealing with this area has emphasised the importance of establishing need as part of the practice of commissioning (see DCLG, 2006; Department for Education and Skills and Department of Health, 2006; Department of Health, 2007; Department for Work and Pensions, 2007; Home Office, 2011). The Audit Commission (2007: 6) places needs assessment at the heart of what they describe as 'Intelligent Commissioning', vitally important to commissioners' understanding of local markets and central to good procurement practice. Effective needs assessment is clearly related to the requirement to develop networks with local providers, and the voluntary sector in particular. The positioning of needs assessment alongside the other elements of the commissioning process is significant, with this activity required before and after the procurement of services. To this end, commissioning is often described as a cyclical process. A dizzying array of cycles is present in the guidance emanating from government, and in the embryonic literature on the subject (see DCLG, 2006; Department for Education and Skills and Department of Health, 2006; Department of Health, 2006, 2007; Department for Work and Pensions, 2007; Home Office, 2011). Primarily, however, they all serve to conceptualise commissioning as an ongoing activity, with service design, procurement, delivery and monitoring all built around the continual assessment of need.

A further element of the commissioning agenda has been the provision of training and support for public sector practitioners. This has been the primary objective of some of the elements of recent government policy and was clear in the implementation of many other areas (see Department of Health, 2006, 2007; DCLG, 2006). Perhaps the most obvious example of this was the then – Improvement and Development Agency's (IDeA) National Programme for Third Sector Commissioning (IDeA, 2008). Under this scheme, public sector employees received formal training in the principles and practice of commissioning services from third-party organisations, normally from a higher education institution. The programme was aimed at the 'top 2000' commissioners from across central government, and had a specific focus on ensuring that public managers were able to understand the value and needs of the voluntary sector, involve VSOs more closely in the commissioning process, and provide support to improve the bidding practice of VSOs. Indeed, on this final point, the success of the agenda was also dependent on relations with the voluntary sector. The Audit Commission (2007: 36) suggests that for commissioning to be successful, specific changes need to take place in local practice, noting that 'capacity building is unlikely to result in a significant expansion in the voluntary sector's share of the service delivery market unless local public bodies accompany this with effective commissioning practice'.

Despite these four pillars of the commissioning agenda, its translation into practice remains unclear. In part, this is an issue of evidence; it is difficult, from the existing body of research, to discuss the implementation of commissioning with any certainty, a situation unlikely to change without further scholarly attention. An examination of commissioning can be instructive as an example of the net effects of change on the relationship between the voluntary sector and the state on both actors. For VSOs, the kinds of relationship with the state that have developed in recent years have brought both dividends and peril. If we believe that the trajectory of government policy is moving towards greater control and coordination of voluntary action, of the kind that Macadam (1934) envisaged, then we might interpret the commissioning agenda as an attempt to ensure the adequate management of public services at a devolved level. If, conversely, it is understood as aligned with attempts to preserve the values and independence of voluntary action which characterised policy in the New Labour era, then it is possible to understand initiatives like commissioning as attempts to reclaim previous relationships, where the complexities of market management and competition between voluntary agencies are less important than the virtues of the providers themselves. There might also be a technocratic explanation for this kind of initiative; perhaps the introduction of commissioning can be best understood as a means of mitigating the demands on public managers, given the changes marketisation has brought to their roles.

In reality, it would be difficult to come to any of these conclusions without an appreciation of the recent history of the voluntary–state relationship because there is a thread running from Macadam to the present day which reflects the concerns of current policy. Tension and debate of the kind prompted by the suggestion of centralised forms of state control over the actions of VSOs, rather than being diluted in recent years, has instead been amplified first by marketisation, and then by the increased policy attention which arose with the partnership agenda. Viewed in abstract, each of these developments can be seen as radical changes in the terms of the relationship. In context, the dilemmas they raise for both the voluntary sector and the state appear as part of a much older set of arguments.

Conclusion: context, continuity and change

The voluntary sector today is not the same as the patchwork of organisations that existed in the interwar period, and the relationship that it maintains with the state must be thought of as distinct from that described by Macadam (1934). Much has changed since Macadam was writing and both the shifts in emphasis on the part of the state described in this chapter (ranging from the market-focused logic of the reforms of the 1980s and early 1990s to the emphasis on partnership-based approaches which came in the New Labour era) have meant that the reach of government, and the tools which govern its relationship with the voluntary sector, do not bear much resemblance to those seen during the interwar period. However, a glance back to earlier periods helps us to interpret current problems and attempts to find solutions. The account of the commissioning agenda provided in this chapter illustrates the value of this kind of activity. Where limited information is available on the application and efficacy of programmes aimed at reforming the relationship between the voluntary sector and the state, then viewing these activities through the lens of past debates encourages different perspectives of their intention and value. It is the continuities, and the differences, between the various periods of development in the relations between the voluntary and public sectors which provides policy-makers and scholars alike with the tools needed to fully understand the kinds of changes which are taking place.

All of the developments sketched in this chapter have brought about a number of challenges for both VSOs and for the public sector itself. The advent of contracting, in particular, has generated concerns about the voluntary sector's ability to retain its independence in an environment where a significant amount of its funding is provided by the state, and then delivered conditionally in a competitive environment. The twin worries of financial insecurity and loss of independence, so familiar in the wider literature, were also to be found in the 1930s and reflected in the concerns that followed the publication of *The New Philanthropy*. Similarly, the changing funding environment is bringing about significant challenges for public managers. New roles are emerging for the public sector, with the development of the commissioning narrative making demands of public managers that a hard-pressed public sector may struggle to fulfil. And yet, by glancing to previous accounts of the relationship between the state and the voluntary sector, we can see that the question of independence from state control is perennial.

It is not surprising, therefore, that the developments sketched out in this chapter seem set to continue for the time being. The election of the Coalition government in 2010 brought with it no dramatic change in the policy focus on the voluntary sector. Instead, VSOs were given an important place in the (now rarely-publicised) 'Big Society' agenda pursued in the early stages of the coalition, and the voluntary sector remains important in the welfare programme pursued since 2010 (Alcock, 2010b). While the long-term impact of recent policy may be uncertain, what is clear is that VSOs continue to be viewed as a significant provider of services by the public sector. Recent rounds of cuts to public spending seem to have cemented the voluntary sector's role, given the unlikelihood of new investment in public sector provision.

We end this chapter as it started. Regardless of the current trajectory of government policy, recent attempts to harness the value of voluntary action have deep roots in the social history of Britain. The efficacy of commissioning, with its aim to tackle some of the unintended consequences of the marketisation of public services, cannot rely on an understanding of voluntary action as something entirely new but must include a sense of the history of the voluntary sector's public service role. Throughout the chapter, we have attempted to present a picture of the development of the relationship between the voluntary sector and the state that is sympathetic to the broader context of voluntary action in the UK. Our contention is that any reading of recent policy without sympathy to this development would be incomplete.

Note

1 In *The New Philanthropy*, Macadam talks at various point of 'control' and 'cooperation' (p. 17), 'organisation' (p. 41), 'supervision' (p. 50) and 'coordination' (p. 56) and even (presciently) 'partnership' (p. 285). The terms are used interchangeably, with 'coordinative' (p. 56) organisations such as the Charities Organisation Society carrying out a similar role to the state in directing voluntary effort.

References

Alcock, P. (2010a) A Strategic Unity: Defining the Third Sector in the UK, *Voluntary Sector Review*, 1 (1): 5–24.
Alcock, P. (2010b) Building the Big Society: A New Policy Environment for the Third Sector in England, *Voluntary Sector Review*, 1 (3): 379–389.
Anheier, H. and Kendall, J. (Eds.) (2001) *Third Sector Policy at the Crossroads: An International Nonprofit Analysis*. London: Routledge.
Audit Commission (2007) *Hearts and Minds: Commissioning from the Voluntary Sector*. London: Audit Commission.
Beveridge, W. (1948) *Voluntary Action*. London: George Allen & Unwin.
Billis, D. and Glennerster, H. (1998) Human Services and the Voluntary Sector: Towards a Theory of Comparative Advantage, *Journal of Social Policy*, 27 (1): 79–98.
Bode, I. (2006) Disorganised Welfare Mixes: Voluntary Agencies and Governance Regimes in Western Europe, *Journal of European Social Policy*, 16 (4): 346–359.
Bovaird, T. (2006) New Forms of Partnership with the 'Market', *Public Administration*, 84 (1): 81–102.
Cabinet Office (2006) *Partnership in Public Services: An Action Plan for Third Sector Involvement*. London: HMSO.

Dacombe, R. (2011) Can We Argue Against It? *Public Money and Management*, 31 (3): 159–166.

Dahrendorf, R. (2001) *Challenges to the Voluntary Sector, Arnold Goodman Lecture, 17th July 2001*. Tonbridge: Charities Aid Foundation.

Deakin, N. (1996) The Devils in the Detail, *Social Policy and Administration*, 30 (1): 20–38.

Deakin, N. (2001) *In Search of Civil Society*. London: Palgrave.

Department for Communities and Local Government (2006) *Strong and Prosperous Communities*. The Local Government White Paper. London: HMSO.

Department for Education and Skills, and Department for Health (2006) *Joint Planning and Commissioning Framework for Children, Young People and Maternity Services*. London: HMSO.

Department of Health (2005) *Commissioning a Patient-Led NHS*. White Paper. London: HMSO.

Department of Health (2006) *Health Reform in England: An Update and Commissioning Framework*. London: HMSO.

Department of Health (2007) *Commissioning Framework for Health and Well-being*. London: HMSO.

Department of Health (2009) *World Class Commissioning: An Introduction*. London: HMSO.

Department for Work and Pensions (2007) *DWP Commissioning Strategy – Interim Report*. London: HMSO.

DETR (2001) *Guidance on the Implementation of the Local Government (Organisations and Standards) Act (2000)*. London: HMSO.

Evers, A. and Laville, J-L. (2004) *The Third Sector in Europe*. London: Edward Elgar.

Ferlie, E., Ashburner, L., Fitzgerald, L. and Pettigrew, A. (1996) *The New Public Management in Action*. Oxford: Oxford University Press.

Ferlie, E., Fitzgerald, L., McGivern, G., Dopson, S. and Bennett, C. (2011) Public Policy Networks and 'Wicked Problems': A Nascent Solution?, *Public Administration*, 89 (2): 307–324.

Finlayson, G. (1994) *Citizen, State and Social Welfare in Britain 1830–1990*. Oxford: Clarendon Press.

Glasby, J. (2012) *Commissioning for Health and Well-Being*. Bristol: Policy Press.

Harris, J. (1993) *Private Lives, Public Spirit: Britain 1870:1914*. London: Penguin.

Home Office (2011) *National Offender Management Services Commissioning Framework*. London: HMSO.

HM Treasury (2002) *The Cross-cutting Review of the Voluntary Sector in Public Service Delivery*. London: HM Treasury.

HM Treasury (2005) *Exploring the Role of the Third Sector in Public Service Delivery and Reform*. London: HM Treasury.

Hood, C. (1995) The 'New Public Management' in the 1980s: Variations on a Theme Accounting, *Organizations and Society*, 20 (2/3): 93–109.

Huxham, C. (1996) *Creating Collaborative Advantage*. London: Sage.

IDeA (2008) *Evaluation of the National Programme for Third Sector Commissioning – Phase 1*. London: IDeA.

Kendall, J. (2000) *The Mainstreaming of the Voluntary Sector into Public Policy: Whys and Wherefores*. LSE: Centre for Civil Society Working Paper No. 2.

Kendall, J. (2003) *The Voluntary Sector*. London: Routledge.

Kendall, J. and Knapp, M. (1996) *The Voluntary Sector in the UK*. Manchester: Manchester University Press.

Knapp, M., Hardy, B. and Forder, J. (2001) Commissioning for Quality: Ten Years of Social Care Markets in England, *Journal of Social Policy*, 30 (2): 283–306.

Kramer, R. (1994) Voluntary Agencies and the Contract Culture: Dream or Nightmare?, *Social Service Review*, 68 (1): 33–60.

Lewis, J. (1995) *The Voluntary Sector, the State and Society in Britain*. Aldershot: Edward Elgar.

Lewis, J. (1999), Reviewing the Relationship between the Voluntary Sector and the State in Britain in the 1990's, *Voluntas*, 10 (3): 225–270.

Lewis, J. (2005) New Labour's Approach to the Voluntary Sector: Independence and the Meaning of Partnership, *Social Policy and Society*, 4 (2): 121–131.

Macadam, E. (1934) *The New Philanthropy: A Study of the Relations between the Statutory and Voluntary Social Services*. London: George Allen and Unwin.

Macmillan, R. (2011) 'Supporting' the Voluntary Sector in an Age of Austerity: The UK Coalition Government's Consultation on Improving Frontline Support for Civil Society Organisations in England, *Voluntary Sector Review*, 2 (1): 115–124.

Milbourne, L. (2009) Remodelling the Third Sector: Advancing Collaboration or Competition in Community-based Initiatives?, *Journal of Social Policy*, 38 (2): 277–297.

Murray, G. (2008) Towards a Common Understanding of the Differences between Purchasing, Procurement and Commissioning in the Public Sector. In *Proceedings of the 3rd International Public Procurement Conference*, Amsterdam, The Netherlands, August 2008.

Newman, J. (2001) *Modernising Governance: New Labour, Policy and Society*. London: Sage.

Osborne, S. and Gaebler, T. (1993) *Reinventing Government*. London: Penguin.

Osborne, S. and McLaughlin, K. (2002) Trends and Issues in the Implementation of Local 'Voluntary Sector Compacts' in England, *Public Money and Management*, 22 (1): 55–64.

Prochaska, F. (1998) *The Voluntary Impulse*. London: Faber and Faber.

Thane, P. (1982) *The Foundations of the Welfare State*. London: Longman.

Unwin, J. (2004) *The Grantmaking Tango*. London: Baring Foundation/JRF.

Ware, A. (1989) *Charities and Government*. Manchester: Manchester University Press.

Webb, S. and Webb, B. (2010 [1912]) *The Prevention of Destitution*. Charleston, SC: Nabu Press.

Whelan, R. (1999) *Involuntary Action: How Voluntary is the 'Voluntary' Sector?*. London: Institute of Economic Affairs.

Wilson, S. and Game, C. (2002) *Local Government in the UK: Beyond the Centre*. London: Palgrave.

5
Deconstructing the Panacea of Volunteering in Criminal Justice

Mary Corcoran and *Jurgen Grotz*

> When someone leaves prison, I want them already to have a mentor in place to help them get their lives back together. I want them to be met at the prison gate, to have a place to live sorted out, and above all someone who knows where they are, what they are doing, and can be a wise friend to prevent them from reoffending. (Grayling, 2012)

The announcement in November 2012 by the Minister of Justice of plans to recruit volunteering organisations as indispensable to his 'rehabilitation revolution' crystallised several favoured policy themes of the coalition government. The speech confirmed the special status that voluntary sector organisations (VSOs) had assumed in governmental thinking about resettling and managing offenders. The proposition that civic-minded volunteers could salvage offenders from lives of crime on a widespread scale was fêted as an idea whose time had come. That appeal resonated with the Big Society project, which promulgated the idea that civil society could play an important, and sometimes more successful, role than the state in tackling entrenched social problems, including crime (Norman, 2010). Within this paradigm, it is claimed that properly trained members of the community and even former lawbreakers are singularly well placed to help offenders to turn their lives around where the prisons and probation system are deemed to have failed (Carter, 2003; Le Grand, 2007). However, underlying the appeal to socially responsible citizenship was the more sombre warning that discharging offenders back to homelessness, social isolation or substance addiction without help would perpetuate their reoffending, to the eventual cost of public safety:

> Solving these problems requires a radically different approach. Our central objective is to make the public safer by breaking the cycle of crime. (Ministry of Justice, 2010: 7, s15)

These ideas bring to the fore assumptions about the utility of volunteering as a prop for a plethora of policy goals ranging from reducing crime to tackling social exclusion by building community resilience. According to Rochester and colleagues (2010: 10) such expectations are projected onto the voluntary sector via a 'dominant paradigm', in which the sector is envisaged as a constituent element of the public welfare apparatus and where volunteering tends to be likened to 'unpaid work'. As a consequence, 'a very high proportion of the discussion about volunteering – by practitioners, policy makers and researchers alike – is concentrated on *one very specific view*', that volunteering is inherently of benefit to individuals and society (Rochester et al., 2010: 10, emphasis added). This chapter links the one-dimensional political perspective of volunteering to the overwhelmingly positive bias in research, academic and charitable sector discourses of the phenomenon. We utilise the term 'benefit fallacy' to describe the self-perpetuating logic whereby the body of evidence which demonstrates the beneficial outcomes of volunteering merely confirms the initial premise of such research that volunteering is inherently a good thing. The widespread emphasis on volunteering as a virtuous circle obscures the potential and actual occurrence of harms that are likely to arise given the nature of the activities undertaken by several VSOs (Grotz, 2010). The purpose of this chapter is to replace the benefit fallacy with a balanced and proportionate appreciation of the consequences of volunteering in penal contexts. Our case is based on the following observations:

1. The pervasiveness of the benefit fallacy is manifested in a general unwillingness to critique the concept of volunteering because it is unwelcome as a message to researchers, policy makers and practitioners. This is underpinned by a skewed presumption in favour of volunteering in the literature.
2. There is an avoidance in many accounts of the specifically penal dimensions of volunteering in criminal justice settings. Much of the current debate glosses over questions of power, legal coercion and involuntary restrictions, which are inescapable facts of operating in the arenas of crime 'control' and offender 'management'.
3. There is insufficient systematic analysis of the capacity for volunteering relationships to convey negative as well as positive social capital. We amend this by taking into account Smith's proposition that scholars consider the 'dark side' of volunteering, that is, 'the potentially or actually negative [and] harmful aspects of these civil society or non-profit sector groups' (Smith, 2008: 2).

4. Volunteering in criminal justice is increasingly constructed as a hazard that needs to be carefully managed with risk assessment and safeguarding regulations. The operative concept of risk that is increasingly applied mirrors narrow, technocratic calculations which are directed at minimizing breaches of security or monitoring relationships between volunteers and clients. Additionally, the responsibility and costs for managing such risks are devolved to VSOs.

In sum, we suggest that the benefit fallacy restricts open deliberation about the negative implications for VSOs – including reputational, legal, financial, moral and human – which derive from participating in offender management and crime reduction programmes. We conclude that the growing impetus to utilise volunteers must be cautiously approached. The powers available to VSOs must be proportionate to their civilian status as well as their legal and ethical responsibilities. Such arguments are intended to clarify the role, function and value of volunteering to all potential beneficiaries including service users, volunteers, penal reformers, policy makers and the public interest. They should also assist in holding policy makers to account when their plans and the evidence they use are uncritically founded on the benefit fallacy.

Great expectations

In recent decades, volunteers have been the subjects of political applause, which conveys a sense both of their sanctified status and their utility value to policy agendas. Before the general election in 2010, the Conservatives summed this up as follows:

> Volunteers are the beating heart of Britain's civil society, an indispensable resource for the voluntary sector and in many public services. Volunteering generates social capital – building the networks that turn mere places into communities. In economic terms, the value of volunteering can be measured in billions of pounds, but its true worth is beyond price. Without volunteers much of what we take for granted in our national life would grind to a halt. (Conservative Party, 2008: 20)

David Cameron's speech summarised the combination of two ideal typical characteristics which derive from the benefit fallacy, to which we add a third. Firstly, volunteers are understood to be a *resource* in the form of a reserve workforce that can supplement the operations of existing public agencies and provide specialist or individualised support to victims or offenders. Such expectations are allied to the rationality that using volunteer organisations brings about cost savings while underlining the political message that tackling the public's fear of crime cannot be undertaken only by the state. Secondly, volunteering is conceived of as a *source* of social capital whereby 'law-abiding' people who work alongside the police, community crime panels, probation or prison services, for example, are valued for facilitating public safety. In this and other volunteering contexts, volunteering is framed as being inherently beneficial in that 'doing good' endows both volunteers and offenders whom they help with social dividends such as trust, communal solidarity, social cohesion and consensus towards the legitimacy of governing institutions. Therefore, our third characteristic entails the importance of volunteers for forming trust relationships with offenders who are alienated from the criminal justice system. Equally, we probe how these trust relationships are functionally valued for steering offenders towards *normative attitudes and behaviours*. These three ideal typical beneficial attributes of volunteering are now critically unpacked.

Volunteering as a resource

The breadth and scale of volunteering with criminal justice agencies are already hugely diverse and growing (Gill and Mawby, 1990; Gojkovic et al., 2011). The number of VSOs working with offenders as their main client group is approximately 1743, with an additional 18,380 organisations that identified offenders as one of their client groups (Gojkovic et al., 2011: 19). These figures only account for organisations that declare themselves to be service providers and thus exclude several other areas of volunteer activism such as membership of reform or advocacy ('lobbying') groups, community-based neighbourhood crime control or restorative justice groups. In addition, under the Ministry of Justice's offender management strategy (2004), a much larger number of private and voluntary sector providers of housing, employment and training, healthcare, drugs and alcohol support, finance benefit and debt, children and families and attitudes, thinking and behaviour are now conceived of as part of a 'penal voluntary sector' (Ministry of Justice, 2004; Corcoran, 2011: 30). It is difficult to quantify the numbers or types of volunteers operating in criminal justice because they are distributed across different organisations with varying relationships to the state, and because of the different levels of statutory power held by volunteers. However, the very wide variation under those criteria is evident if one compares the formal roles of magistrates, lay members of Parole Boards, Youth Justice Boards or Special Constables, for example, with volunteers offering various kinds of 'gift relationships' (Titmus, 1970) such as befriending, motivational, counselling or social welfare. For the purposes of precision, this chapter largely refers to volunteering in community-based projects that are focused on rehabilitation and resettlement.

Furthermore, the term 'volunteer' refers to social activities that comply with the five following features: (a) the prevailing definition of volunteering is that it is 'of benefit'; (b) it is useful as service or productive work, not purely enjoyment for its own sake; (c) it is directed to other people outside the immediate family/household; (d) volunteering must be non-compulsory, thus, not coerced or forced externally by law, contract or other powerful social influences; and (e) while volunteers may receive some reimbursement or payment, it is not done primarily for monetary gain, and the payment is usually less than the economic value of the volunteering work done (Home Office, 2004; United Nations, 2001; Volunteering England, 2008).

Economic benefits

An obvious appeal of volunteering at a time when public spending is contracting is that it makes a major economic contribution by extending the capacities of national welfare and local public services. 'Valuable practical services . . . are accomplished in the community that can reduce municipal costs and taxes or can improve municipal efficiency' (Smith, 2000: 203). Nationally, the amounts involved are substantial. In England, for example, the total of 1.9 billion hours contributed by volunteers in 2003 was equivalent to the time put in by 1 million full-time workers and, at the national average wage, was worth around £22.5 billion (Home Office, 2004). Volunteer programmes are attractive to local government or statutory contractors because they relieve the strain on overstretched governmental and non-governmental organisations, as well as filling gaps left where public services are reduced or withdrawn (Brown and Ross, 2010: 32). Volunteers may also be deployed to alleviate the caseload of statutory agencies by 'allowing "professional" time to be deployed elsewhere' (Boyce et al., 2009: 12). Volunteer programmes can and do displace local paid posts. This has occurred where local authorities or Police and Crime Commissioners have been driven by economic considerations to replace some public policing and crime services with small grants to voluntary sector providers (*BBC NEWS*, 2013; Harman, 2013; *Western Morning News*, 2013).

Although pragmatic gains can be made from using volunteers to fill gaps, there is disquiet among the voluntary sector that governmental motivation for promoting volunteerism is linked with scaling back public services. Precisely because government is promoting volunteering as leverage for reducing public services, the unions representing the police, probation and prison staff are hostile to the potential threat to their jobs (NAPO, 2013). However, there seems to be little appetite among VSOs to replace state services. For example, Greater London Volunteering said that '[l]ike-for-like substitution of volunteers for paid staff is as unacceptable as redundant staff being replaced by new staff in the same role' (Greater London Volunteering, 2010: 5.1), while Baroness Neuberger's review of volunteering in criminal justice clearly stated that volunteering 'is in no way about services being provided on the cheap' (Neuberger, 2008: 3).

In answer to the tacit expectation that the voluntary sector represents a cheap substitute for public services, voluntary organisations contend that recruiting, training and managing volunteers are complex and costly efforts, and that governments are mistaken if they believe they are harnessing a free resource (Read et al., 2011). On the contrary, training and supporting skilled volunteers in areas such as victim support, sexual or domestic violence services, legal or welfare advice, police or prison custody monitoring, or suicide prevention, for example, is costly and labour-intensive. Therefore, volunteer organisations have to recover their investment by setting high expectations of the levels of commitment they demand from volunteers. Some voluntary organisations are vulnerable to the 'poaching' of skilled or experienced volunteers by 'rivals'. Anecdotal evidence indicates that, in the current period of austerity and underemployment, volunteers are discontinuing their purely volunteering roles to take up opportunities to obtain paid roles in their own and other organisations. Although students may offer a potential pool of volunteers who are closer in age, and purportedly in outlook, to younger offenders, their life experience can be more limited and there is also a question mark over the length of time that they are available for the work (Buck et al., 2015: 19). Other problems with recruiting and retaining suitable volunteers occur because of the unsocial hours that may be involved (especially for night-time or out-of-hours work). VSOs can underestimate the time and effort involved in operating within the routine restrictions that apply to secure environments, and are subsequently deterred by delays in obtaining security clearance or access to people in custody (cf. Mills and Meek, chapter seven, this volume). The nature of work with some vulnerable people can be so demanding and complex, at least in some aspects, that volunteer interventions such as mentoring are insufficient to meet offenders' needs (Hucklesby and Wincup, 2014; Buck et al., 2015). Indeed, the difficulties of evidencing these observations, which are recognised by practitioners and researchers, is indicative of the sensitivities involved in publicly acknowledging the pressures to properly utilise and retain volunteer time and labour as a valuable commodity.

Social capital and well-being

According to the literature, one of the principal attributes that volunteering generates is an increase in social capital. This may be broadly defined as 'investment in and use of embedded resources in social relations for expected returns' (Lin, 2000: 786). From this perspective, volunteering is held up as generating primary gains for participants in the form of enhanced well-being, which in turn contributes to secondary benefits such as personal resilience, reciprocity and social cohesion. Accordingly, volunteering enables individuals to gain confidence and self-esteem while developing knowledge and skills which, for some, will improve their employability or career prospects. Others highlight the impact on the volunteer's quality of life (Ockenden, 2007), such as higher levels of satisfaction and contentment (Pancer and Pratt, 1999), improved educational performance (Parkin and McKeganey, 2000) and better physical and mental health (Casiday et al., 2008). In addition, the Home Office Citizenship surveys show a strong correlation between rates of volunteering in an area and the extent to which residents felt that other people in the neighbourhood could be trusted (Kitchen et al., 2006). Criminologists have also identified linkages between fostering well-being and social capital as preconditions to 'making good' on the part of offenders (Maruna, 2001; Farrall, 2002). Indeed, proponents of voluntarism attach particular efficacy to involving prisoners and offenders because volunteering is thought to constitute a unique opportunity to bring about self-transformative effects for themselves (Porteous, 2007; Fletcher et al., 2009). Particular attention has been paid to voluntary peer support programmes, for example, because they are claimed to create a 'multiplier effect' whereby 'benefits that accrue to individuals from their work as Peer Advisors are matched by benefits to the recipients of their advice' (Boyce et al., 2009: vi). Organisations that are operated by former offenders claim that their work is ultimately more meaningful and implicitly more successful because service users are more receptive to somebody who has been through the same experience. One former offender turned mentor exemplified the argument:

> Having a mentor meant that when I got released I knew I had some-
> one to talk to and tell how I felt. He was an ex-prisoner, so he has
> been through the system himself. He knows what it's like and he
> knows the struggles. (BBC, *Today Program*, 20 November 2012).

Additionally, peer-based volunteering is thought to have the potential to correct the more condescending effects of professional interventions by serving 'as a counterbalance to the widespread belief that
programmes are something that is "done" to offenders by specialists'
(Boyce et al., 2009: vi).

Whilst research in areas as diverse as health, education and neighbour-
liness have found enhanced social capital among volunteers, one must
be sceptical towards claims that this is ipso facto beneficial. A distinction
should be drawn between the research findings which often emerge from
discrete, small-scale case studies, and the manner in which these findings
have been cumulatively marshalled as evidence by commentators with
different ideological, intellectual or policy agendas. For example, sum-
maries of the evidence often belie crucial analytical differences between
theorists who view social capital as cross-cutting social hierarchies to
establish shared social norms and values (Etzioni, 1994) and those who
believe that social capital is linked to formations of privilege, power and/
or exclusion along class (Bourdieu and Wacquant, 1992), gender or ethnic lines (Lin, 2000). These respective theories are significantly different in their understanding of citizen power, with the former focused
on mobilising the strengths of informal, community-based networks in
the fight against social ills such as crime (ODPM, 2005), while the latter
implies that communities should also concern themselves with inequality and exclusion as part of the aetiology of crime.

Trust and legitimacy

Although social relationships are significant in working with offenders,
VSOs also lay claim to the uniqueness of their comparatively informal
approaches which focus on building strengths rather than correcting deficits. Programmes offering befriending, counselling, emotional or confidential listening and peer supports are founded on the principle that
volunteers' contributions should be qualitatively different from those
which paid staff bring (Levenson and Farrant, 2002). Volunteers, for
example, are claimed to elicit greater trust and confidence from offenders

and prisoners who may prefer to turn to sources that are not associated with 'the system' (Parkin and McKeganey, 2000: 301). Paradoxically, however, state agencies such as probation or the police champion volunteering precisely because they hope that it will channel offenders into engaging with state agencies (Youth Justice Board, 2007: 4). Similarly, volunteers are expected to mediate between lawbreaking individuals and the 'moral community' (Crawford, 1999: 509) in the hope that it will 'lead to greater public confidence in the . . . system' (Youth Justice Board, 2007: 4). Concurrently, volunteers are imagined to convey powerful communicative impressions by getting service users 'to understand the consequences of their actions on others in their area' (Youth Justice Board, 2007: 4).

The enthusiasm among statutory bodies for volunteering is supported by the preferential focus in the research literature on the benefits of volunteering to volunteers, VSOs, beneficiaries and society at large. There are complex explanations for this positivity and the paucity of critical perspectives in the volunteering literature. One explanation points to the predominance of evaluative research in the field, which tends to be small-scale, localised studies of individual projects over short periods of time, and therefore not generalisable (Colley, 2001: 178). Secondly, evaluative research tends to comply with prescribed investigative remits and requirements that the 'positive impact' of programmes can and must be scientifically demonstrated as prerequisites to obtaining funding to continue their work. A third explanation lies with the tendency to withdraw poor or negative results for fear of losing reputation or future funding (cf. Hedderman and Hucklesby, chapter six, this volume). McCord (2003: 26), for example, argued that the failure to report negative outcomes of crime prevention programmes in the United States, for example, contributed to a false positive picture:

Evidence about adverse effects from social program[me]s is hard to find, in part because of a strong bias against reporting adverse effects. . . . Authors of studies that fail to produce evidence of beneficial outcomes sometimes do not bother to submit their reports for publication.

Propagation of the benefit fallacy is not confined to academics or policy makers. VSOs can themselves subscribe to the wider sense of urgency about crime and reoffending by bringing issues to the fore 'with the aim to induce an immediacy to act' (Richter and Norman, 2010: 225). In a competitive funding climate, there is an increasing tendency to perpetuate credence regarding the efficacy of volunteer programmes by showcasing their superior outcomes in comparison with commercial or public sector projects.

The 'dark side' of volunteering

Against the prevailing tide, a very small number of scholars have broached the prospect that volunteering may foster harmful relationships between volunteers and offenders, while still fewer have focused on the exposure of volunteers themselves to harm (Scandura, 1998; Devilly et al., 2005). However, volunteering organisations are no less susceptible than businesses or state agencies to crime, fraud, malpractice or discriminatory practices by staff or volunteers (Thomas, 2012). Even where such harms are thought to be low, 'the consequences of a lack of attention to these risks . . . [are] potentially significant for public trust and confidence in that charity and the sector in general' (Thomas, 2012: 4). Thus, a more considered and balanced appraisal is required which takes account of the 'dark side' of volunteering (Smith, 2008), that is, 'all kinds of deviance and misconduct by community sector/non-profit groups and individuals', involving 'formal and informal volunteers, paid staff, officers, [and] board members' (Smith, 2008; 2). Importantly, consideration of the 'dark side'

> does not imply condemnation. . . . Potential harmful or negative effects are *not actual* harmful or negative effects, but it is wise to know about such potentials. Moreover, there are virtually no human activities, including [those] as group members or participants, which do not have their negative aspects. (Smith, 2008: 2, emphasis in the original)

It is indicative of the fact that volunteer organisations may suffer from mismanagement or poor relationships among clients, staff and volunteers that many have policies in place to discipline volunteers. The Institute for Volunteering Research (1998) found that three quarters of 547 organisations surveyed had procedures for disciplining volunteers. According to Volunteering England (Brown, 2013), the circumstances under which volunteers may be disciplined include persistently bad timekeeping; taking on tasks which go outside the agreed remit; failure to respect client/customer confidentiality; failure to respect their dignity, independence and individuality; breaches of health and safety regulations or agreements; misuse of the organisation's equipment or facilities; theft and discrimination on grounds of disability, race, gender or other factor. Of course, VSOs are subject to civil, contractual, criminal and regulatory codes as incorporated legal bodies (Restall, 2005). But in actual practice, the contribution of volunteers does not always fit neatly within the scope of legal frameworks such as employment law, for example. Rather, the practical problem of reconciling their dual roles as individuals discharging legally accountable public functions 'opens up the possibility of messy disciplinary issues, especially if there is already confusion over the boundaries between roles' (Restall, 2005: 61).

In contrast to pervasive claims about the benefits of volunteering for enhancing confidence and self-esteem, the potential for being emotionally harmed as a result of volunteering was identified during the Volunteer Rights Inquiry for Great Britain (Volunteering England, 2010: 7). Witnesses to the inquiry reported how their formal volunteering experience left them 'physically and mentally in pieces' as they had been 'continually harassed, bullied, and worn down' (Third Sector, 8 July 2010). Additionally, the Interim Report for the inquiry (Volunteering England, 2010) collected 'numerous' reports from volunteers narrating 'stories of bad management, poor governance, bullying and improper behaviour', and cited incidents of verbal abuse, intimidation and sexual harassment (Third Sector, 2010). Although a comparatively small proportion of all volunteers, two thirds of complainants to the enquiry submitted evidence of 'serious' allegations including bullying, conflicts arising from new management structures and practices, breaches of trust, including the leakage of confidential information about themselves and exploitation of volunteers' goodwill (Volunteering England, 2010: 10). Moreover, victims of inappropriate behaviour encompassed all strata of workers from trustees to volunteers and involved the intimidation of managers by their volunteers and inappropriate behaviour by clients (Volunteering England, 2010: 7–11). The inquiry concluded that many organisations still lacked appropriate procedures for dealing with problems, complaints and disputes. It recommended that a framework of good practices for identifying conflict, early intervention, transparency and independent arbitration should be developed and applied to the whole sector (Volunteering England, 2010).

Unlike some other countries, incidents of occupational death, injury or crimes involving volunteers are not centrally recorded in the United Kingdom, so that the picture of occupational risk in the course of volunteering is patchy. A few studies have investigated harmful physical or psychological effects such as post-traumatic stress disorder among volunteer fire fighters (Bryant and Harvey, 1996) or among volunteers working with people with HIV/AIDS (Ross et al., 1999), for example. Indeed, Thoits and Hewitt (2001: 128) point out that the health benefits associated with volunteering may be more dependent on the conditions under which they volunteer than the fact that they are being altruistic: 'perhaps doing volunteer work is less important for well-being than the particular conditions of the work that is done'. Some prosecutions have been taken on behalf of the Health and Safety Executive against charities for liability contributing to the death of an employee. In 2010, the charity Mental Health Matters was fined £30,000 and ordered to pay £20,000 costs after admitting failure to protect an employee, Ashleigh Ewing, 22, who was stabbed to death by a client in the client's home (*BBC NEWS*, 2010). The tribunal concluded that a 'simple risk assessment may have averted [the] incident'. The narrow focus on human error and the apparent failure or non-existence of safety procedures is problematised in a later section of this chapter ('Volunteering as security risk'). At this point, however, these incidents highlight broader issues relating to the practice of sending lone volunteers into certain settings and the dilemmas that are presented for charities in terms of their legal duties of care. With the exception of a few serious, publicised cases, it is striking that volunteering seems to be disregarded as a specific area of concern in the field of occupational safety regulation, notwithstanding the general principle that legal protections as well as liabilities ought to apply to all sectors (Restall, 2005).

Negative social capital

Broadly conceived, negative social capital refers to factors which convert social interactions that are meant to be vehicles for integration and trust-building into occasions for controlling, regulating or excluding individuals or social groups by inducting them into exploitative, dependent or disrespectful relationships. The concept draws on Bourdieu's theory of social capital, which summarises the economic, social, cultural and symbolic resources that accrue for an individual by virtue of their membership of a social group. The more powerful and well-resourced an individual or group is, the greater their capacity to convert the value of one form (such as 'cultural' capital) into another (such as 'economic' capital), while conversely, the more a group or individual is dispossessed, 'the lower the value of that particular social capital' (Wacquant, 1998: 28). According to this formulation, everyone possesses the capacity for both 'positive' and 'negative' forms of social capital.

In his seminal study of volunteering in the United States, Putnam (2000: 22–23) distinguished between *bridging social capital*, which fostered relationships across diverse social groups, and *bonding social capital*, in which groups were conjoined by mutual interest only. Whereas the former facilitated altruistic networks, negative social capital amassed in the latter as single-interest, mono-cultural groups developed exclusive and even discriminatory tendencies towards 'outsiders' (Putnam, 2000: 350–363). Smith (2008) elaborated on this finding to suggest that negative social capital might be transmitted through an individual's or group's attachment to voluntary institutions or subcultures. Likewise, he postulated that harmful social influences were conveyed through several types of groupings. For example, 'gang' membership demonstrated how individuals gain social capital by embracing stigmatised roles by bonding with like-minded peers and adhering to group norms, even if they are deemed to be 'deviant or unacceptable' (Smith, 2008: 28).

Criminological 'strain' theories have long recognised the propensity for weak and selfish social relationships to transmit negative social capital (Agnew, 2001). Because volunteering involves complex, and to some extent tentative and open-ended, interactions, it can become a conduit for undesirable and harmful, as well as positive, effects. Peer mentoring or befriending programmes, for example, may reinforce a sense of self-justification for past crimes on the part of the mentee. Whilst such programmes have shown results such as improved self-esteem or social capital, they are unable to confirm hypotheses that personal changes convert into reduced criminal activity on the part of an individual (Jolliffe and Farrington, 2007). At best, the effect of mentoring on recidivism may be tangential in so far as participation can help to diminish 'high-risk' behaviours which are deemed to be related to offending (DuBois et al., 2002; Tolan et al., 2008). Indeed, some quantitative studies found evidence of increased offending among participants on peer-mentoring programmes (Blechman et al., 2000). Moreover, the initial appeal of being mentored by those who have travelled the same road diminishes over time as other needs or priorities arise for mentees (Jaffe, 2012: 222–235). Other commentators question whether the intended beneficiaries, the mentees, gain as much from the process as their mentors or even mentoring organisations (Scandura, 1998; Colley, 2001; Hucklesby and Wincup, 2014). Research has pointed to hidden forms of exploitation in volunteer–service user relationships where volunteers may be enlisted by programmes to monitor or discipline offenders' behaviour, especially with individuals whose participation on programmes is part of a court order or probation supervision (Goddard, 2012). Still others hold that the literature largely glosses over questions of inequality and power between service users and volunteers (Singh, 2012), so that volunteer interventions reinforce or normalise social inequalities to the point where they mask participants' understanding of 'structural disadvantage and discrimination' (Colley, 2001: 180).

The claims and counterclaims in the wider research about the supposedly real value of volunteering interventions reveal the underlying problem that we are raising in this essay. That is to say, the fixation on whether volunteering programmes 'work' or 'do not work' connotes a prior assumption that they ought to work because volunteering is already deemed to be inherently beneficial. At best, the findings can only suggest that gains from volunteer involvement seem to be qualitative, primary rather than secondary, and specific to individual recipients. Volunteering continues to elude categorisation as a reliable method for reducing offending because 'the valuable features and most promising approaches cannot be stated with any certainty' (Finnegan et al., 2010: 8). This is in contrast with the Ministry of Justice's measures for funding volunteer groups on the basis of payment by results and 'what works', which are construed on the basis that interventions will or will not reduce offending. However, these calculations do not always factor in neutral or null hypotheses, that is, where volunteering interventions may produce no impact or even adverse effects.

NIMBYism versus legitimacy

The tensions between building solidarity and social integration on the one hand and the protection of property or the status quo on the other reveal how volunteering is an anomalous force, capable of creating cohesion but also of sowing divisiveness. Volunteering with neighbourhood watch groups is encouraged as a vital component in achieving 'stronger and safer' communities, for example. Equally, however, local campaigns often emerge as manifestations of informal involvement in opposition to local plans, such as the siting of drugs and alcohol support centres or housing for ex-offenders (Rossendale Free Press, 2011; South Wales Evening Post, 2012). While such campaigning is sometimes heralded as a return of power to the community, it is also associated with NIMBYism, a neologism for 'Not in My Back Yard'. Similarly, Aldrich and Crook's paper *Trailers in Post-Katrina New Orleans* (2008) showed how civil society actors worked simultaneously to bring citizens together while mobilising them against the 'threat' of temporary trailer parks in their neighbourhoods for those made homeless by that extreme weather event. It is now widely recognised that activating residents to protect their localities from crime or disorder can accentuate the polarisation of 'law-abiding' residents from so-called 'offenders' (Crawford, 1999;

Shapland, 2007). It must be acknowledged that a campaign expressing one view may result in a counter movement, leading to counterproductive or unintended consequences. Examples of the complexity of these issues may be seen from the 'dark side' of the victims' rights movement, which, in setting out to redress dereliction in the criminal law or practice with regard to victims, has intentionally or not lent moral weight to the ratcheting up of punitive or authoritarian measures, and even to retaliation and vigilantism, in the interests of 'the community' (Ministry of Justice, 2011).

Managing volunteering as a security 'risk'

Up to this point, the discussion has focused on those aspects of volunteering which are not, but perhaps should be, comprehended as potentially or actually harmful for participants. The final section will focus on one obvious exception to the wider oversight of questions of harm. This is where volunteering with offenders has become a field in which volunteers are construed as innate *bearers of risk* requiring vigilant management, necessitating the pervasive application of screening and safeguarding procedures. The operative concept of 'risk' that applies here mirrors narrow, technocratic calculations which are directed at minimising breaches of security or monitoring relationships between volunteers and clients. The narrow formulation of risk in this context reflects actuarial governing rationalities which are characterised by a general avoidance of complex questions of ethics and power by reducing them to technical problems that may be resolved procedurally rather than substantially (cf. Mills and Meek, chapter seven, this volume). Thus an expanding, but under-researched, aspect of state regulation converges on the extension of the security gaze to the activities of VSOs.

Risk management policies have become pervasive in the domain of crime prevention and it is now obligatory for all agencies working in a criminal justice framework to install procedures for ascertaining risks posed by certain clients, as well as assessing and managing their potential conduct. As a consequence, VSOs are obliged to develop procedures for individualised risk prediction and safety management (O'Malley, 2010) as well as situational preventive measures that apply to volunteers and service users.

Volunteer projects must meet the security and risk assessment requirements of statutory criminal justice agencies. In order to gain accreditation from the National Offender Management Service (NOMS) they must also develop protocols governing the screening of volunteers and staff, information sharing, adherence to data protection legislation and confidentiality agreements. In general, their procedures are often made more stringent by the requirements of statutory partners or funders who are focused on the security dimensions of volunteer behaviour and influence on offenders. One obvious response is that volunteer organisations scale up their in-house risk assessment and volunteer-training procedures, develop joint training programmes or hand over part of the training to their statutory partners. We conducted a content and discourse analysis of the guidelines issued by the prison service (Prison Service, 2002, 2010) and the training and induction materials devised for volunteers working in custody settings that are in the public domain (Clinks, 2012; Independent Custody Visiting Association 2013) and others that are not available to the public. This analysis identified those areas where volunteers are instructed in explicit and detailed scenarios about what to do during the various following events:

- A volunteer is assaulted by a prisoner.
- An offender makes a disclosure amounting to a concern related to the safety of a minor or vulnerable person.
- An offender attempts to coerce a mentor into doing something illegal, 'turning a blind eye' to something they have done or said.
- A prisoner is suspected of obtaining/using drugs or alcohol, passing or receiving a package.
- Any incident that may put the mentor or prisoner at risk, for example, a member of the public approaches/attacks the prisoner.
- An offender is 'inappropriate' (open to interpretation) with a mentor or member of the public.
- A client commits (or is suspected of committing) a crime during time out.
- A prisoner absconds or attempts to abscond.

Without making general scientific claims from these readings of induction and training materials, what becomes apparent is the elision of 'safety' and 'security' discourses and the semantic slippages between risks presented *by* volunteers and hazards *to* which they are potentially susceptible.

We do not assert that risk assessment or security procedures are unnecessary intrusions, and concede that they are instituted to prevent harm to either volunteers or others, to minimise disruption to prison establishments and to discharge statutory duties towards public safety. However, our focus is on the means by which risk and security logics enter into volunteering contexts from the initial stages of training and preparation. The construction of volunteers as carriers of risk is reinforced through stringent procedures for obtaining security clearance or the screening for criminal disclosure. In this context, volunteers are socialised into the mores and modes of self-policing behaviours that govern those of professional, paid criminal justice staff.

It is evident that working in prisons and with probation creates 'security creep' as volunteers become inculcated into the attitudinal and behavioural boundaries which professional criminal justice workers have long been taught to guard against. One classic preoccupation in the prison service is the danger of staff becoming 'conditioned' (manipulated by means of intimidation or coercion) or overfamiliar with clients (through inexperience or other cause). Moreover, even when volunteers obtain clearance to work with prisoners, that permission is highly contingent and volunteer organisations continue to report their sudden exclusion from access to clients on the grounds that they disrupt security or the prison routines or undermine the professional authority of staff.

The pattern of sharing responsibility for the routine monitoring of risk and undertaking to report concerns to statutory authorities brings VSOs in line with prevailing risk management approaches in criminal justice. These primarily characterise volunteers as risk carriers and oblige VSOs to take more responsibility for these risks. Far from lacking awareness about potentially negative moral and ethical consequences of deploying volunteers in working with vulnerable groups, we suggest that considerations of harm are dominated by a 'risk paradigm' which emphasises utility, adherence to legal and security requirements and breaches of protocols. The risk paradigm underpins the need for prior screening of volunteers and service users, training in conducting risk assessments, and minimising criminal or civil legal liability (Health and Safety Executive, 2013).

This is a narrower purview of safety than that adopted by many VSOs which customarily build precautionary practices from more holistic models which focus on safeguarding vulnerable adults or children, developing lone working policies, safe recruitment procedures, responding to whistle-blowers, managing allegations against staff and volunteers, and emphasising the dignity and respect of clients. Finally, the effects on volunteers' motivations and attitudes towards clients are unclear. However, practices for inducting volunteers in a manner which frames *their* work in terms of risks and dangers may reinforce a sense of alienation from service users as well as mandating volunteers to act as the 'eyes and ears' of prison, or probation services. Singh (2012: 283) suggests, for example, that 'the framing of offenders as threatening goes hand in hand with the privileging of disciplinary tactics and constructions of mainstream program[me]s as appendages of the criminal justice system'. It is difficult to assert that the problem is widespread. More research is needed into the processes by which volunteers may or may not absorb risk management dispositions or are influenced by criminogenic frames of references.

Summary and conclusion

This chapter has argued that the field of volunteering has been skewed by normative assumptions which insist on its inherent beneficence. We have suggested that a benefit fallacy arises from observations based on the shallower and visible end of research on volunteering. By contrast, the paucity of data on the 'dark side' can be related to the under-researched and unmeasured, and hence less visible or empirically validated, knowledge about the risks and hazards. Three main dangers arise from the failure to apprehend (and possibly manage) the known potential for volunteering to generate harms or inequalities. Firstly, the reluctance to openly discuss the potentially negative as well as positive aspects of volunteering may lead to a future backlash. If the desire to promote volunteering leads to a lack of candour about all its facets, the greater the public backlash is likely to be when difficulties occur. Secondly, by endeavouring to maximise the engagement of volunteers without taking account of negative impacts, policy making is seriously unbalanced in its apprehensions of the benefits and costs. Finally, organisations or statutory bodies which wittingly or unwittingly continue to subscribe to the benefit fallacy put not only volunteers and clients at risk but potentially their reputations and legitimacy as well.

Several commentators have raised concerns that official discourse and some VSOs have created conflicting ideas about the purpose of volunteering in criminal justice–related work. One consequence is that concepts of volunteers as embodying reserves of citizen goodwill are deployed interchangeably with references to an untapped labour force for supplementing the work of statutory criminal justice services. Such constructions conflate instrumentalist ideas about the voluntary 'alternative arm of the penal state' (Haney, 2010: 211) with the virtuous appeal of restorative solidarity that underpins normative discourses of community justice. We have suggested that these ideals not only permeate academic, public, media, charitable and political discourses, but contribute to a confusion of purpose about the benefits of volunteering. This manifests in the ways in which policy makers and spokespeople for the voluntary sector seek to demonstrate the utility of volunteering in so far as it contributes to wider policy goals for reducing crime or reoffending. The well-documented failure to halt the revolving door through which many offenders are admitted and readmitted to the courts and prisons attests to the importance of exploring viable alternatives, including the greater use of community-based, volunteer-led interventions. But it is contentious to assume that the value of volunteering is weighted primarily in terms of its adherence to utilitarian political agendas, whether fiscal or related to law and order.

Indeed, there is evidence that the actual conditions of undertaking voluntary work are already counteracting the benefits fallacy. For example, many VSOs do not wish to replace statutory services and few seem to be eager to assume powers of sanction or adopt higher thresholds of coercion. Furthermore, many are worried about undertaking work that will absorb their workforces, paid and volunteer, in complicated and expensive procedures. Such practices necessarily divert resources to the upkeep of regulatory regimes, and involve tangible as well as qualitative shifts towards the formal management of staff, volunteers and service users. The final comments of this chapter lay out some constructive and proportionate proposals for creating a framework of due diligence that will accommodate a pluralistic culture of social justice, that is, one which accommodates the ethos and values of VSOs and their relationship with for-profit and statutory partners.

The first principle entails adopting a cognisance of harm, that is, a conscious acknowledgement of the avoidable harms that may be perpetuated by volunteering, ensuring that these are made more visible, and that accountability is prioritised so as to advance their social mission with integrity. It is stressed that a cognisance of harm is not the same as predicting risks or hazards to which the answer to date has been proliferating regulation. Nor is it the same as cost/benefit calculations regarding the utility of involving or not involving volunteers, although in practice these will inform agencies' decisions about pursuing service contracts.

Secondly, a prominent concern relates to penal drift, that is, the migration of practices founded on concerns with security and control from statutory to voluntary bodies, which potentially has significant consequences for VSOs and their service users. This trend may be ameliorated if VSOs routinely applied a 'legitimacy test' when contemplating taking on work where elements of coercion or monitoring breach of sentence orders are involved. Such a legitimacy test would involve comparing the voluntary sector's aims and mission with the terms of their service contracts and also with assessing the goals and disposition of partner organisations, especially where they have statutory duties to implement breach proceedings or formal sanctioning powers.

Thirdly, explicit, sector-wide guidelines could be published in the form of an ethical code between VSOs and the police, courts, prisons or probation agencies which clarify the responsibilities of each partner and the opportunities for either party to review practices against the guidelines.

Fourthly, a principle of subsidiarity or non-coercive/non-penal intervention could be incorporated into Commissioner's codes of practice so that VSOs are not penalised by actions related to breach of contract or downgraded in future funding competitions if they indicate clearly and in advance those areas where they are unwilling to perform certain tasks (such as reporting offenders where breach of sentence procedures might ensue).

Finally, volunteers should be made aware of the consequences of their involvement in working with victims and offenders, and be discouraged from identifying with penal rationalities. Volunteers (and perhaps paid staff) ought to be allowed to withdraw from activities which exceed pastoral thresholds or which they perceive to be unacceptably coercive. Managers ought to be able to take decisions that would minimise adverse outcomes for service users.

While it is possible that, as the available evidence suggests, the benefits of volunteering outweigh the problems, it is untenable to continue in the belief that an activity in which millions of people participate every day is without negative impacts.

References

Agnew, R. (2001) Building on the Foundation of General Strain Theory: Specifying the Types of Most Likely to Lead to Crime and Delinquency, *Journal of Research in Crime and Delinquency*, 38 (4): 319–361.

Aldrich, D. P. and Crook, K. (2008) Strong Civil Society as a Double-Edged Sword: Siting Trailers in Post-Katrina New Orleans, *Political Research Quarterly*, 61 (3): 379–389.

BBC NEWS (2010) *Mental Health Charity Fined over Employee Knife Death*. [Online] 1 February. Available from: http://news.bbc.co.uk/1/hi/england/8491026.stm [accessed 13/10/13].

BBC NEWS (2013) *Leicestershire Police Cuts: Hundreds of Officers Face Axe, Says Union*. [Online] 21 August. Available from:http://www.bbc.co.uk/news/uk-england-leicestershire-23777236 [accessed 23/08/13].

BBC (2012) *Today*, Radio 4, 20 November 2012. Available from: http://news.bbc.co.uk/today/hi/today/newsid_9771000/9771025.stm [accessed 13/10/13].

Blechman, E. A., Maurice, A., Buecker, B. and Helberg, C. (2000) Can Mentoring or Skill Training Reduce Recidivism? Observational Study with Propensity Analysis, *Prevention Analysis*, 1 (3): 139–155.

Bourdieu, P. and Wacquant, L. (1992) *An Invitation to Reflexive Sociology*. Chicago: University of Chicago Press.

Boyce, I., Hunter, G. and Hough, M. (2009) *The St Giles Trust Peer Advice Project: Summary of an Evaluation Report*. London: King's College.

Brown, P. (2013) How Do You Reprimand a Volunteer or Take Issue with their Behaviour When they're Giving their Time Freely?, *Volunteering England*. [Online] Available from: http://www.volunteering.org.uk/resources/goodpracticebank/Core + Themes/dealingwithproblems/howdoyoureprimandavolunteerortakeissuewiththeirbehaviourwhentheyregivingtheirtimefreely.htm [accessed 20/11/13].

Brown, M. and Ross, S. (2010) Mentoring, Social Capital and Desistance: A Study of Women Released from Prison, *Australian and New Zealand Journal of Criminology*, 43 (1): 31–50.

Bryant, R. A. and Harvey, A. G. (1996) Posttraumatic Stress Reactions in Volunteer Fire Fighters, *Journal of Traumatic Stress*, 9 (1): 51–62.

Buck, G., Corcoran, M. S. and Worrall, A. (2015) Gendered Dynamics of Mentoring. In: Brayford, J. and Deering, J. (eds) *Women and Criminal Justice: from the Corston Report to Transforming Rehabilitation*. Bristol: Policy Press: 157–175.

Carter, P. (2003) *Managing Offenders, Reducing Crime: A New Approach*. London: Cabinet Office Strategy Unit.

Casiday, R., Kinsman, E., Fisher, C. and Bambra, C. (2008) *Volunteering and Health: What Impact Does It Really Have?*. London: Volunteering England.

Clinks (2012) *Volunteer Peer Support: A Volunteering and Mentoring Guide*. London: Clinks.

Colley, H. (2001) Righting Rewritings of the Myth of Mentor: A Critical Perspective on Career Guidance Mentoring, *British Journal of Guidance and Counselling*, 29 (2): 177–197.

Conservative Party (2008) *A Stronger Society: Voluntary Action in the 21st Century, Responsibility Agenda, Policy Green Paper No. 5*. London: Conservative Party.

Corcoran, M. S. (2011) Dilemmas of Institutionalisation of the Penal Voluntary Sector in England and Wales, *Critical Social Policy*, 31 (1): 30–52.

Crawford, A. (1999) Questioning Appeals to Community within Crime Prevention and Control, *European Journal on Criminal Policy and Research*, 7 (4): 509–530.

Devilly, G. J., Sorbello, L., Eccleston, L. and Ward, T. (2005) Prison-based Peer Education Schemes, *Aggression and Violent Behaviour*, 10: 219–240.

DuBois, D. L., Holloway, B. E., Valentine, J. C. and Cooper, H. (2002) Effectiveness of Mentoring Programs for Youth: A Meta-analytic Review, *American Journal of Community Psychology*, 30 (2): 157–197.

Etzioni, A. (1994) *The Spirit of Community: The Reinvention of American Society*. New York: Touchstone.

Farrall, S. (2002) *Rethinking What Works with Offenders*. Cullompton: Willan.

Finnegan, L., Whitehurst, D. and Deaton, S. (2010) *Models of Mentoring for Inclusion and Employment, a Thematic Review of Evidence on Mentoring and Peer Mentoring*. London: MOMIE/Centre for Economic and Social Inclusion.

Fletcher, R. C., Sherk, J. and Jucovy, L. (2009) Mentoring Former Prisoners: A Guide for Re-entry Programs, *Public/Private Ventures*. Available from: http://www.aecf.org/KnowledgeCenter/Publications.aspx?pubguid = {22DC48C8-E9D1-442C-8686-0BB48348AC27} [accessed 04/10/13].

Gill, M. and Mawby, R. (1990) *Volunteers in the Criminal Justice System*. Milton Keynes: Open University Press.

Goddard, T. (2012) Post-welfarist Risk Managers? Risk, Crime Prevention and the Responsibilization of Community-based Organisations, *Theoretical Criminology*, 16 (3): 347–363.

Gojkovic, D., Mills, A. and Meek, R. (2011) Scoping the Involvement of Third Sector Organisations in the Seven Resettlement Pathways for Offenders. *Working Paper 57.* Third Sector Research Centre, University of Southampton.

Grayling, Right Hon C. (2012) *Rehabilitation Revolution: The Next Steps.* [Online] Available from: http://www.apccs.police.uk/fileUploads/Rehabilitation_Revolution_Rt_Hon_Chris_Grayling_Speech_201112.pdf [accessed 20/10/13].

Greater London Volunteering (2010) *Principles of Volunteering.* [Online] Available from: http://greaterlondonvolunteering.files.wordpress.com/2011/02/principles ofvolunteering.doc [accessed 21/11/13].

Grotz, J. (2010) When Volunteering Goes Wrong: Misconduct in Volunteering. In *16th NCVO/VSSN Researching the Voluntary Sector Conference*, 6–7 September 2010, University of Leeds, UK.

Haney, L. (2010) *Offending Women: Power, Punishment and the Regulation of Desire.* London: University of California Press.

Harman, S. (2013) Dorset Police Stations Will Have to Close, Crime Commissioner Tells Police, *Daily Echo*. [Online] 21 August. Available from: http://www.bournemouthecho.co.uk/news/10631025.Police_stations_will_have_to_close__crime_commissioner_tells_meeting/ [accessed 23/08/13].

Health and Safety Executive (2013) *Voluntary Organisations: Managing Low Risk.* Available from: http://www.hse.gov.uk/voluntary/index.htm [accessed 21/11/13].

Home Office (2004) *2003 Home Office Citizenship Survey: People, Families and Communities.* London: Home Office.

Hucklesby, A. and Wincup, E. (2014) Assistance, Support and Monitoring? The Paradoxes of Mentoring Adults in the Criminal Justice System, *Journal of Social Policy*, 43 (2): 373–390.

Independent Custody Visiting Association (2013) *TACT Student Manual*. London: ICVA.

Institute for Volunteering Research (1998) *Issues in Volunteer Management – A Report of a Survey.* Available from: http://www.ivr.org.uk/researchbulletins/bulletins/issues-in-volunteer-management-a-report-of-a-survey [accessed 13/10/13].

Jaffe, M. (2012) *Peer Support and Help Seeking in Prison: A Study of the Listener Scheme in Four Prisons in England.* A Thesis Submitted in fulfilment of the Requirements of Keele University for the Degree of Doctor of Philosophy.

Jolliffe, D. and Farrington, D. (2007) *A Rapid Evidence Assessment of the Impact of Mentoring on Re-offending: A Summary.* London: Home Office.

Kitchen, S., Michaelson, J., Wood, N. and John, P. (2006) *2005 Citizenship Survey: Active Communities Topic Report.* London: Department for Communities and Local Government.

Le Grand, J. (2007) *The Other Invisible Hand: Delivering Services through Choice and Competition.* Oxford: Princeton University Press.

Levenson, J. and Farrant, F. (2002) Unlocking Potential: Active Citizenship and Volunteering by Prisoners, *Probation Journal*, 49: 195–204.

Lin, N. (2000) Inequality in Social Capital, *Contemporary Sociology*, 29 (6): 785–795.

Maruna, S. (2001) *Making Good: How Ex-convicts Reform and Rebuild their Lives.* Washington, DC: American Psychological Association.

McCord, J. (2003) Cures That Harm: Unanticipated Outcomes of Crime Prevention Programs, *Annals of the American Academy of Political and Social Science*, 587: 16–30.

Ministry of Justice (2004) *National Action Plan for Reducing Re-Offending*. London: HMSO.

Ministry of Justice (2010) *Breaking the Cycle: Effective Punishment, Rehabilitation and Sentencing of Offenders*. London: Ministry of Justice.

Ministry of Justice (2011) *Victims' Commissioner Responds to Plans for Sentencing Reform*. Available from: http://www.justice.gov.uk/news/press-releases/victims-com/vcnewsrelease210611 [accessed 13/10/13].

NAPO (2013) *NAPO Discussion Forum*. Available from: http://www.napo2.org.uk/phpBB3/viewtopic.php?f=2 andt=177 [accessed 20/11/13].

Neuberger, J. (2008) *Volunteering Across the Criminal Justice System*. London: Home Office.

Norman, J. (2010) *The Big Society: The Anatomy of the New Politics*. Buckingham: University of Buckingham Press.

O'Malley, P. (2010) *Crime and Risk*. London: Sage.

Ockenden, N. (ed.) (2007) *Volunteering Works: Volunteering and Social Policy*. London: Institute for Volunteering Research and Volunteering England.

ODPM (2005) *Citizen Engagement and Public Services: Why Neighbourhoods Matter*. London: ODPM.

Pancer, M. and Pratt, M. (1999) Social and Family Determinants of Community Service Involvement in Canadian Youth. In: Yates, M. and Youniss, J. (eds) *Community Service and Activism in Youth*. Chicago: University of Chicago Press: 32–55.

Parkin, S. and McKeganey, N. (2000) The Rise and Rise of Peer Education Approaches, *Drugs, Education Prevention and Policy*, 7(3): 293–310.

Porteous, D. (2007) The Rise and Fall of Mentoring in Youth Justice, *Prison Service Journal*, 170: 20–24.

Prison Service (2002) *Strategy for Working with the Voluntary and Community Sector Prison Service Order 4029*. London: NOMS.

Prison Service (2010) *Security Vetting Prison Service Instruction 43*. London: NOMS.

Putnam, R. D. (2000) *Bowling Alone, The Collapse and Revival of American Community*. New York: Simon and Schuster.

Read, J., Thompson, D., Tomczak, P. and Tufail, W. (2011) *The Third Sector in Criminal Justice: A Critical Relationship? Report of the First Seminar on 'The Third Sector in Criminal Justice*. Leeds: University of Leeds.

Restall, M. (2005) *Volunteers and the Law*. London: Volunteering England.

Richter, L. M. and Norman, A. (2010) AIDS Orphan Tourism: A Threat to Young Children in Residential Care, *Vulnerable Children and Youth Studies*, 5 (3): 217–229.

Rochester, C., Ellis Paine, A. and Howlett, S. (2010) *Volunteering and Society in the 21st Century*. Basingstoke: Palgrave Macmillan.

Ross, M. W., Greenfield, S. A. and Bennett, L. (1999) Predictors of Dropout and Burnout in AIDS Volunteers: A Longitudinal Study, *AIDS Care*, 11 (6): 723–731.

Rossendale Free Press (2011) *Decision to House Sex Offenders at Centre a 'Slap in the Face' for Village*. [Online] 14October. Available from: http://www.rossendale-freepress.co.uk/news/loc al-news/decision-house-sex-offenders-centre-1705603 [accessed 13/10/13].

Scandura, T. A. (1998) Dysfunctional Mentoring Relationships and Outcomes, *Journal of Management*, 24 (3): 449–467.

Shapland, J. (ed.) (2007) *Justice, Community and Civil Society: A Contested Terrain.* Cullompton: Willan.

Singh, R. (2012) When Punishment and Philanthropy Mix: Voluntary Organizations and the Governance of the Domestic Violence Offender, *Theoretical Criminology*, 16 (3): 269–287.

Smith, D. (2008) Accepting and Understanding the 'Dark Side' of the Nonprofit Sector: One Key Part of Building a Healthier Civil Society. Annual conference of the *Association for Research on Nonprofit Organizations and Voluntary Action*, 20–22 November 2008, Philadelphia, PA.

Smith, D. H. (2000) *Grassroots Associations.* Thousand Oaks, CA: Sage.

South Wales Evening Post (2012) *Llanelli Residents Vow to Fight Ex-offenders Hostel Plan.* [Online] 21 June. Available from: http://www.thisissouthwales.co.uk/Residents-streets-oppose-ex-prisoners-home/story-16425078-detail/story.html#ixzz2dkogfXNN [accessed 13/10/13].

Third Sector (2010) *Interim Results of Volunteer Rights Inquiry Reveal 'Shocking Stories'.* [Online] 8 July. Available from: http://www.thirdsector.co.uk/news/1014899/ [accessed 13/10/13].

Thoits, P. A. and Hewitt, L. N. (2001) Volunteer Work and Well-Being, *Journal of Health and Social Behavior*, 42 (2): 115–131.

Thomas, D. (2012) *The Charity Sector and Financial Crime Risks.* London: Thomson Reuters/Accelus.

Titmus, R. M. (1970) *The Gift Relationship: From Human Blood to Social Policy.* London: George Allen & Unwin.

Tolan, P., Henry, D., Schoeny, M. and Bass, A. (2008) Mentoring Interventions to Affect Juvenile Delinquency and Associated Problems, *Campbell Systematic Reviews*, 1–16.

United Nations Volunteers Report (2001) Prepared for the *UN General Assembly Special Session on Social Development*, Geneva: United Nations.

Volunteering England (2008) *Volunteering England Information Sheet: Definitions of Volunteering.* London: Volunteering England.

Volunteering England (2010) *Volunteer Rights Inquiry: Interim Report.* London: Volunteering England.

Wacquant, L. J. D. (1998) Negative Social Capital: State Breakdown and Social Destitution in America's Urban Core, *Netherlands Journal of Housing and the Built Environment*, 1: 25–40.

Western Morning News (2013) *Police Boss Launches Cash Safety Grants.* [Online] 20 August. Available from: http://www.thisiscornwall.co.uk/Police-boss-launches-cash-safety-grants/story-19680603-detail/story.html#axzz2cnVy0wwX [accessed 23/08/13].

Youth Justice Board (2007) *Volunteering in the Youth Justice System: Guidance for Youth Offending Teams and Secure Establishments.* London: Youth Justice Board for England and Wales.

6
When Worlds Collide: Researching and Evaluating the Voluntary Sector's Work with Offenders

Carol Hedderman and *Anthea Hucklesby*

Government and statutory sector agencies gain considerable value from securing voluntary sector involvement in the delivery of services to marginalised, hard-to-reach groups. Meanwhile, many voluntary sector organisations (VSOs) accept government and statutory sector funding because it provides a level of financial security which (in theory) ensures a reliable service to their clients. Until 2014, in the case of services for offenders in England and Wales, this was usually achieved by contracting out specific aspects of service provision to VSOs. From now on it is more likely that VSOs will be the junior partners in commercially led consortia or subcontractors to such consortia. In either situation, the funding services provided by VSOs are increasingly requiring evidence of success and effectiveness, which many VSOs are ill-equipped to provide. This chapter considers some of the consequences of the new requirements for VSOs to 'prove' their worth. It argues that the very characteristics which make involving the voluntary sector in service delivery attractive to funders also make them hard to evaluate in the sorts of ways which government and other funders increasingly require.

In the remainder of this chapter, we consider why there is such a mismatch between common practice in the voluntary sector and the way the statutory sector (and private companies) thinks about evidencing value, by examining differences in their organisational constraints, demands, aspirations, cultures, structures, caseloads, working practices and reporting requirements. The chapter goes on to discuss some of the challenges which arise for evaluators and VSOs when doing or commissioning research. The chapter draws primarily on two recent examples, both of which were evaluations of pilots funded by government and run by VSOs (Hedderman et al., 2008; Hucklesby, 2011). The Effective Bail Scheme (EBS) provided accommodation and support to defendants on bail (Hucklesby, 2011) whilst the Together Women Project (TWP) ran community interventions for women who had or were at risk of offending (Hedderman et al., 2008). The chapter concludes by considering how these differences in approach by state and voluntary sectors can be accommodated more effectively in future evaluations and research. First, we set the chapter in context before highlighting the different approaches to research and evaluation which can arise between VSOs and researchers particularly when they are independent of the organisation being researched.

Current context

The terms 'voluntary' or 'third' sector are often used interchangeably to refer to organisations which are not part of the public or the private sector. Their defining feature is that their actions are inspired primarily by social values rather than being either a statutory duty or a desire to make a commercial profit. In some cases this means they do not generate an income surplus; in others it means that any profits are reinvested to support and expand their activities. Aside from this distinguishing feature, organisations within the sector vary in terms of form and size from loose local affiliations of a few like-minded individuals who donate their time to a good cause, through social enterprises and cooperatives, to large-scale registered charities employing thousands of people across the world.

Research activity in the voluntary sector is wide-ranging and encompasses research, evaluation and monitoring that is carried out in, for and by VSOs. This chapter is based largely on our experiences of doing evaluative research in VSOs but many of the issues also apply to research activities. It encompasses activities as diverse as in-house evaluation, research conducted by individuals often undertaking university qualifications, practitioners or academics linked to the organisation in some way, for example, as trustees and outside research organisations, or academics being commissioned to undertake an evaluation. Who carries out research and the nature and extent of the enquiry is usually dictated by the available resources and results in a trade-off between the robustness of the research and its independence. The nature of research which is carried out is usually a compromise between what the organisations really would like to do and what they can afford.

VSOs have relied on many different funding sources over time. Historically only a limited number of these have required robust evaluation of the services provided and of outcomes as a requirement of funding. Generally, grant-awarding bodies have been relatively relaxed about evaluation regimes and many VSOs have hitherto obtained funding with no such requirements. Increasingly, however, VSOs are accessing funding which demands a greater level of accountability and more concrete measurement of outputs and outcomes as well as evidence of effectiveness before future funding is confirmed. Primary amongst funders in the criminal justice field are government and statutory agencies that have increasingly commissioned services from VSOs over the last two decades. In 2010, a survey of VSOs reported that 70 per cent of those with a criminal justice focus received public sector funding. This was true of 59 per cent of those who worked mainly with offenders. For a quarter of these organisations, this was the largest source of funding (Clifford et al., 2010). The same study also found that the smaller the organisation, the more likely it was to be mainly reliant on public sector support. At the same time, grant-awarding bodies have found themselves under scrutiny in terms of the funding they provide to organisations and are increasingly expected to insist that VSOs demonstrate that they provide value for money. In addition, other funding sources including European Union institutions such as the European Social Fund (ESF) have become important to VSOs and these often come with requirements for monitoring information and detailed feedback on outcomes (for example, Cole et al., 2007).

The requirement that VSOs should demonstrate their value in terms of the effectiveness of the services they provide is likely to grow rather than diminish. The UK coalition government sought to cut around a quarter of Ministry of Justice expenditure between 2010 and 2014 (HM Treasury, 2010) and subsequently made plans for a further 10 per cent reduction in 2015/16 (HM Treasury, 2013). This was partly to be delivered by encouraging the voluntary sector to 'shape and provide innovative, bottom-up services where *expensive* state provision has failed' (HM Government, 2010: 3, emphasis added). In other words, the voluntary sector was and still is being expected to replace the statutory sector while doing better for less. Meanwhile, the *Transforming Rehabilitation* (TR) agenda will see VSOs becoming more deeply involved in services funded by public money. Underpinning this policy is that part of the fee for work they will provide with offenders will be on a payment-by-results basis (Ministry of Justice, 2013a), which requires being able to define, estimate and measure impact (Fox and Albertson, 2011). While the strategy recognises that this is likely to disadvantage smaller VSOs, and minor adjustments to the bidding process have been made to address this,[1] there is a clear expectation that VSOs will usually be employed by commercial companies as subcontractors (tier two and three providers), rather than being commissioned directly by central government (tier one providers) (Clinks, 2013; Ministry of Justice, 2013b). Leaving aside the wider implications of these changes for the supervision of offenders, they have two important implications for monitoring and evaluating the work of VSOs. First, the pressure for such organisations to prove their value will increase as they seek to compete for even scarcer resources; and second, they will have to prove their value, not only in terms that the government funders require but also in a way which meets the expectations of the (mostly) private sector 'primes' (i.e. the main contractors for whom they will subcontract). In this new context, price and value for money are likely to assume an even higher degree of importance because these are key to private sector success.

All public sector bodies are obliged to operate with efficiency and financial transparency, to secure cost-effective delivery and to make decisions based on reliable, comprehensive and comparable information (NAO, 2011). Contracting out service provision does not absolve the public sector of these responsibilities, but requires them to obtain information from contractors to monitor performance against these benchmarks. While there have been numerous attempts over the last decade to ensure that such monitoring requirements are proportionate (e.g. HM Treasury, 2002; NAO, 2005; Cabinet Office, 2010), it remains true that, on average, public funders impose a heavier monitoring burden on VSOs than do other funders (NAO, 2009: 7). Even meeting the comparatively more modest monitoring requirements of other funding bodies carries some cost as every pound spent on monitoring requirements is one less spent on service delivery. The resultant pressure has led to a considerable amount of effort being invested by VSOs in monitoring and evaluation, although little of this has generated robust results because these generally small-scale operations lack both the capacity and expertise to do either task well. Moreover, monitoring and evaluation requirements may themselves influence the work carried out by VSOs as has been demonstrated in the statutory sector (Hucklesby and Wincup, 2007, 2014). As Harlock (2013: 20) has suggested, '[t]here are growing concerns that funders' and commissioners' requirements are shaping and dominating approaches to impact measurement in the voluntary sector over the needs of service users, beneficiaries and VSOs themselves'.

The purpose of research in the voluntary sector

On one level all parties would agree that research and evaluation in the voluntary sector is about providing robust evidence which demonstrates which services are effective and which are not. Of course, these are not simple questions and there is a huge literature on how such evaluations may be done which will not be revisited here (see, e.g., Pawson and Tilley, 1997). What this section does is to identify some fundamental differences in the ways in which independent researchers and VSOs may view the purpose of research which has significant implications for what type of evidence is produced. In common with any such exercise the lines between approaches are more blurred in reality than are portrayed here.

Independent researchers would usually approach the evaluation by finding out how an intervention works by undertaking a process evaluation and then identifying outcomes. There may also be an action research element in which blockages and problems are identified and ways are sought to overcome them whilst the evaluation is under way. In practice, criminal justice examples of action research are rare.[2] The purpose of such research is to provide a clear picture of what is taking place and an assessment of its value in terms of the aims of the project. Inevitably it involves uncovering activities and practices which demonstrate positive and negative aspects of a project's work and in doing so provides evidence to improve the implementation of the intervention or indeed might suggest that the activity should cease. By contrast, some VSOs adopt an alternative approach, which is based on values and beliefs rather than concrete evidence. They view the role of research and evaluation as validating an approach which they intuitively know works. Consequently, they become uncomfortable when researchers begin to uncover negative aspects of the services provided and, as a result, question their work. The stance taken by VSOs is understandable because the stakes are high. They have expended considerable time and resources in setting up and operating the service(s). The organisation's reputation may be in the balance as well as personal reputations, careers and jobs of those providing the service. The result can be a mismatch between the expectations of researchers (and, increasingly, funders) on the one hand and of VSOs on the other.

Delivering criminal justice services: contrasting the statutory and voluntary sectors

A further distinction can be drawn between how the voluntary and statutory sector work with criminal justice populations and how they perceive and describe such work. One illustration of this is that, when working with those who have offended, VSOs are likely to refer to clients, service users or customers and to treat them as people being offered help and choices, whereas statutory sector agencies usually refer to offenders and their role often involves controlling and demanding certain behaviours from those they supervise. Of course, in practice, clear distinctions and boundaries between the sectors do not necessarily exist in these terms. The reality is much more opaque with blurred and intersecting working practices. This is particularly pertinent given the blurring of the boundaries between the sectors brought about primarily by the current direction of policy and the movement of managers and staff between sectors and organisations.

The extent of both the powers and responsibilities of statutory criminal justice agencies is defined in, and constrained by, law, and their budgets are set accordingly. As the demand for their services usually outstrips their budgetary capacity, priorities and performance targets are usually set by senior managers even when they are not fixed by legislation or through central government directives. While other staff usually have some degree of professional autonomy, this is too often subject to statutory regulation, such as the national standards governing probation work (NOMS, 2011). In either case, discretion is limited. It rarely extends to allowing them to expand their remit or to work with those who fall outside it. The restrictions requiring staff to focus on certain cases and particular aspects of them (e.g. reducing reoffending) tend to encourage a view of service users as 'cases' to be processed and quickly resolved rather than rounded individuals whose needs may not fit neatly within organisational boundaries. This is most evident when 'offenders' are also 'victims' such as women who are involved in sex work who have been trafficked (Anti-Trafficking Monitoring Group, 2013). In contrast, because VSOs are more likely to focus on people, they accept a greater degree of complexity and work on the multiple needs of their clients. Sometimes this is done in-house directly; in other cases it is achieved by tapping into other statutory sources of funding (e.g. related to drug addiction, mental health or unemployment), or by referrals to other VSOs who have appropriate expertise or resources.

In performing their duties, statutory agencies are required to consider the (potentially competing) interests of victims, suspects, defendants, offenders and the wider public.[3] For example, the Code for Crown Prosecutors (Crown Prosecution Service, 2013: 2) requires that they make the decision to prosecute 'fairly, impartially and with integrity help to secure justice for victims, witnesses, defendants and the public' and 'must always act in the interests of justice and not solely for the purpose of obtaining a conviction'; and the National Offender Management Service (NOMS, 2013: 2) justifies its role in 'helping offenders to reform their lives' by arguing that in doing so they 'protect the public'. In contrast, far from being obliged to take account of the competing interests of other groups or of the general public interest, many VSOs exist specifically to champion the needs of a particular client group. For example, Victim Support makes no mention of the rights of defendants in their statement of vision, purposes and values; and the Clinks Manifesto[4] focuses exclusively on the rights of prisoners and their families. These organisations are not tasked by anyone with such objectives but have chosen to focus on them. To this extent they are like the private sector, although they are motivated primarily by achieving social goals rather than profits.

Historically, the obligation to deal equally and impartially with all citizens, combined with the need to keep public spending to a minimum, has also shaped the way statutory criminal justice agencies operate when working with defendants and offenders. Quite properly, given that convicting individuals and imposing and enforcing a criminal punishment is probably the worst thing any state can do to its citizens, any hint of discrimination or unfairness is subject to scrutiny and challenge. As a result, a 'one size fits all' approach tends to prevail with equality of application rather than outcome being the approach. This is also the cheapest way to provide a service enabling large numbers of individuals to be processed as efficiently as possible. While the personalisation agenda, which has begun to significantly reshape service provision in the social care sector, has gained little traction in criminal justice to date (Fox et al., 2013), evidence on effective (and cost-effective) approaches to reducing reoffending has led to the introduction of a degree of individual tailoring into the way offenders are dealt with post sentence over the last two decades. This is often where the voluntary sector has something to offer. Their greater operational flexibility enables them not only to deliver individually tailored responses but also reportedly to innovate (NAO, 2005; NOMS, 2008). This may be facilitated by the fact that many are small-scale organisations with relatively flat management structures which lack the inefficiencies some view as inherent in more hierarchical and bureaucratic organisations.[5]

Statutory sector agencies have no option but to work with all offenders who fall within their remit and in most cases they would be 'involuntary clients' (Trotter, 1999). Their caseload is not negotiable whereas the voluntary sector has to date had more discretion about which clients it accepts and how long it works with them. Furthermore, offenders have traditionally had a choice, albeit constrained, about whether to engage with the services provided by the voluntary sector (the EBS (Hucklesby, 2011) and drug treatment services (Hucklesby and Wincup, 2010) are exceptions).

Traditionally, the work of the voluntary sector has focused on working with lower-end, less risky offenders whereas the statutory sector has no choice but to work with the full range of offenders. Consequently, the composition of the client base, and the motivation of those with whom they work, is likely to differ between the two sectors. These distinctions are now even more pronounced after the implementation of the *TR* agenda has begun. High-risk offenders are supervised by the National Probation Service, which remains a statutory sector agency, whilst medium- and lower-risk offenders are the responsibility of Community Rehabilitation Companies (CRCs) which are operated under contract by private or voluntary sector providers or consortia (see https://www.gov.uk/government/uploads/system/uploads/attachment_data/file/389727/table-of-new-owners-of-crcs.pdf).

Professionalisation of the statutory sector has been a key development in the post-war period (May, 1991; Newburn, 2008; Mair and Burke, 2012). Increasingly statutory agencies have been required to ensure that their work meets quality thresholds and internal and external procedures have been put in place to ensure consistency and accountability including oversight by the central government and inspectorates (Morgan, 2007; NAO, 2014). Staff within the agencies have become accustomed to recording their work and being accountable for their decisions and it is viewed (grudgingly in some cases) as an integral part of their job. Such moves have been largely absent from the voluntary sector and a culture of accountability or monitoring and evaluation does not routinely pervade organisations (Hucklesby and Worrall, 2007). The issue is especially acute when VSOs rely on volunteers. Quite reasonably, volunteers (and sometimes paid workers) tend to view their role as working with defendants/offenders and, having given up their time freely, do not view completing paperwork as a priority. This often results in poor compliance with requests to do so. Consequently, the framework for such activities including a skills base has not really existed within the voluntary sector (Sampson, 2002).

Differences in their responsibilities, size and context mean that statutory criminal justice agencies and VSOs operate with different reporting requirements. Like all other public bodies (as noted above), statutory sector agencies are required to demonstrate that they have used their resources efficiently and cost-effectively, and that their decisions are based on reliable, comprehensive and comparable information (NAO, 2011). The nature of these requirements ensures that such organisations collect, value and report on quantitative data on 'cases' and have the infrastructure to do so including secure and reliable IT schemes. In the case of criminal justice agencies such as the police, Crown Prosecution Service

(CPS), courts and National Offender Management Service (NOMS), while delivery may be local, the data to be collected are specified at a national level. The data required are quantitative and generally, but not exclusively, relate to processing decisions and key performance targets (KPTs) (NOMS, 2014b). When qualitative data are included in reports on their operations, this information is used to put a human face on these data rather than being used in its own right as important and valuable evidence. In contrast, the voluntary sector's focus on people, rather than cases, encourages a recognition of, and response to, differences rather than similarities and this is much more easily and appropriately captured through recording individual case history narratives. Even when VSOs seek to record quantitative data, the scale of most such organisations, combined with the lack of infrastructure and skills, means that they rarely have the resources or in-house expertise to buy, create or maintain accurate and reliable quantitative data systems.

A less obvious, but equally important problem is that the case histories VSOs collect are rarely of a standard to constitute qualitative evidence of impact but are usually little more than personal anecdotes collected on an ad hoc basis by staff. Even when they have sought to maintain their impartiality, they will be perceived as having a vested interest in portraying their work with service users, and progress made, in a favourable light. Indeed the approach of the voluntary sector to research tends to be validating an approach which they intuitively believe 'works' but for which there is no independent evidence. This is particularly the case in organisations which focus on a single activity on which their whole existence depends. Case studies are a useful tool for this exercise because it is likely that in any organisation there will be a small number of exceptional cases which 'prove' that the approach works. However, case studies do not provide the quality or breadth of evidence which is increasingly required by funders.

In the next section, we consider how these tensions play out when voluntary sector agencies deliver services to defendants and offenders and funders require evidence of impact and independent evaluators are commissioned.

Aims, objectives and theories of change or lack of them

As a consequence of the commissioning process, providers often inflate targets and state their aims in terms of ambitions to reduce reoffending, reduce prison populations, divert offenders from custody and so on. Setting aside for the moment problems with measurement, such approaches rarely go further and explain how the goals are going to be achieved and the theory of change which is being relied upon.

For example, the Corston Review (2007) recommended the development of community-based services for women in order to reduce their involvement in the criminal justice system and to divert them from custody. This led the government to sponsor what was described as a 'national demonstration project' which involved the Ministry of Justice spending £9 million to support three VSOs in setting up and running five 'Together Women' centres[6] in the North of England over a three-year period (see Hedderman et al., 2008, 2011; Jolliffe et al., 2011). These were expected to provide a holistic response to socially deprived women who were either 'offenders' or 'at risk' of offending. While the response was influenced by the way other similar centres worked, there was no agreed underlying 'model of change' of the sort underlying offending behaviour programmes accredited for offenders in prison or on probation. Thus, the three organisations were free to create their own approaches.[7]

Similarly, the EBS (Hucklesby, 2011) was funded by the Treasury to provide accommodation and support to defendants awaiting trial to divert defendants from custody and increase compliance with bail conditions, court attendance rates and the use of non-custodial sentences if defendants were convicted. Some of the activities of the project were clearly linked to these aims such as providing or paying for transport to get defendants to court but for others, such as requiring defendants to attend meetings with workers, the link between them and the aims of the project was more tenuous. This was particularly the case if meetings were used purely for reporting. Yet this does not mean that such activities were without utility – ensuring that defendants reported and so could be recorded as present was important because one of the stated objectives of the project was to meet with defendants three times a week so defendants complied and the project met its KPTs. What would or should happen at these meetings was never articulated, nor was how they linked to the aims of the project. Similarly, mentoring was an integral part of the project but how this activity fulfilled the aims of the project was never made clear (Hucklesby, 2011; Hucklesby and Wincup, 2014). In another project evaluated by one of us, the aim of the resettlement project was to improve the employability of prisoners but not only are there many ways to measure this, it became clear that there was no agreed understanding of what employability meant (Hucklesby and Wincup, 2007). For some it meant getting offenders into actual work; for others it was getting them more 'job ready', which again had several different interpretations.

Abstract, high-end aims are one problem but there are also examples of projects run by VSOs (and others) in which aims are not clearly articulated, are too abstract or are unobtainable. Concepts are often used in stated aims for which there is no consistent understanding. For instance, even something as fundamental as what constituted an 'offender' was not defined in advance in the TWP. Indeed, the label was only used by Together Women when reporting on contractual issues as they had targets concerning the number of 'offender' service users. Thus, 'offenders' sometimes included those currently involved in the criminal justice system, even if they had not been convicted. At other times it referred to those who had only offended many years earlier. The use of 'at risk' in TWP is also illustrative. Data from the Women Centres suggested that women were labelled 'at risk' if they had two or more social needs but did not have either a history of offending or current involvement in the criminal justice system. Confusingly, when Together Women staff talked about 'risk' they meant risk of harm to self or others rather than 'risk of offending'. 'Needs' is another concept which is widely used but for which there is no agreed definition as TWP and the EBS illustrate. Both projects created plans (called either supervision or action plans) by interviewing service users about their needs and completing assessment forms which differed even within the TWP. The three VSOs in the TWP, the EBS and resettlement initiatives (Hucklesby and Wincup, 2007) evaluated by us were all free to devise their own measurements of what constituted a need and the severity of the need. At the same time, it was clear that concepts such as 'criminogenic needs' are increasingly framing the ways VSOs construct the concept of needs and their work with defendants/offenders.

Once needs have been identified, services have to be put in place to try and alleviate them. There are different models adopted for doing this within and between projects. In the case of Together Women Centres, services generally reflected needs associated with risk of offending among women (Hedderman, 2004; Blanchette and Brown, 2006; Hollin and Palmer, 2006) including life skills and self-confidence, education and training, housing, previous and current victimisation, mental health, finance, physical health, and substance abuse. However, the level of support provided, and whether this was commissioned from other local agencies or delivered in-house, varied from site to site and according to the skills set of each centre's staff and locally available services. The three VSOs were also free to devise their own measurements of what constituted levels of service and outcomes to be achieved. In the EBS, as with an increasing number of other VSO projects, mentors were an integral part of service provision (Hucklesby, 2011; Hucklesby and Wincup, 2014). Project staff would refer all defendants to the in-house mentoring service regardless of whether a need for a mentor had been identified because this was a measureable outcome of the project. This meant that they had ticked the box that the services had been provided to satisfy the funder, whilst leaving the type and level of assistance given up to individual mentors. In reality, this often meant that no contact took place between defendants and mentors, or that contact was over the phone or was limited to a single meeting in a coffee shop or fast food restaurant rather than a sustained relationship over a period of time (Hucklesby and Wincup, 2014).

Such practices are not necessarily problematic when projects are set up as pilots or demonstration projects specifically to test out new ways of working or working with different groups of offenders as with both the TWP and the EBS. However, evaluations of such initiatives are often required to measure their effectiveness in terms of high-end aims. In the case of TWP, NOMS (NOMS, 2006) designated Together Women a 'national demonstration project' and commissioned an evaluation to measure the effectiveness of the overall project in terms of diverting women 'at risk' from offending, diverting women who had offended from reoffending and diverting women out of the criminal justice system (especially from custody). In other words, having encouraged the centres to tailor support to each service user, they then set three very simple pass or fail tests of success. In this context, the lack of a common underlying model of how the TWP was expected to bring about change and what success would look like, and that each location and, in some cases, each key worker was free to use the same terms ('at risk', 'offender', 'needs', 'service') to mean different things from case to case became over time highly problematic. For example, NOMS wished to see the value of the approach tested for 'offenders' and those 'at risk of offending' but, as noted, the terms were neither clearly defined nor operationally meaningful, with the result that the evaluation team identified at least six potentially distinct groups among Together Women service users rather than just these two:

1. 'At risk' of self-harm or being victimised, with no documented history of offending;
2. 'At risk' of self-harm or being victimised, with a documented history of offending;
3. 'At risk' of offending, with no documented history of offending;
4. 'At risk' of offending, with a documented history of offending;
5. 'Current' offenders with no documented criminal history;
6. 'Current' offenders with a documented criminal history.[8]

When there is no clear articulation of aims or clear understanding of the inputs of the project, the measurement of outcomes is made impossible. In these circumstances what replaces outcomes is often a concentration on the measurement of processes (for example, how many offenders had an action plan created) or actions/outputs (for instance, that offenders attended a group session). Processes are more easily measured than outcomes and morph into ends rather than means. Examples include projects focusing on getting referrals rather than what they do with defendants/offenders once they are service users or counting referrals to outside agencies but with no follow-up to assess the engagement of the service users with those services. The problems associated with measuring engagement with services and high-end outcomes such as reducing reconvictions are not of course confined to VSOs. For example, an evaluation of the government-funded Basic Skills Pathfinder, which sought to address the literacy deficits of offenders, found that only 194 (19 per cent) of 1003 offenders who were screened as probably needing basic skills subsequently attended a full assessment because of this lack of follow-up (McMahon et al., 2004).

Where many VSOs are at a disadvantage compared to statutory sector agencies is a lack of an infrastructure to facilitate the collection of data. Most VSOs have created their own system for recording information, often at considerable expense. These bespoke databases created by specialist software companies are costly to maintain and amend and are often incompatible with data analysis packages. In some cases, such as the TWP, this means that each of the VSOs involved in a project collected data in different ways making comparisons difficult. This problem is likely to be exacerbated when consortia are made up of several partners involved in running CRCs. In some organisations, especially smaller ones and those who use volunteers, there is still a reliance on paper-based records requiring significant investment on the part of the VSOs or researchers to transform records into data which are usable and analysable.

Also, to be able to assess an intervention's effect on reconviction requires being able to say what would have happened in the absence of that intervention ('the counterfactual'). Historically, most VSOs have not had access to such a group and, even if they did, would not have the necessary information to compare the samples. Recognising this problem, the Ministry of Justice has created the 'Justice Data Lab' to facilitate reconviction analysis (http://www.justice.gov.uk/justice-data-lab). The aim is to provide reconviction data on service users of VSOs and control groups but only in aggregate form. The project is in its early stages but there are some indications that VSOs are having difficulties in providing the Ministry of Justice with the necessary data for the lab to be used (NOMS, 2014a). Questions also remain about how accurate or meaningful the results will be. In one example we are aware of, significant gaps and errors were found in the data provided. Certainly, reconviction analysis on several projects we have been involved in suggests that matching service users to Police National Computer (PNC) records is a hit or miss affair, making the results of dubious value. Furthermore, in the case of the TWP, the Justice Data Lab would only be useful for 'current' offenders. Consequently there was simply no way of saying whether, but for Together Women, those 'at risk' (sic) would have offended.

These should not be regarded as a criticism of the Together Women Centres. While the lack of clear criteria about what constituted a serious or minor problem, and inconsistencies in record keeping, created major difficulties when trying to conduct a post hoc outcome evaluation, this probably had no effect on the help women received as individual workers tended to know their clients very well. Certainly feedback from service users suggested that the centres provided more consistent and effective support than any previously received (see Hedderman et al., 2011). What this does reflect is the fact that professional evaluators were involved too late in the day, and that the mismatch in what central government required as evidence, and what was being collected, was identified too late for the situation to be retrieved without the centres being furnished with much more professional evaluation support and resources. Even then it is questionable whether central government expectations about what the centres would achieve in terms of reductions in reoffending were realistic given what the centres were doing, who they were doing it with and the scale they were doing it on. As noted in the first and final evaluation reports (Hedderman et al., 2008; Jolliffe et al., 2011), it was never entirely clear whether the projects were intended to support offenders who happened to be women or socially excluded women who happened to be offenders.

It is also worth noting that the centres worked with the evaluators to devise and agree on a common set of alternative outcome measures when it became clear that our ability to assess the value of Together Women's impact on reoffending was going to be severely limited. Although when NOMS specified the content of the final impact report, it showed no interest in this information. However, subsequent analyses of one centre's data, carried out for the Corston Coalition of Funders, have shown that for well over half the women for whom this information was recorded, needs were partly or fully met. For example, reduced needs were recorded in two out of every three cases who were said to have substance misuse, accommodation and ETE (Education, Training and Employment) needs (Hedderman and Jolliffe, 2013).

The four data challenges: availability, timeliness, quality and quantity

In this section we examine some of the challenges for researchers and evaluators in accessing and working with data relating to the work of the voluntary sector.

The period of time available in which to evaluate the work of VSOs is often limited. Much of their work is funded on 'soft money' and rarely extends for more than a few years (and sometimes is for a year or less). The relatively short-term nature of the projects usually means that there is little time to evaluate the service as it was envisaged it would operate. Significant time is spent setting up projects during which any research is likely to be measuring implementation and not a fully operational service. Likewise, as projects near the end of their funding, uncertainties about whether further funding will be found will inevitability lead to staff looking for other jobs and/or leaving and the service winding down. Receiving follow-on funding for existing services can also present challenges for researchers. Changing funders might necessitate redefining the service provided alongside its aims and objectives. Yet, whether these changes are appreciated by workers, service users or others who have contact with the service is sometimes questionable and can lead to problems for evaluators researching a service with operational aims which differ from its stated aims.

A further difficulty which is regularly encountered is that evaluation teams are rarely appointed until some months after a project has been commissioned or even after it has begun operating. As a result, evaluation requirements have not been built into implementation delivery but are tacked on as an afterthought. This leads to data collection being a cumbersome and time-consuming chore for project staff because the infrastructure, for example an electronic database to support an outcome study, has not been put in place. In one evaluation, records were kept in paper-based case files and not transferred to an electronic database until many months into the project and after the initial evaluation report was completed (Hucklesby, 2011). Even if an electronic database is created challenges arise because it usually has a dual purpose – as a case management system and an evaluation tool. Understandably, the first role tends to take precedence over the second, especially if evaluators are appointed once the implementation process has begun. Consequently, databases tend to focus on process matters (such as sources of referral and actions planned and taken) and outputs (e.g. numbers referred to other agencies). Even when databases are in place, challenges remain. Data are often mis-recorded and lack standardised definitions of matters as central as 'needs' resulting in inconsistent data recording. To the extent that outcomes are recorded they tend to rely on self-report by service users and/or the judgement of workers rather than externally validated measures. Key pieces of information required for outcome measures such as PNC numbers are often inconsistently recorded or missing completely sometimes because these data are not provided by statutory agencies when defendants/offenders are referred to the services. We have also found that record completion is of variable quality. For example, in TWP, one centre's database had fields for recording substance abuse, but this information was not always completed in cases where records showed work on substance use had been conducted. Also, the categories available to record substance abuse did not distinguish the actual level of use (units of alcohol, type and quantity of drug) from the extent to which a service users defined themselves as having a problem. Thus, records showing 'problematic' use could include those who consumed a relatively small amount of alcohol or drugs but found this problematic (e.g. because they were trying to hold down a job or they had mental health problems) and exclude others who did not regard consuming very high quantities of substances as problematic because it was such a routine and long-standing feature of their daily existence. Another problem for evaluators is that much data is recorded as 'free text' rather than in drop down boxes resulting in significant challenges when transferring databases into analysable formats.

There are a number of potential reasons for data quality issues and many of these are not unique to VSOs. But we have found evidence that the voluntary sector may have particular challenges because of the context in which it provides services. Some staff are resistant to spending time recording their work with service users because they believe that it keeps them away from their 'real work' (Hucklesby, 2011). Such beliefs are likely to be more strongly held by volunteers who give up their time freely to help people rather than spend time on paperwork. The leverage available to projects to insist on volunteers recording data is limited as they are not 'employed' by the organisation. As we see it, this is a major challenge for VSOs commissioned by the government or private sector providers under the *TR* agenda that will be required to provide data to support payment by results (PbR).

Coming into an evaluation after the commencement of projects may also raise ethical issues. In our experience, rarely have service users been asked for their consent for their data to be used for research purposes. Even when they have been asked, such consent is generally too limited to be useful. For example, they may have been asked if the project can use or disclose information for research purposes anonymously, but often researchers need identifying information in order to link project data to other sources such as the PNC. If the evaluation is proposing to use historical data relating to ex-service users this can be a hurdle which cannot be overcome and data may be lost, resulting in missing data and small numbers of cases. Trying to gain consent retrospectively results in its own challenges – service users are often difficult to find but more problematically they may have 'gone straight' and contacting them again may open up old wounds and alert new friends, families and employers to their past.

Many VSOs are relatively small and even many of the larger ones work on local or regionally funded projects, which can mean that the number of service users they work with during the lifetime of a specific project is quite small. Consequently, researchers may struggle to ensure that they have sample sizes which are large enough to undertake statistical analysis which will lead to robust results. Working with subgroups of service users to examine important factors such as how effectively projects work with diverse or minority populations (often a target group for the work of VSOs) or how effectively a resettlement project works with ex-prisoners in the community may exacerbate the issues. In addition, many of those using a particular service will also be receiving other interventions. In these circumstances it is not usually possible to disentangle the outcomes of a specific project, particularly when in our experience some service users do not realise the differences between individuals and projects and may be unable to identify which help was useful.

The final issue discussed in this section concerns data security and management in the context of a mixed economy of criminal justice. Increasingly evaluators are going to be required to use data from multiple sources which are provided to the VSOs being evaluated for non-research purposes. Examples might include OASyS assessments and pre-conviction records. It is often not clear who owns such data. The ethical question this raises is whether researchers are able to access these sensitive documents without gaining the express permission of the organisations which passed them to the VSO. By way of example, in one evaluation we were involved in this would have necessitated applications and negotiations with all of the major statutory criminal justice agencies and both the Ministry of Justice and the Home Office! In another evaluation of a resettlement project we needed to access prison files which included a significant amount of sensitive information unrelated to the project or the evaluation. Access was granted by two prisons but not the third, resulting in a significant gap in data with which to compare the project's work with different constituencies of prisoners.

Dissemination

Dissemination of research is a highly charged topic and one in which criminological researchers have grappled with continuously over many years. In our experience, the VSO approach to dissemination ranges along a broad spectrum. On the one hand, we have been commissioned by funders to write specific publications to disseminate our research and, on the other hand, we have been informed that research reports will be kept confidential to a few individuals within the VSO. Generally, however, we have found a reluctance to disseminate findings widely both within and outwith organisations. Supporting research in an organisation takes up many individuals' time, especially those who have participated in the research. From the point of view of researchers, it is important for these people to know that their views are reflected in the subsequent report. However, VSOs appear to be concerned that their employees (and volunteers) may be demoralised if the research does not demonstrate conclusively and unequivocally that the project is successful and, as we know, this type of evidence is rarely available.

Evaluation and research reports often highlight areas which could have been dealt with more effectively as well as best practice. Such findings are particularly useful to other organisations, especially those who are working in similar areas or projects or indeed those who take over a project from another organisation. However, because research findings are often not disseminated, opportunities for learning are lost. The reasons why VSOs are reluctant to disseminate research findings are complex, and often appear to stem from a limited understanding of the nature of research. What seems clear to us is that some of these reasons are going to grow in importance given the current policy environment. Organisations are likely to become more concerned about the potential for reputational damage of mixed findings, even when research reports are unlikely to be read in that way. Commercial (sic) confidentiality is of heightened significance in a marketised criminal justice system as competition has the effect of stifling dissemination and the sharing of good practice (see, for example, http://www.express.co.uk/news/uk/305391/Probation-ordered-off-prison-site). But the stakes are higher – more short-term contracts with multiple providers means that lessons learnt in one project are less likely to be passed on to subsequent providers so problems and mistakes may be repeated.

Conclusions

Involving the voluntary sector in the delivery of criminal justice services has a number of advantages: they tend to be pragmatic and flexible, trusted by hard-to-reach communities and relatively cheap. However, funders of voluntary sector services are increasingly requiring evidence of success and effectiveness. That pressure is likely to increase as the *TR* Strategy takes hold, and work which was previously conducted by the public probation service is outsourced to private providers either in consortia with voluntary organisations or those employing voluntary sector agencies as subcontractors.

Few VSOs have the expertise to create monitoring systems which will sustain a high-quality outcome or impact study using quantitative measures. While many include service user stories these tend to be in the form of anecdotes from hand-picked clients. To demonstrate the value of any intervention or support service in a way which is likely to impress government sponsors (and private sector companies), VSOs would be well advised to begin by recording exactly what they intend to do and how they intend to do it (a model of change). Assessing whether they are meeting their objectives is something which can be done in-house only if the audience for that information is exclusively internal and future funding decisions are not resting on the results. Like it or not, the standard of work provided in-house does not usually stand up to external scrutiny and is unlikely to be sufficient to secure future funding. Those running and working in VSOs are experts in helping, but they rarely have the skills to monitor and evaluate. The moment a VSO wants to claim that its service makes a difference or is good value for money, they need professional research advice. This must come at a very early stage. By the time advice was sought on TWP data requirements, decisions about what information to collect had already been made locally by centre managers who were highly skilled in delivery but untrained in devising monitoring systems on which to base a national evaluation. Despite evaluation being a requirement of funding for the EBS, the VSO had not put in place a systematic procedure for data collection and data remained in paper files long after the project began. Involving researchers who understand the field will inform strategies for gathering information that will be needed further down the line (such as

PNC identifiers needed in reconviction studies), as well as agreeing what style and type of data analysis are feasible and will be most informative, and what ethical issues are likely to arise in the course of the evaluation.

Approaches to research are often dictated by available funding. Whilst funding for research and evaluation is usually a low priority whatever the sector, the broader funding challenges facing VSOs mean inevitability that funding for research activities are squeezed. One of the ways in which they might increase their research capacity is to take serendipitous opportunities as they arise. This may involve allowing University students access when they approach projects to undertake research for their Master's dissertations or a PhD thesis. This may seem like a cheap or easy option but it can backfire. Whether the advantages are realised depends on ensuring that students are closely supervised, that the evaluation objectives and methods are agreed and feasible, and that the available timescales and resources are appropriate. It is also important for those delivering or receiving frontline services not to suffer 'evaluation fatigue'. For example, in one evaluation we were involved in, two students were interviewing offenders about the service provided to them by the organisation only a few months before we were due to speak to them as part of the formal evaluation. Other relatively cheap options which may be more fruitful include contacting a local university researcher to see if they would be interested in doing a small-scale evaluation in return for access to the data. Universities sometimes have small grants available for this sort of work, particularly if the results might be used to make a bid to a Research Council for a larger study.

Any evaluation depends on the reliability and validity of the data so the involvement of professional researchers in the management of data collection, including data sampling and data audit, over the duration of an evaluation will produce better quality data than if the data gathering is left unattended. However, if funds are tight, paying a researcher for a few days of consultancy to help design a data collection system, to check data quality midway and to help in analysing the results is better than having no professional research advice at all.

The use of consistent, and preferably standardised, assessment tools to measure need and outcome is important, not just for evaluation purposes, but for accurate case management records. Beyond evaluation, the use of standardised measures allows for clear comparison between areas and also with other populations. On a practice level it would also provide the VSO with clear information about the added value of using a particular service or approach when trying to encourage referrals. At first sight, this suggestion may seem to conflict with the move towards local autonomy. In fact, such standardisation would relieve local projects from wasting resources (i.e. collecting information that would not be useful for evaluation) and even increase their chances of making successful bids for funding, by providing potential funders with stronger and more robust evidence on needs' profiles and local impact.

Finally, VSOs have a good record of cooperation and partnership with the statutory sector: to date this has been one of its strengths. Yet, VSOs are often reluctant to share the findings of research and evaluation for fear of reputational damage and concerns about the impact of future funding. The new landscape of marketisation in offender management makes dissemination of research more challenging given that the stakes are arguably now higher. Yet, the benefits of the research and evaluation for the organisation and for others working in the field are clear and will ultimately lead to better, more appropriate and responsive service provision. Doing high-quality research and sharing research findings, via comprehensive dissemination strategies, are key elements for the sustainability of a vibrant and effective voluntary sector.

Notes

1 The government's response to the public consultation exercise (Ministry of Justice, 2013a) includes promises to spend £500,000 building VSO capacity to compete and training to improve bidding skills.
2 Both the EBS and TWP were intended to follow this approach. In the event, this aspect of the TWP evaluation was not realised. An element of action research was undertaken in the EBS evaluation but it was not completed fully.
3 The extent to which this actually happens is contentious, of course (see, for example, Cook, 2006).
4 Clinks is an umbrella organisation which represents and campaigns for Third Sector organisations working with offenders. See http://www.clinks.org/resources/about-clinks.
5 Gojkovic et al. (2011) found that 61 per cent of third sector organisations whose *main* beneficiaries are offenders, ex-offenders and their families have an annual income of less than £100,000 and that 27 per cent of such TSOs reported having no income at all compared to 17 per cent of all TSOs.
6 One organisation ran three centres, and the other two ran one centre each. In some cases, Together Women was based at an existing Women's Centre with a wider remit; in other cases, they were created as standalone resources.
7 Subsequently, two members of the evaluation team (Hollin and Palmer) were commissioned to create a model of change but this was produced halfway through the project's life and was not adopted by the projects.
8 Even within this grouping, 'current' did not necessarily mean convicted.

References

Anti-Trafficking Monitoring Group (2013) *In the Dock: Examining the UK's Criminal Justice Response to Trafficking.* London: ECPAT UK. http://www.ecpat.org.uk/sites/default/files/in_the_dock_atmg_2013.pdf

Blanchette, K. and Brown, S. L. (2006) *The Assessment and Treatment of Women Offenders: An Integrative Perspective.* Chichester: John Wiley & Sons.

Cabinet Office (2010) *The Compact: The Coalition Government and Civil Society Organisations Working Effectively in Partnership for the Benefit of Communities and Citizens in England.* London: Cabinet Office.

Clifford, D., Rajme, F. G. and Mohan, J. (2010) *How Dependent is the Third Sector on Public Funding? Evidence from the National Survey of Third Sector Organisations.* Working Paper 45, Birmingham: Third Sector Research Centre. Available from: http://www.tsrc.ac.uk/Publications/tabid/500/Default.aspx

Clinks (2013) *Clinks Briefing on the Competition Stage of the Transforming Rehabilitation Reforms.* London: Clinks. Available from: http://www.clinks.org/sites/default/files/basic/filesdownloads/Members%20Briefing%20-%20Competition%20stage%20of%20the%20TR%20reforms%20FINAL.pdf

Cole, A., Galbraith, I., Lyon, P. and Ross, H. (2007) PS Plus: A Prison (Lately) Probation-based Employment Resettlement Model, in: Hucklesby, A. and Hagley-Dickinson, L. (eds) *Prisoner Resettlement: Policy and Practice.* Cullompton: Willan Publishing: 121–143.

Cook, D (2006) *Criminal and Social Justice,* London: Sage

Corston, J. (2007) *The Corston Report: A Review of Women with Particular Vulnerabilities in the Criminal Justice System.* London: Home Office.

Crown Prosecution Service (2013) *Code for Crown Prosecutors.* London: CPS. Available from: http://www.cps.gov.uk/publications/code_for_crown_prosecutors/index.html Fox, C. and Albertson, K. (2011) Payment by Results and Social Impact Bonds in the Criminal Justice Sector: New Challenges for the Concept of Evidence-based Policy?, *Criminology and Criminal Justice,* 11 (5): 395–413.

Fox, A., Fox, C. and March, C. (2013) Could Personalisation Reduce Re-offending? Reflections on Potential Lessons from British Social Care Reform for the British Criminal Justice System, *Journal of Social Policy,* 42 (4): 721–741.

Gojkovic, D., Mills, A. and Meeks, R. (2011) *Scoping the Involvement of Third Sector Organisations in the Seven Resettlement Pathways for Offenders.* Working Paper 57, Birmingham: Third Sector Research Centre. Available from: http://www.tsrc.ac.uk/Publications/tabid/500/Default.aspx

Harlock, J. (2013) *Impact Measurement Practice in the UK Third Sector: A Review of emerging evidence.* Working Paper 106, Birmingham: Third Sector Research Centre.

Hedderman, C. (2004) The 'Criminogenic' Needs of Women Offenders, in: McIvor, G. (ed.), *Women Who Offend.* London: Jessica Kingsley: 227–244.

Hedderman, C. and Jolliffe, D. (2013) *Analysing the Needs, Change in Needs and Reconvictions of Women Accessing a Woman's Centre: A Report for the Corston Independent Funders' Coalition* (unpublished).

Hedderman, C., Palmer, E. and Hollin, C. (2008) *Implementing Services for Women Offenders and Those 'At Risk' of Offending: Action Research with Together Women.* Ministry of Justice Research Series 12/08. London: Ministry of Justice.

Hedderman, C., Gunby, C. and Shelton, N. (2011) What Women Want: The Importance of Qualitative Approaches in Evaluating Work with Women Offenders, *Criminology and Criminal Justice,* 11 (1): 3–19.

HM Government (2010) *Building a Stronger Civil Society: A Strategy for Voluntary and Community Groups, Charities and Social Enterprises*. London: Cabinet Office. Available from: https://www.gov.uk/government/uploads/system/uploads/attachment_data/file/78927/building-stronger-civil-society.pdf

HM Treasury (2002) *The Role of the Voluntary and Community Sector in Service Delivery*. London: Treasury.

HM Treasury (2010) *Spending Review 2010*. London: TSO. Available from: https://www.gov.uk/government/uploads/system/uploads/attachment_data/file/203826/Spending_review_2010.pdf

HM Treasury (2013) *Spending Round 2013*. London: TSO. Available from: https://www.gov.uk/government/uploads/system/uploads/attachment_data/file/209036/spending-round-2013-complete.pdf

Hollin, C. R. and Palmer, E. J. (2006) Criminogenic Need and Women Offenders: A Critique of the Literature, *Legal and Criminological Psychology*, 11: 179–195.

Hucklesby, A. (2011) *Bail Support Schemes for Adults*. Bristol: Policy Press.

Hucklesby, A. and Wincup, E. (2007) Models of Resettlement Work with Prisoners, in: Hucklesby, A. and Hagley-Dickinson, L. (eds) *Prisoner Resettlement: Policy and Practice*. Cullompton: Willan Publishing: 43–66.

Hucklesby, A. and Wincup, E. (eds) (2010) *Drug Interventions in Criminal Justice*. Maidenhead: Open University Press.

Hucklesby, A. and Wincup, E. (2014) Assistance, Support and Monitoring? The Paradoxes of Mentoring Adults in the Criminal Justice System, *Journal of Social Policy*, 43 (2): 373–390.

Hucklesby, A. and Worrall, J. (2007) The Voluntary Sector and Prisoners' Resettlement, in: Hucklesby, A. and Hagley-Dickinson, L. (eds) *Prisoner Resettlement: Policy and Practice*. Cullompton: Willan Publishing: 174–198.

Jolliffe, D., Hedderman, C., Palmer, E. and Hollin, C. (2011) *Reoffending Analysis of Women Offenders Referred to Together Women (TW) & the Scope to Divert from Custody*. London: Ministry of Justice.

Mair, G. and Burke, L. (2012) *Redemption, Rehabilitation and Risk Management: A History of Probation*. Cullompton: Willan Publishing.

May, T. (1991) *Probation: Politics, Policy and Practice*. Milton Keynes: Open University Press.

McMahon, G., Hall, A., Hayward, G., Hudson, C. and Roberts, C. (2004) *Basic Skills Programmes in the Probation Service*. Online Report 14/04. London: Home Office.

Ministry of Justice (2013a) *Transforming Rehabilitation: A Strategy for Reform*. London: Ministry of Justice.

Ministry of Justice (2013b) *Transforming Rehabilitation Competition*. London: Ministry of Justice. Available from: http://www.justice.gov.uk/transforming-rehabilitation/competition

Morgan, R. (2007) Probation, Governance and Accountability, in: Gelsthorpe, L. and Morgan, R. (eds) *The Handbook of Probation*. Cullompton: Willan Publishing: 90–113.

National Audit Office (NAO) (2005) *Working with the Third Sector*. London: National Audit Office.

National Audit Office (NAO) (2009) *Intelligent Monitoring: An Element of Financial Relationships with Third Sector Organisations*. London: National Audit Office.

National Audit Office (NAO) (2011) *Annual Report*. London: National Audit Office.

National Audit Office (NAO) (2014) *Probation: Landscape Review*. Report to the Comptroller and Auditor General, HC 1100 Session 2013–14. London: NAO.

Available from: http://www.nao.org.uk/wp-content/uploads/2014/03/Probation-landscape-review.pdf

National Offender Management Service (NOMS) (2006) *Women's Offending Reduction Programme: 2006 Review of Progress*. London: NOMS.

National Offender Management Service (NOMS) (2008) *Working with the Third Sector to Reduce Re-offending: Securing Effective Partnerships 2008–2011*. London: Ministry of Justice.

National Offender Management Service (NOMS) (2011) *National Standards for the Management of Offenders, 2011*. London: Ministry of Justice. Available from: https://www.gov.uk/government/uploads/system/uploads/attachment_data/file/217252/national-standards-management-offenders-2011.pdf

National Offender Management Service (NOMS) (2013) *How the National Offender Management Service Works*. London: Ministry of Justice. Available from: http://www.justice.gov.uk/downloads/about/noms/noms-org-chart.pdf

National Offender Management Service (NOMS) (2014a) *Justice Data Lab Statistics*, November 2014. Available from: https://www.gov.uk/government/uploads/system/uploads/attachment_data/file/373676/justice-data-lab-statistics-nov-2014.pdf

National Offender Management Service (NOMS) (2014b) *NOMS Annual Report and Accounts (2013–14)*. London: HM Stationary Office. Available from: https://www.gov.uk/government/uploads/system/uploads/attachment_data/file/322699/NOMS_AR_2014_web.pdf

Newburn, T. (2008) Models of Policing, in: Newburn, T. (ed.) *The Handbook of Policing*. Cullompton: Willan Publishing: 17–46.

Pawson, R. and Tilley, N. (1997) *Realistic Evaluation*. London: Sage.

Sampson, A. (2002) Principles and Pragmatism: Surviving Working with the Prison Service, in: Bryans, S., Martin, C. and Walker, R. (eds) *Prisons and the Voluntary Sector*. Winchester: Waterside Press: 130–137.

Trotter, C. (1999) *Working with Involuntary Clients: A Guide to Practice*. London: Sage.

Part II

7
Voluntary Work in Prisons: Providing Services in the Penal Environment

Alice Mills and *Rosie Meek*

The role of voluntary sector organisations (VSOs) is well established and rapidly developing, both in prison settings specifically and in criminal justice more broadly. In this chapter we examine the role of volunteers as service providers in prisons in England and Wales. We contextualise this field of study with some of the policy changes that have been introduced in England and Wales in recent years, and then present data derived from a national study of VSOs working in criminal justice based on interviews with over 250 offenders, criminal justice staff and VSO representatives. We focus in particular on the benefits and limitations of voluntary work in prisons from the perspectives of those directly affected by such work, as well as exploring the specific features and challenges of the partnerships between VSOs and criminal justice personnel that evolve in such prison settings. We examine how these in turn can impact upon both voluntary sector work and prison cultures, for example, in the perceived legitimacy of voluntary sector services. Although in this chapter we make reference to 'voluntary sector organisations' (VSOs), it is important to note that many of these organisations will have paid employees, if only in small numbers, who are employed to provide support to volunteers. Where a situation or experience that is specific to unpaid volunteers is discussed, they will be described as 'volunteers'. Where the context requires a discussion of both paid employees and volunteers, they are referred to as 'VSO staff' or 'VSO workers'.

The policy context of voluntary work in prisons

The voluntary sector has a long history of providing services to prisoners, ex-prisoners and their families in England and Wales. For example, in the early 19th century, Elizabeth Fry and The Ladies' Association for the

Improvement of the Female Prisoners in Newgate campaigned for better prison conditions and provided education and religious instruction, food, clothing and assistance on release to prisoners (Carey and Walker, 2002). In 1862, Discharged Prisoners' Aid Societies were attached to individual prisons and could be paid up to £2 per prisoner to aid their resettlement. In 1935, these organisations, which had since extended their remit to prisoners' families, were brought into a National Association of Discharged Prisoners' Aid Societies, which acted as a link between the societies and the prison authorities. Much of the work in prisoner welfare and resettlement was handed over to the Probation Service in the 1960s (Carey and Walker, 2002), and the role of the sector subsided with the development of the welfare state in the post-war period (Gill and Mawby, 1990). However, it has continued to play a significant role in service provision, coinciding with a shift away from faith-based approaches to more secular and professionally run services (Carey and Walker, 2002). Today, VSOs provide a variety of services to prisoners, ex-prisoners and their families. Such services include assistance with resettlement such as training, employment and housing advice, pastoral and faith-based support, substance misuse treatment and support, mentoring and advice services, and services for prisoners' families such as the provision of visitors' centres. In England and Wales, they also perform a watchdog function in the form of Independent Monitoring Boards in prisons; panels of independent volunteers, including local magistrates, who monitor day-to-day life in prisons and ensure the maintenance of care and decency in addition to dealing with problems and complaints that prisoners have been unable to resolve through the usual internal channels.

Establishing the number of VSOs currently working with offenders in England and Wales is 'a complex and challenging task' (Meek et al., 2013: 341), which depends on the sources of information used and understanding what constitutes 'working with offenders'. An analysis of the 2008 Charity Commission database identified 769 organisations which classified prisoners or offenders as their main beneficiary groups or recognised prisoners/offenders in their aims and objectives (Meek et al., 2013). In contrast, the National Survey of Charities and Social Enterprises (NSCSE) found in 2010 that 1475 organisations identified offenders, ex-offenders and their families as one of their main client groups, and 13,586 organisations reported that offenders, ex-offenders and their families are one of their client groups (Cabinet Office, 2011). Although the majority of organisations working with offenders are small and locally based,[1] the heterogeneity of the sector should not be overlooked. At the other end of the scale, a small number of national organisations have multimillion-pound annual incomes, 4 per cent have over 100 paid employees and just under half have an income of over £150,000 (Centre for Social Justice, 2013). Volunteers still play a substantial role in providing services; 24 per cent of organisations which work with (ex)offenders and their families have no paid employees at all and therefore rely on a volunteer workforce (Cabinet Office, 2011).

VSOs are said to have a number of strengths that contribute to the desirability of their increased role in the criminal justice system. These include cost-effectiveness; independence from the criminal justice system, which may mean that offenders view them as more trustworthy; links with local communities; and the ability to use local knowledge to develop and provide services. VSOs are also seen to be less hampered by bureaucratic demands, and to have, therefore, the aptitude to devise innovative solutions to difficult social problems (Gill and Mawby, 1990; Bryans et al., 2002; Ministry of Justice (MoJ)/National Offender Management Service (NOMS), 2008a; New Philanthropy Capital, 2009; Silvestri, 2009; Centre for Social Justice, 2013).

Several jurisdictions have emphasised the need to work in partnership with the voluntary sector, particularly in relation to solving the hitherto intractable problem of reducing reoffending which, it is suggested, state correctional services are not realistically able to tackle alone. For example, in New Zealand, prisoner reintegration services have long been contracted out to voluntary sector, often faith-based, providers and recent proposals to reduce reoffending by 25 per cent by 2017 have made it clear that this cannot be done without the voluntary sector (New Zealand Ministry of Justice, 2012). In the United States, the challenges of prisoner resettlement (or 'reentry') are particularly severe, given the country's exceptionally high rates of incarceration and recidivism. Programme devolution, a component of 'new federalism', has seen a shifting of responsibility for some aspects of correctional services from the federal government to the state level. As administrators look beyond the state for solutions, VSOs are increasingly responsible for providing re-entry services, including long-term shelter, job training, substance abuse treatment, and mentoring for ex-offenders and their families. In England and Wales during the New Labour government, services to promote successful resettlement and help to reduce recidivism[2] were originally due to be commissioned from the voluntary sector and other providers by Directors of Offender Management (MoJ, 2008; MoJ/NOMS, 2008a, 2008b), though these were swiftly superseded by a central commissioning team as a result of the restructuring of the National Offender Management Service (NOMS) due to public expenditure cuts. At this time, and based on the recommendations of the Corston report,[3] VSOs were also funded to provide community support projects for women at risk of going to prison or at risk of offending. Additionally, two VSOs (Turning Point and Catch 22) were successful in winning two prison contracts in conjunction with Serco, an international service delivery company and private prison provider.

Amid some controversy the coalition government in the United Kingdom sought to continue the expansion of the involvement of the voluntary sector in England and Wales, as part of a broader neo-liberal marketisation of criminal justice. This is especially evident in the UK government's policy of privatising probation services in England and Wales. Since June 2014 a variety of voluntary sector providers working in conjunction with private sector partners have been providing probation services and post-release support for low- and medium-risk offenders, whilst work with high-risk offenders remains in the public sector under the National Probation Service (NPS). Payment by results has been implemented alongside these organisational changes to bring out 'the diverse skills from all sectors' (MoJ, 2010: 41) in efforts to reduce recidivism. Following a programme of prison privatisation, the UK government has at the time of writing recently announced its intention for the core custodial functions of state prisons in England and Wales to remain in public hands for the time being. Resettlement and other ancillary services, however, were put out to tender from the private and voluntary sectors (MoJ, 2012; Chambers, 2013), and such organisations will continue to work in partnership with – as well as in competition with – public and private prison providers.

These drives to increase the involvement of the voluntary sector in criminal justice services, however, have been made on the basis of rather weak evidence as to the effectiveness and strengths of voluntary sector providers. Although individual service evaluations often contain the views of services users, little is known about whether offenders themselves value voluntary sector services in general, and those provided specifically by volunteers. Much of the existing literature either comes from the sector itself or consists of policy documents seeking to appeal to the sector, and hence tends to eulogise the strengths of voluntary sector work with offenders, with minimal discussion of the limitations of such work, particularly within the controlled environment of a prison.[4] Such difficulties can include deep-seated cultural barriers between criminal justice and voluntary sector staff and the potential for conflict between the differing priorities and approaches of the more person-centred voluntary sector and the criminal justice system, which prioritises the security of the prison, control of offenders and risk management (Mills et al., 2011).

The study

These issues will be addressed in this chapter by drawing on a two-year study that examined the role of the voluntary sector in work with offenders in England and Wales, carried out as part of a larger programme of research undertaken at the Third Sector Research Centre, funded by the Economic and Social Research Council, Barrow Cadbury Trust and Office for Civil Society. The study had several aims including an assessment of the level of awareness and use of VSO services in prisons, examining the role and impact of the sector in the reintegration of prisoners, and exploring relationships between VSOs' staff and criminal justice professionals to examine the operation of partnership working and the impact of any cultural barriers. To meet these aims, 254 qualitative interviews were carried out with offenders who were users of VSOs' services ($n = 102$), with criminal justice staff ($n = 74$) and with VSO representatives ($n = 78$) in eight prisons.[5] The research sites were chosen to incorporate a range of different populations (juvenile/young offenders/adults, male/female), different security classifications (closed/open) and different criminal justice statuses (remand/short sentence/long sentence). Two of the prisons were operated by private providers. The interviews were carried out face to face or, in the case of a small number of VSOs, over the telephone. The data from the interviews were analysed using framework analysis (Ritchie and Spencer, 1994), with the quotes presented here being representative of the themes which emerged from this analysis. Additionally, an offender survey was carried out in each prison to gauge the awareness and use of VSO services provided there. In total, 680 prisoners completed surveys; a response rate was obtained of just 12 per cent of the total offender population of the research prisons, which whilst low is fairly typical for self-completed surveys (Fazel and Danesh, 2002). The sample of prisoners was broadly representative of the prison population at the time of the survey although Black, Asian and Minority Ethnic (BAME) groups were slightly over-represented (see Meek et al., 2013 for full details of the survey methodology, administration and sample). Together these methods provided a picture of the nature and extent of VSO work with offenders but also offender, staff and VSO perspectives of that work.

'Added value' or just another service provider? Benefits and limitations of voluntary sector work in prisons

In addition to the various strengths of VSOs noted above, the existing literature has stressed the 'added value' that VSOs bring to their work and the services they provide (Hooper, 2002; NOMS, 2007; Neuberger, 2009). However, there is little robust evidence (NOMS, 2007) or even articulation as to what this 'added value' might consist of. All interviewees included in the research were asked what they felt the benefits were of offenders receiving services from VSOs and what the 'added value' was that VSOs could bring to their services. Most prisoners felt the main strength of the sector was the ability of its workers (both paid and volunteers) to take the time to listen to them, to understand their problems and needs and to build up relationships with them. Services from VSOs were seen as 'more personal' (Offender Interview 9, Prison B) than services from other providers. Whilst this might be expected of VSOs that seek to promote emotional health such as the Samaritans, and those engaged in addiction work, this benefit was associated with a range of VSOs' services including housing, mentoring and employment training. Both staff and prisoners recognised the value of empathetic VSO workers, particularly those who had similar experiences to offenders, who were more likely to be perceived as non-judgemental, making prisoners feel more comfortable and giving them a 'common ground' which they could 'relate to' (Offender Interview 11, Prison C).

In addition to being a 'non-statutory, experienced, confidential and caring listening ear which transcends the institutional setting' (Hooper, 2002: 104), volunteers in particular were recognised as bringing something special to the work that they did. Their commitment and willingness to give up time to come and talk to prisoners were deeply appreciated, particularly as it was agreed that prisoners were likely to be perceived as an undesirable set of clients. Prisoners and staff spoke of volunteers as doing their job 'from the heart' rather than for any obvious reward or monetary recompense. That people were prepared to come and talk to them, when they had been shunned by many others, had a powerful effect on prisoners who as a result were more likely to engage with volunteer services and engage in a more meaningful way. This effect was also noticed and highly respected by prison staff:

> They volunteer to do it because they want to do it and that's a whole different ball game. That definitely makes a difference in the eyes of offenders. In terms of added value they can reach people on a different level that we just can't. (Staff Interview 2, Prison 1)

This commitment was thought to be central to the 'added value' of VSOs' services and was what demarcated them from other civilian providers such as private companies or local authorities. Like Neuberger (2009: 16), we found that prisoners reported being more willing to talk to volunteers and to be honest with them. Volunteers were not led by criminal justice priorities or the constraints of a custodial role and routine and were seen as having little obligation to do the job, all of which ensured they were perceived to be substantially more trustworthy than other agencies:

> They bring in a fresh perspective. They are not in the system, they are less biased, whereas prison staff are first and foremost loyal to the system. (Offender Interview 3, Prison X)

Being seen as independent has been acknowledged as a critical reason for the effectiveness of VSOs (Centre for Social Justice, 2013). In our study volunteers were valued for their impartiality and their ability to relate to prisoners in ways in which prison officers may be prohibited from doing by prison cultures and the demands of the job. Staff also recognised that at times volunteers could work with prisoners more easily as they were not coming into prison 'to control them, tell them what to do or make them follow the regime' (Staff Interview 7, Prison E), whereas prison staff, even those who worked in areas associated with rehabilitation such as drug treatment, were still associated with control and punishment:

> They're [volunteers] not seen as threatening in any way. Quite often an issue that we have with prison officers in uniform working with prisoners on resettlement-related issues [is that] they're still seen as Mr Bad Guy instead of Mr Good Guy who's trying to help them. (Staff Interview 3, Prison D)

Crewe (2007) notes that whilst uniformed staff are now no longer seen to embody penal power (see also Warr, 2008; Crewe, 2009), prisoners perceive civilian specialists such as psychologists and probation officers as part of a repressive and powerful network of disciplinary knowledge which holds substantial influence in the prison. Despite prisoners in his study being encouraged to be open and honest with probation and psychology staff, they felt unable to do so, knowing that such honesty carried risks. It could demonstrate non-compliance with the regime and the expectations upon them, leading to them being 'killed off on file' (having negative comments placed on their record) (Crewe, 2007: 263), with potentially damaging consequences for their treatment in prison or jeopardising their chances of obtaining early release. In contrast to this, prisoners may view volunteers as relatively powerless, thus ensuring the formation of more honest and better-quality relationships, although it should be noted that prisoners may not always be aware whether the individuals they engage with are volunteers or paid VSO workers. Being seen as separate from the system and potentially even as 'amateurs' rather than professionals could reap substantial benefits for the work of volunteers in prisons.

The kind of help volunteers offered was also seen as preferable to that offered by criminal justice agencies. One prisoner described the guidance he received from a volunteer as what he had 'always needed', and contrasted this with his relationship with probation:

> He [volunteer support worker] works alongside me and tries to direct me the best way forward. . . . That's the kind of support I've always needed and for ten years I've had none. Plenty of times I've gone and sat with probation and tried telling them my problems and I'm not coping right and it's just with them, 'Oh we'll see how you're doing next week then. Take care'. (Offender Interview 8, Prison Z)

VSOs, particularly their volunteers, were seen to engage in more substantial 'person work' with offenders, building up relationships with them and focusing on them as individuals, something which prison and probation officers may be increasingly less able to do due to a lack of time, but also historically reluctant to do because of the need to maintain a professional distance. Paradoxically, the ability to develop meaningful relationships is recognised as being central to the promotion of desistance (Maruna, 2001; Burnett, 2004), an approach that is increasingly publicly subscribed to by those responsible for prisoner resettlement (Ministry of Justice, 2010).

It could be assumed that by the very nature of entering into the volunteering relationship, offenders choose whether to engage with voluntary sector services rather than being coerced to do so, a choice that ought to result in empowering offenders to take responsibility for their own resettlement. However, within the setting of a prison, the notion of 'choice', at least for some groups of prisoners, may be something of a misnomer. Non-engagement with certain services and courses such as employment training could affect their treatment in the prison system and during the early release or parole process, and offenders may not necessarily be readily able to distinguish between a caseworker from a volunteer service and, for example, a representative from a mandatory resettlement activity.

In earlier work, we noted the trend, particularly in larger organisations, towards the professionalisation of the VSO workforce (Mills et al., 2012). At its simplest, professionalisation occurs when a service or an activity ceases to be delivered by volunteers (Geoghegan and Powell, 2006).[6] In response to the growth of contract funding, the wider voluntary sector is increasingly utilising paid staff, and engaging more in the formal, bureaucratic and managerialist practices traditionally associated with the business sector, often in order to obtain large contracts or grants from the state and charitable foundations (Hwang and Powell, 2009; see also Geoghegan and Powell, 2006). Such an approach may assist VSOs in gaining and retaining contracts, but if an implication of this is a reduction in the number of volunteers, VSOs not only risk becoming less cost-effective but also losing a degree of the informality and commitment and therefore the 'added value' that volunteers currently bring to their work with offenders.

In line with Gill and Mawby's (1990) study of volunteers in probation, for criminal justice staff, such as prison officers and probation officers working in prisons, the most commonly cited benefit of VSOs was their connections to the community. Such links could offer several identified advantages. Firstly, they could enable the provision of 'through the gate' services'. VSOs were thought to be better able to provide these services because they were more likely to be based in the particular localities where offenders may live on release, and thus had local knowledge of, and often also connections to, available services. Such work was seen to be not only out of the remit of criminal justice staff, particularly for offenders sentenced to less than 12 months who at the time of the research were not subject to any post-release supervision, but also out of their comfort zone. In contrast, VSOs were perceived as 'not scared of working with people on release' (Staff 12, Prison X). Secondly, in being independent from the criminal justice system, volunteers in particular could help to bring the community into the prison, represent the community to prisoners and break down misconceptions about prisons and prisoners, thereby helping to improve confidence in the system:

> Many volunteers in the community have negative perceptions about prison, and prison volunteers are really the only people who can change that perception because they come in voluntarily and they bring the communities closer to the prison. (Staff Interview 13, Prison X)

This is supported by research in Hong Kong which found that prison volunteers genuinely believe their work can effect change in the lives of prisoners, and argued that prison volunteering can cultivate positive attitudes towards offenders (Chui and Cheng, 2013), although evidence for the degree to which these attitudes actually extend into the wider community was not offered. Thirdly, by allowing prisoners contact with civilians in the community, VSOs could assist in the integration of prisoners into community groups and structures, even when these offenders had not felt well integrated before they came to prison:

> In terms of what offenders will take from that situation and what it offers them, it's the opportunity to be engaging with the real world and to start to integrate themselves into the wider community because a lot of offenders are very much on the peripheral (sic) and generally not well-integrated into the structures of society. (Staff Interview 9, Prison Y)

This was a particular strength of groups such as Circles of Support and Accountability,[7] but also other faith-based groups and the Women's Institute, which had recently started a branch in one of the women's prisons in the study. VSOs have built up connections in the community through the use of volunteers and strong relationships with other organisations, including local authorities, housing providers and employers (see also Centre for Social Justice, 2013). Fundamentally, VSOs can utilise their social capital in order to facilitate the resettlement of offenders but may also assist offenders to develop their own social capital by helping them to gain employment and integrate socially into their communities.

Knowledge and suitability of VSO services

Despite the benefits of VSOs' and volunteers' work with offenders, it is important to note that this work can be limited in its impact and this may be exacerbated by the independence of VSOs from the criminal justice system. The prisoner survey in our study revealed that one of the main limitations of VSOs is a lack of awareness of their services. In each of the eight sites, surveys provided participants with a list of VSOs working in the prison and asked them to indicate their awareness and use of their services. At the time of the research, the prisons had an average of 20 VSOs working in each prison (ranging between 15 and 31) and most respondents had been in their respective prisons for an average of three months, suggesting they were likely to have a reasonably good idea of the services available to them. However, on average, prisoners were aware of just four VSOs in the prison and engaged with only one. Levels of awareness did vary between prisons with a better awareness among long-term male adult prisoners. This may be because they had more time to accumulate knowledge and experiences of VSOs' services on offer and how to access them. The most common reason indicated by prisoners for not using VSOs' services was that they felt the services could not help them. In almost half of all survey responses, offenders reported having heard of an organisation but not engaging with it. The next most substantial response was that prisoners simply did not know anything about VSOs working in their prison (Meek et al., 2013). This issue was repeated by several of the prisoners during interviews, who suggested that some of the services provided by volunteers were wholly ineffectual and did not meet their needs:

> You have organisations like [name of VSO] who are there to, ahem . . . 'build our confidence'. So much money goes out of the prison's pot for what? So that we can draw pics and shout words at each other? And they are like 'Oh we are so successful in turning your lives around'. [. . .] There's others like [name of VSO]. They teach us to wear baby pink and yellow and stop looking like 'tramps', which is how they think we look. What a load of b..locks! It wasn't my choice of colours that got me here in the first place! (Offender Interview 4, Prison B)

Historically, VSOs' services in prison developed in a rather ad hoc, incremental fashion, based on which VSOs were willing to offer their services to prisoners and had the resources to be able to do so rather than being based on an assessment of prisoner need in any coordinated way (Padel, 2002), or even on the needs of the prison. For some prisoners, the services they received were only of limited use. Where this was the case and the organisation was named, the overwhelming majority of these were housing organisations. In these cases, VSOs were often unable to help either because the prisoner did not meet the statutory criteria for classification as 'homeless' (Mills et al., 2013: 44) or match the criteria to qualify for support from a particular housing provider.

Other limitations

In general in our interview study, prisoners were substantially more reluctant to identify the limitations of volunteer services. Some did acknowledge that the lack of power held by volunteers in prison was a double-edged sword. Whilst on the one hand it helped prisoners to trust volunteers, as noted earlier, it also meant that volunteers could do little to affect the treatment of prisoners or improve prison conditions.

> Sometimes if you do want to know anything, if you want to really know any information you have to speak to somebody who's actually in the system. (Offender Interview 17, Prison X)

This lack of power and the dependency of VSOs on prison staff to access prisoners meant VSOs struggled to advocate for prisoners' interests with prison management in the same way that they did with banks, housing providers, Jobcentre Plus and other outside organisations. One volunteer from an organisation contracted by the prison to do advocacy work noted the negative reaction of staff whenever they tried to engage in advocacy:

> We're often asked to do advocacy work in [name of prison] but . . . there are some members of staff who actually really like to have us in the prison but really don't like it when we bring up any kind of problems. (VSO interview 1, Prison X)

Despite the overwhelmingly positive view of volunteers amongst prisoners, the ability of volunteers to build relationships with prisoners should not be taken for granted. Because of the need for time to commit to a volunteering role, many prison volunteers were from a drastically different demography than the prisoners, notably older, white and middle class, which could lead them to have difficulties engaging with prisoners:

> The problem is that the people who can afford to volunteer tend to be very middle class, 90% of the time that's what they are, white, middle class. [. . .] They're lovely people but they sometimes don't understand why they can't connect with the women. [. . .] And essentially, they are so different to the women in terms of their age, in terms of their ethnicity and their background. (Staff Interview 6, Prison X)

As a consequence of this, some VSOs were not seen to be 'grass roots' enough to be accepted by prisoners (Offender Interview 6, Prison X) or alternatively were most likely to be accepted by those who, like themselves, were white and middle class.

Prison staff registered their substantial frustration at VSOs, which, they felt, could promise offenders more than they could deliver but then left the prison staff to pick up the pieces when this did not come to fruition. Funding difficulties, often as a result of short-term contracts or grant funding, could exacerbate the likelihood of this happening:

> I'm constantly aware when people say, 'Oh, I've got funding for this', I'm always saying to them, 'That is great. What happens when that funding stops?' It doesn't help anybody in the long term when the money goes. (Staff Interview 1, Prison C)

Since the research took place in 2010–2011, VSOs have faced increasing funding difficulties, with a growing number relying on their reserves to survive and the majority of organisations believing this situation is likely to persist (Clinks, 2013). This indicates that prison staff will continue to endure the challenges of short-term VSO-provided services. Staff also felt that VSOs could overpromise what they could provide on release, and were not honest with prisoners about the difficulties they were likely to face due to structural barriers and discrimination, notably in relation to obtaining jobs and accommodation after release. Instead, prison staff believed that VSOs told them what they wanted to hear in an effort to win them over.

> You've got an organisation coming in making reams of promises about what they can do when you're released. There's no, or very little, evidence of that being available prior to release, it's not actually there that job, that training. (Staff Interview 4, Prison D)

Realities and insecurities of partnership working in the prison environment

VSO versus prison priorities and the nature and operation of volunteer services

Despite the rhetoric of partnership working between criminal justice agencies and VSOs, and the drive to substantially increase the involvement of VSOs in criminal justice service provision, the experience of VSO staff working in an environment which prioritises security and control has generated little discussion in the literature. Prisons and VSOs have different primary goals and strong cultural differences arising from these. The voluntary sector has tended to favour more rehabilitative, relational approaches to working with offenders, whilst prison staff are likely to be concerned first and foremost with security and risk management of prisoners. The research interviews revealed a variety of challenges which indicate the insecurity of doing voluntary work in secure, highly controlled settings and which can affect the nature and operation of VSOs' services in prisons. Although many VSOs that also provide services in the community are able to adapt their services to fit the prison environment, the high stress placed on security in prisons can hinder the kind of services that can be provided. For example, one prison officer recounted his experiences of having to turn away services from a volunteer disability organisation which were not suitable for the prison environment, explaining that due to security issues 'things that you would do outside in a care home or a person's house, you can't do here' (Staff Interview 2, Prison Z). In other instances, VSOs were unable to bring in certain equipment due to security concerns:

> We had a Buddhist gentleman and he was bringing in all sorts of goodies . . . there were blank CDs for them to put chanting on and incense and everything, but he didn't understand the implication of bringing a recordable item into a prison. (Staff Interview 1, Prison C)

The requirements of the prison could also place substantial restrictions on who can volunteer in prison. Notwithstanding the potential benefits for prisoners of talking to people with a history of prior offending, who have been described as 'uniquely credible' in their work with offenders (Centre for Social Justice, 2013: 22), several of the prisons in which we conducted the research had banned them from coming into the prison at all. This could have a substantial impact on the quality of 'through the gate' schemes which involve offenders being mentored by reformed ex-offenders, recently promoted by a UK Justice Minister (Grayling, 2013). It may also lead to increased chances of reoffending amongst those who have started volunteering in prison and have enjoyed having this meaningful role, when they are unable to continue on release (Neuberger, 2009).

The nature of services that could be provided may also be affected by the prison's need to be seen as punishing prisoners. Following negative media publicity about a party in a women's prison and a stand-up comedy club in HMP Whitemoor, a maximum security prison, a 'public acceptability test' was introduced in 2009. Governors are now required to consider the possible public reaction to activities with a view to avoiding those which would produce indefensible criticism and undermine public confidence in the service (Prison Service Order 0500 cited in Liebling et al., 2011: 15). As a result of this, prisoners could miss out on what staff perceived to be highly worthwhile training opportunities provided by VSOs:

> We had a great opportunity . . . with the [name of VSO] Boxing Squad [that] wanted to come in and teach boxing up to Level 1 standard, with the view to getting 10 to 20 inmates (sic) a year going out and working [in] community gyms. [. . .] At national level they blew it out. They said that you can't do boxing because it promotes fighting, which is complete and utter rubbish. Drugs, alcohol and gangs promote fighting. Boxing is a sport, but I guess there'll be people the other side of the argument, but I'm adamant on that. (Staff interview 1, Prison E)

Getting access to prisoners could also be difficult due to the restricted timetable of the prison regime but also security incidents which led to prison-wide 'lockdowns' where volunteers are unable to see any prisoners. This could be the source of considerable inconvenience and frustration, particularly if volunteers had travelled substantial distances to get to the prison and the prison had made no effort to contact them to inform them of their inability to access prisoners.

Influence of staff culture and relations: still naive 'do-gooders'?

It was also acknowledged that, at times, the inaccessibility of prisoners could be affected by staff whim rather than any security concerns:

> Some staff aren't willing to unlock for them [VSOs]. Can't be bothered being honest with you, but it depends what member of staff is on that wing from day to day. (Staff Interview 6, Prison Z)

Traditional prison officer culture is thought to be characterised by a degree of 'them and us' in relation to outsiders who seek to help prisoners (Crawley and Crawley, 2008), negative attitudes towards prisoners and prison managers, and a preoccupation with the maintenance of safety (Liebling, 2008). Prison staff may not share the same set of values around the treatment of offenders as those held by VSOs, and perceive VSOs' personnel to be 'on the side of the prisoners', making it appear that they are opposed to the work of the prison (Hucklesby and Worrall, 2007). Volunteers have traditionally been viewed in derogatory terms as naive 'do-gooders', interfering 'busy bodies' or 'carebears':

> There's a culture in prison which is if you haven't worn a uniform, you don't know anything about a prison. [. . .] I think the third sector is still perceived as interfering do-gooders who don't do nothing else but [cause] trouble. (Staff interview 8, Prison B)

This was noted by VSOs who recognised that in the eyes of prison officers they could be nothing but a nuisance:

> Clearly we are seen as sort of interfering do-gooders at times. We're a security risk, we just get more people in the prison that have to be controlled and watched and looked after. You get that kind of resistance from the old guard who just sort of want to bang people up. (VSO interview 10, Prison C)

Within this culture, prisoners may be perceived as 'less eligible' subjects who are not deemed worthy of services that can help them (Scott, 2008), although this hostility may also be born from a sense of frustration with their own job and/or the fear that VSO staff may replace prison officers or take away the more enjoyable aspects of their job (Bryans et al., 2002; Hooper, 2002; Padel, 2002; Neuberger, 2009). However, prison staff cultures are complex, changing and variable. Their nature and form can differ substantially depending on the age, experience and commitment of officers, the history and role of the prison and relations with senior management. Liebling (2008: 118) argues that in prisons where staff largely adhere to the traditional prison officer culture, showing care for prisoners may be culturally unacceptable, leading to hostility and potentially affecting VSOs' access to prisoners. By contrast, in prisons with more positive staff cultures, officers are likely to work more cooperatively with specialists, viewing them as a source of support (Liebling, 2008: 119), and welcoming them into the prison. The threat of privatisation and the consequent declining power of the Prison Officers' Association is contended to have eroded some of the 'traditional sources of indifference and disengagement among uniformed staff' (Crewe, 2009: 100). Many interviewees, both criminal justice and VSO staff, argued that negative attitudes towards VSOs and volunteers were limited to small groups of older officers who did not accept that rehabilitation was now part of their role. In a handful of cases, officers also confirmed they felt actively threatened by voluntary sector work in the prisons because they felt that it had removed some of the more enjoyable and varied tasks of a prison officer's job:

> If you want the blunt, honest answer, I'm sure once upon a time there was money, and there were people in prisons in a uniform that did these sort of jobs. But I have seen the officer's role shrink back from these outside agencies to be basically just looking after the prisoners on the wings. (Staff Interview 1, Prison C)

Negative attitudes towards VSOs could affect the treatment of volunteers in the prison, ensuring that they felt less than equal partners with the prison staff. They could also influence offenders' access to VSOs' services as this can be dependent on criminal justice staff informing offenders of these services and passing on referrals from offenders who put in requests in writing to access them (Mills et al., 2011). A small number of VSOs expressed concerns that they were not receiving referrals because of a perceived lack of enthusiasm from prison staff who did not publicise their services. One noted that the peer mentoring scheme they ran did not operate on as many wings as it should have done 'because of the non-participation or uptake of the programme by staff' (VSO Interview 8, Prison Y).

In spite of such attitudes, many VSO respondents stressed the good relationships they had with the prisons, felt that they made a valued contribution and praised the work of prison staff in helping them to access prisoners. Similarly, staff who participated in this research were highly supportive of the work of VSOs, recognising that if prisons were to rehabilitate, rather than just contain, prisoners, they could not do this alone, but actively needed the participation of other agencies. In some cases, interviewees refuted the idea that the prison and VSOs had different priorities, suggesting instead that 'we are all very much out for the same aims' (VSO Interview 2, Prison B), which substantially contributed to the positive relationships they enjoyed. In one case, a paid VSO employee, who was part of a small team with two prison officers, described the accommodation between the differing priorities of prison staff and VSOs which enabled them to work together:

> I've had some interesting debates (laughter) because [name of prison officer] and [name of prison officer] who work for the team are funny because they're like, 'you're just so optimistic'. They just see the same people coming back to prison time and time and time again but you forget about Joe Bloggs that only came in once, somebody got a house for him and he got his messed up future sorted out and he never came back. All you ever remember is people who came back time and time again, and they always say 'you're not going to break us' and I'll say 'you're not going to break me' (laughter). And we just keep having this sort of dialogue. (VSO Interview 3, Prison Z)

Despite the potential for conflict between the optimism of VSOs and the cynicism of prison staff, co-existence was common and exchanges such as the one described above were seen as part of the general banter of prison life. However, where VSOs enjoyed positive relations with staff, their value could still be questioned by the perceived unprofessionalism of individuals in their relationships with prisoners, and in particular by the naivety of volunteers who could become complacent about issues of security and leave themselves open to being 'conditioned' by prisoners:

> Prisoners are very manipulative so I had one lady come in and say, 'Oh this gentleman's really interested in his music, I thought I'd bring

him a music magazine in. Can I send it to you [name]?' 'No, because you're not going to send in a music magazine, you know you can't do that', and then you sit and explain. (Staff Interview 1, Prison C)

Although the central strengths of volunteers are that they are not seen as part of the system, are not constrained by criminal justice priorities and are more willing to build up relationships with offenders, staff raised the concerns about this approach and its conflict with security protocols. They particularly distrusted organisations which they saw as wilfully overstepping the boundaries of a professional relationship, threatening security and disrespecting the priorities of the prison:

> Some organisations, like [name of VSO] hog offenders . . . just behave sometimes like these offenders are just there to talk to them all day long [slight laughter]. Also a couple of times it happened that they kept prisoners past the lockup time without letting anyone know and the whole prison went on lockdown until we found those girls [sic] and [name of VSO] behaved like we were being silly! . . . They forget that they are *in a prison*. (Staff Interview 9, Prison X, our emphasis)

For criminal justice volunteers to gain access to their service users, they have always needed to behave in such a way as to retain the confidence of prison staff and management (Tennant, 2007). Staff recounted a number of incidents in which VSO staff, often volunteers, had been persuaded to break prison rules by manipulative prisoners, including asking volunteers to do their washing, post letters for them, make phone calls and bring items into the prison for them. Volunteers did not seem to always understand the need for such rules or grasp the unique issues that arise when working in a secure environment. In their desire to help prisoners and build up relationships with them, they did not always exercise appropriate caution or respect the appropriate boundaries, potentially endangering not only the security of the establishment but also relations with prison staff. Despite the rhetoric of partnerships, VSOs are still required to act as guests in a host environment with requisite standards of behaviour (Mills et al., 2012).

Power and risk management

Crewe (2009: 23) has argued that, since around 2002, public protection has become the central concern of the penal system, whilst other objectives such as resettlement have been forced to take a back seat. As a result of this, civilian specialists such as probation officers and psychologists, who may have previously engaged in work to address offenders' difficulties and encourage rehabilitation, have instead transformed prisoners' individual needs such as mental health problems and substance misuse into 'risks' that require careful management rather than treatment (see also Hannah-Moffat, 2005). In contrast, VSOs have remained welfare-orientated and much less bound up in the discourse of public protection. Criminal justice staff in our research confessed that the differing priorities of the VSOs left them feeling anxious and uneasy about the degree to which information pertaining to risk management was shared and VSOs engaged in risk assessment and management procedures, potentially jeopardising prison staff's ability to perform their statutory responsibilities to manage risk and to protect the public. Guidance to VSOs to encourage rigorous risk assessment procedures has been issued (NOMS, 2010), but volunteers in prison do not currently have obligations for risk management under any legal contract (Neuberger, 2009: 19). This may lead to inevitable tensions within the risk-averse setting of a prison and the increased likelihood that poor data-sharing practices become a barrier to the effective involvement of VSOs, or even a justification for their exclusion from the delivery of core rehabilitative services.

Relations with providers

If the traditional prison officer culture does negatively affect the treatment of 'outsiders', better relations might be expected in prisons managed by the private sector, where officers may lack the experience of their public sector counterparts, but have been found to demonstrate more positive attitudes towards prisoners (Shefer and Liebling, 2008), and are consequently less cynical about the possibility of rehabilitation (Crewe et al., 2011). Several VSOs in our sample had worked on a regional basis in both a public sector (Prison D) and a privately run prison (Prison A). In the interviews, they made some striking contrasts about the way they were treated by both establishments.

> Prison A wins hands down. Probably as [co-worker] and myself are respected members of staff with a good record for delivery. We work regularly with A and are always looking to support them as they are with us. . . . D are a disgrace, we can pick out two members of staff that support us. . . . I feel they are then outcasts to their peers for their positive relations with us. . . . I think they feel we are a threat and therefore keep everything close to their chest. We have had terrible issues with staff, including senior management, in trying to establish and work in partnership. (VSO Interview 7, Prison A/12, Prison D)

I know A very well . . . the system is solid and due to the comfort and relationships I have built over the years I do feel A is a very inspirational place to be. [With] D . . . I often feel a power issue is at hand, I don't feel trusted, but have been clinical towards my actions to provide support towards all requests and tasks. I can and do ensure young people and service are at the forefront of my actions, but for the last two visits I have not been able to see the young people. (VSO Interview 5, Prison A/11, Prison D)

Crucially, respondents felt they also did not have the support of senior prison management in prison D, which can be essential in supporting the integration of volunteers (Neuberger, 2009: 21). Due to this lack of staff support, one VSO felt that this meant that prisoners were in greater need of their support, as they did not seem to be supported by the prison. In contrast, the partnership with the private prison was felt to be one of mutual support and respect. Firm conclusions about the differences in relationships between VSOs and public/private prison providers cannot be drawn from such a limited sample. Nevertheless, relationships between private criminal justice providers and VSOs remain under-theorised and worthy of further consideration, particularly when considering the trend towards the marketisation of criminal justice and the willingness of both private and public providers to work in partnership with VSOs when bidding for contracts to manage prisons and probation services. In private prisons, the work of VSOs could conflict with the organisational and management priorities of the prison provider rather than just the needs of the criminal justice system.

[Name], which is our parent company have many requirements from us. And VSOs may not necessarily share those values as well, and it's just bridging these things together. It's a very fine line to tread and it's something they'll have to do every day, as part of their work. (Staff Interview 14, Prison X)

VSOs who also had experience of working with public providers noted the closer monitoring of their activities by the private company, the adjustment to which they found challenging. In this particular prison, a strong emphasis on cost-effectiveness led to several services that had been run by VSOs, including housing and debt advice being taken over by the prison. Any potential 'added value' offered by the VSOs which ran these services was dismissed for the sake of improving efficiency and cutting costs.

Discussion: the strengths and future of VSO work in prison

The research evidence presented here indicates that VSOs have a number of unique strengths that they can bring to their work with offenders. VSOs' staff, particularly volunteers, are seen to offer more personal, individual and independent services than other agencies, and the commitment of volunteers appears to add value as both prisoners and staff respect their willingness to give up their free time to perform their role, so that offenders are more likely to be responsive to them as a consequence. Despite the fact that many VSOs are funded by prison providers or other parts of the criminal justice system, VSOs' staff, especially volunteers, have thus far been able to maintain an 'outsider' status in the eyes of prisoners which absolves them of any association with the operation of penal power. Similar to prisoner views of other 'outsiders' such as education and chaplaincy staff in Crewe's (2009) study, the offenders in our research appreciated VSOs staff's orientation towards welfare and genuine care and concern. At a time when the impact of managerialism is being felt in prisons in England and Wales, and prison officers' relationships with prisoners risk becoming emotionally barren (Liebling et al., 2011) as the 'relational' model of such relationships is deprioritised (Liebling and Crewe, 2013), VSOs' staff, both paid and volunteers, may simply give prisoners the time and space to talk, which is lacking elsewhere.

However, despite these strengths and the continual language of partnership between the voluntary sector and criminal justice providers, the work of VSOs and volunteers can be limited in various ways. Voluntary sector services at the very least need to be better publicised, and due to low levels of reported prisoner engagement, thought should also be given to a reconfiguration of voluntary sector services to ensure that prisoners' needs, rather than the needs of the prison/criminal justice system or even VSOs themselves, are met. This may involve bringing in VSOs which support broader sections of the community and may be better able to assist with reintegration and linking ex-prisoners and their families to services in the community. Furthermore, the partnership between VSOs and prison providers remains unequal and, at times, somewhat uneasy as in most prison environments, voluntary sector workers remain fairly powerless and are able to fulfil their service remit only with the consent of the prison management and staff.[8] Such powerlessness is a strength of their work with offenders, but can leave them in a highly vulnerable position and subject to the whim of uniformed prison staff who still have considerable discretion as 'street-level bureaucrats' (Lipsky, 1980) in their implementation of penal policies and their treatment of those without power in the penal environment. The different traditions, resources and practices of the two sectors often give the appearance that they have different goals (Martin, 2002). Yet despite the cultural and ideological differences between the VSO and criminal justice staff evident in our research, many interviewees agreed on the common goal of reducing reoffending and suggested the two groups could and did work together productively in order to try and achieve this. Prison staff often appreciated the expertise and knowledge that VSOs could bring, particularly to resettlement, and recognised that VSO workers could take considerable pressure off prison staff. Nonetheless, further work could be done on relationships between the voluntary sector and criminal justice staff to ensure that VSOs' workers are more conscious of the implications of working in a secure environment where, for prison staff at least, security and control remain paramount. This could help to dispel suspicions and hostility amongst prison staff, including senior management, and facilitate volunteers' and VSOs' workers' access to prisoners.

The potentially increasing role of VSOs running core criminal justice services, as exemplified by their involvement in the provision of Probation services, may represent a time of increasing opportunities for the VSO but also inherent dangers. As has been well documented, smaller, volunteer-led VSOs whose financial vulnerability has already been heightened by the decrease in grant funding may lose out on public contracts because they do not have the finance or expertise to negotiate complex contracting and monitoring procedures. VSOs which are contracted to provide services may be vulnerable to 'incremental colonisation' by criminal justice concerns (Mythen et al., 2012: 363), losing the flexibility and personable approach of their services. Mythen et al. (2012) note that in being drawn into becoming key criminal justice providers through the marketisation of probation and prisons, in a time of scarce funding, smaller VSO providers in particular may end up accepting the

> dominant discourse of risk where measures of reconviction and value for money come to supersede the principle of 'moral good' that has historically underpinned activities and policymaking in the sector. (Mythen et al., 2012: 364)

As such VSOs may only target those offenders who are less likely to reoffend and more likely to help them meet their targets, excluding the harder cases (Bell, 2011: 121). This is in contrast to the history of many VSOs which have often worked with 'hard-to-reach' groups and those at high risk of reoffending who have been excluded from other services, such as prisoners serving sentences of under 12 months. In the criminal justice context, risk management also refers to the maintenance of public protection. As the role of VSOs in the provision of services within the criminal justice expands, like probation officers and psychologists before them, volunteers may become increasingly co-opted into wider machinery of risk management and the network of disciplinary knowledge, jeopardising their much-valued independence and trustworthiness and their welfare orientation.

Since 2007, prisons have experienced what Liebling and Crewe (2013) call 'managerialism minus' – a period of economic rationalism which is dominated by frugality and efficiency and appears more emotionally barren and morally denuded. This style of penal management may lead to the disappearance of some VSOs from prisons as prison managers seek to rationalise their spending, and may push VSOs to engage in processes of professionalisation to demonstrate their ability to win and maintain contracts. 'Managerialism minus' appears to lack an appreciation for the finer qualities of the voluntary sector's work discussed in this chapter. As Corcoran (2011) has noted, voluntary (lay) traditions have been 'consigned to a paternalistic, unaccountable and outmoded realm unsuited to consumerist relations with service users' (2011: 45). Even for the VSO itself, empathy has been 'sidelined' as the focus is now on the market rather than on the people (Clive Martin cited in James, 2014). In such an environment, the humanitarian strengths of VSOs and their volunteers may be excluded from prisons if the services they offer are not aligned with criminal justice goals, or they may be reduced, or at worst eliminated, by notions of efficiency, cost-effectiveness as VSOs become merely another competitor in the criminal justice market. They risk not only losing their perceived and actual independence and the commitment shown by their volunteers, but also their credibility within communities, possibly endangering their potential to help offenders form community links and build up their social capital. In short, VSOs are in danger of becoming nothing more than 'biddable service providers' (Corcoran, 2009: 32), losing their 'added value', their uniqueness which makes their service attractive to offenders, just when developments in penal policy suggest their humanising approach is most needed due to the erosion of human relationships elsewhere in the prison system. Although the precise impact of the challenges discussed here will necessarily vary between VSOs depending on a number of factors, including their reliance on government funding and the values and management of the organisation, despite their long history of work with prisoners and their families, the future of volunteers in the penal system currently looks unpredictable and uncertain.

Notes

1 Sixty-one per cent of organisations in the NSCSE carried out their activities on a local level, 33 per cent on a regional level and 21 per cent nationally. These figures add up to more than 100 per cent as organisations were allowed to tick more than one option in the survey (Cabinet Office, 2011).

2 These services were split into seven resettlement 'pathways': accommodation; employment, education and training; health; drugs and alcohol; finance, benefit and debt; children and families; and attitudes, thinking and behaviour. An additional two pathways were formed for female offenders: domestic and partner abuse and sex work.

3 The Corston report is a review into vulnerable women in the criminal justice system by Baroness Corston (2007). It highlighted the need for a holistic, women-centred approach to improve services for female offenders and those at risk of offending.

4 For a brief exception to this trend, see Hooper (2002).

5 The study also included one probation area which will be the subject of future publications.

6 In using the term 'professionalisation', we do not in any way seek to imply that volunteers are somehow 'amateurs' or 'unprofessional'.

7 Circles of Support and Accountability is a community-based initiative which aims to reduce sex offending by helping sex offenders to develop healthy adult relationships and maximise their chances of reintegrating into society successfully after their release from prison. Each 'Circle' consists of four to six volunteers and one 'Core Member' (the offender). The group meets regularly to provide practical, physical, emotional and spiritual support and volunteers also help the Core Member to recognise behaviours and attitudes that could lead to their reoffending (Circles UK, 2014).

8 The exception to this may be Independent Monitoring Boards which are charged with ensuring that proper standards of decency and care are maintained within prisons, and can draw keys to the establishment and talk to prisoners at any time (MoJ, 2013).

References

Bell, E. (2011) *Criminal Justice and Neoliberalism*, Basingstoke: Palgrave Macmillan.

Bryans, S., Martin, C. and Walker, R. (2002) The Road Ahead: Issues and Strategies for Future Joint Working, in: Bryans, S., Martin, C. and Walker, R. (eds) *Prisons and the Voluntary Sector*, Winchester: Waterside Press: 162–173.

Burnett, R. (2004) One-to-One Ways of Promoting Desistance: In Search of an Evidence Base, in: Burnett, R. and Roberts, C. (eds) *What Works in Probation and Youth Justice*, Cullompton: Willan Publishing: 180–197.

Cabinet Office (2011) *National Survey of Charities and Social Enterprises: Overall Report – National Results*, http://www.nscsesurvey.com/download/2010/Overall. pdf [accessed 01/02/14].

Carey, M. and Walker, R. (2002) The Penal Voluntary Sector, in: Bryans, S., Martin, C. and Walker, R. (eds) *Prisons and the Voluntary Sector*, Winchester: Waterside Press: 50–62.

Centre for Social Justice (2013) *The New Probation Landscape: Why the Voluntary Sector Matters If We are Going to Reduce Reoffending*, http://www.centreforsocial justice.org.uk/UserStorage/pdf/Pdf%20reports/landscape.pdf [accessed 01/02/14].

Chambers, M. (2013) *Expanding Payment by Results: Strategic Choices and Recommendations*, London: Policy Exchange, http://www.policyexchange.org. uk/images/publications/expanding%20payment%20by%20results.pdf [accessed 01/02/14].

Chui, W. H. and Cheng, K. K. (2013) Effects of Volunteering Experiences and Motivations toward Prisoners: Evidence from Hong Kong, *Asian Journal of Criminology*, 8 (2): 103–114.

Circles UK (2014) *What is a Circle of Support and Accountability*, http://www.circles-uk.org.uk/about-circles/what-is-a-circle-of-support-and-accountability [accessed 03/06/14].

Clinks (2013) *The State of the Sector October 2013*, http://www.clinks.org/sites/ default/files/Clinks%20State%20of%20the%20Sector%20-%20Full%20Report. pdf [accessed 01/02/14].

Corcoran, M. (2009) Bringing the Penal Voluntary Sector to Market, *Criminal Justice Matters*, 77 (1): 32–33.

Corcoran, M. (2011) Dilemmas of Institutionalization in the Penal Voluntary Sector, *Critical Social Policy*, 31 (1): 30–52.

Corston, J. (2007) *The Corston Report: A Review of Women with Particular Vulnerabilities in the Criminal Justice System*, London: Home Office.

Crawley, E. and Crawley, P. (2008) Understanding Prison Officers: Culture, Cohesion and Conflict, in: Bennett, J., Crewe, B. and Wahidin, A. (eds) *Understanding Prison Staff*, Cullompton: Willan: 134–152.

Crewe, B. (2007) Power, Adaptation and Resistance in the Late-Modern Prison, *British Journal of Criminology*, 47 (2): 256–275.

Crewe, B. (2009) *The Prisoner Society: Power, Adaptation and Social Life in an English Prison*, Oxford: Oxford University Press.

Crewe, B., Liebling, A. and Hulley, S. (2011) Staff Culture, Use of Authority and Prisoner Quality of Life in Public and Private Sector Prisons, *Australian and New Zealand Journal of Criminology*, 44 (1): 94–115.

Fazel, S. and Danesh, J. (2002) Serious Mental Disorder in 23000 Prisoners: A Systematic Review of 62 Surveys, *The Lancet*, 359 (9306): 545–550.

Geoghegan, M. and Powell, F. (2006) Community Development, Partnership Governance and Dilemmas of Professionalization: Profiling and Assessing the Case of Ireland, *British Journal of Social Work*, 36 (5): 845–861.

Gill, M. L. and Mawby, R. I. (1990) *Volunteers in the Criminal Justice System*, Milton Keynes: Open University Press.

Grayling, C. (2013) *The Opportunities for the Voluntary Sector in Criminal Justice*, London: Centre for Social Justice, 23 July 2013.

Hannah-Moffat, K. (2005) Criminality, Need and the Transformative Risk Subject: Hybridizations of Risk/Need in Penality, *Punishment and Society*, 7 (1): 29–51.

Hooper, R. (2002) The Contribution of Volunteers in the Penal System, in: Bryans, S., Martin, C. and Walker, R. (eds) *Prisons and the Voluntary Sector*, Winchester: Waterside Press: 92–105.

Hucklesby, A. and Worrall, J. (2007) The Voluntary Sector and Prisoners' Resettlement, in: Hucklesby, A. and Hagley-Dickinson, L. (eds) *Prisoner Resettlement: Policy and Practice*, Cullompton: Willan Publishing: 174–196.

Hwang, H. and Powell, W. W. (2009) The Rationalization of Charity: The Influences of Professionalism in the Nonprofit Sector, *Administrative Science Quarterly*, 54 (2): 268–298.

James, E. (2014) Criminal Justice Reforms: 'Empathy has been Sidelined, *The Guardian*, 8 January 2014. Available from: http://www.theguardian.com/society/2014/jan/08/clive-martin-criminal-justice-reforms-reoffending [accessed 10/01/14].

Liebling, A. (2008) Why Prison Staff Culture Matters, in: Byrne, J. M., Hummer, D. and Taxman, F. S. (eds) *The Culture of Prison Violence*, New York: Pearson: 105–122.

Liebling, A. and Crewe, B. (2013) Prisons Beyond the New Penology: The Shifting Moral Foundations of Prison Management, in: Simon, J. and Sparks, R. (2012) *The Sage Handbook of Punishment and Society*, London: Sage: 283–308.

Liebling, A., Arnold, H. and Straub, C. (2011) *An Exploration of Staff-Prisoner Relationships at HMP Whitemoor – 12 Years On*, Ministry of Justice/University of Cambridge Prisons Research Centre, https://www.gov.uk/government/uploads/system/uploads/attachment_data/file/217381/staff-prisoner-relations-whitemoor.pdf [accessed 10/01/14].

Lipsky, M. (1980) *Street Level Bureaucracy: Dilemmas of the Individual in Public Services*, New York: Russell Sage Foundation.

Martin, C. (2002) Recent Progress in Community-Based Voluntary Sector Work with the Prison Service, in: Bryans, S., Martin, C. and Walker, R. (eds) *Prisons and the Voluntary Sector*, Winchester: Waterside Press: 63–73.

Maruna, S. (2001) *Making Good: How Ex Convicts Reform and Rebuild Their Lives*, Washington: American Psychological Association.

Meek, R., Gojkovic, D. and Mills, A. (2013) The Involvement of Non-profit Organizations in Prisoner Reentry in the UK: Prisoner Awareness and Engagement, *Journal of Offender Rehabilitation*, 52 (5): 338–357.

Mills, A., Meek, R. and Gojkovic, D. (2011) Exploring the Relationship between the Voluntary Sector and the State in Criminal Justice, *Voluntary Sector Review*, 2 (2): 193–211.

Mills, A., Meek, R. and Gojkovic, D. (2012) Partners, Guests or Competitors: Relationships between Criminal Justice and Third Sector Staff in Prisons, *Probation Journal*, 54 (4): 391–405.

Mills, A., Gojkovic, D., Meek, R. and Mullins, D. (2013) Housing Ex-prisoners: The Role of the Third Sector, *Safer Communities*, 12 (1): 38–49.

Ministry of Justice (MoJ) (2008) *Third Sector Strategy: Improving Policies and Securing Better Public Services through Effective Partnerships 2008–2011*, London: Ministry of Justice.

Ministry of Justice (MoJ) (2010) *Breaking the Cycle: Effective Punishment, Rehabilitation and Sentencing of Offenders*, London: Ministry of Justice.

Ministry of Justice (MoJ) (2012) *Next Steps for Prison Competition*, https://www.gov.uk/government/news/next-steps-for-prison-competition [accessed 01/02/14].

Ministry of Justice (MoJ) (2013) *About the Independent Monitoring Board*, http://www.justice.gov.uk/about/imb [accessed 31/01/14].

Ministry of Justice (MoJ)/NOMS (2008a) *Working with the Third Sector to Reduce Re-Offending: Securing Effective Partnerships 2008–2011*, London: Ministry of Justice.

Ministry of Justice (MoJ)/NOMS (2008b) *NOMS Third Sector Action Plan: Securing Effective Partnerships to Reduce Re-offending and Protect the Public 2008–2011*, London: Ministry of Justice.

Mythen, G., Walklate, S. and Kemshall, H. (2012) Decentralizing Risk: The Role of the Voluntary and Community Sector in the Management of Offenders, *Criminology and Criminal Justice*, 13 (4): 363–379.

National Offender Management Service (NOMS) (2007) *Volunteers Can: Towards a Volunteering Strategy to Reduce Re-offending*, London: NOMS.

National Offender Management Service (NOMS) (2010) *Guidance for the Voluntary and Community Sector: Working with NOMS to Manage the Risk of Serious Harm*, London: Ministry of Justice.

Neuberger, B. (2009) *Volunteering Across the Criminal Justice System*, London: The Cabinet Office.

New Philanthropy Capital (2009) *Breaking the Cycle: Charities Working with People in Prison and on Release*, London: New Philanthropy Capital.

New Zealand Ministry of Justice (2012) *Delivering Better Public Services: Reducing Crime and Re-Offending Result Action Plan*, Wellington: Ministry of Justice.

Padel, U. (2002) Voluntary Sector Provision in the Penal System, in: Bryans, S., Martin, C. and Walker, R. (eds) *Prisons and the Voluntary Sector*, Winchester: Waterside Press: 82–91.

Ritchie, J. and Spencer, L. (1994) Qualitative Data Analysis for Applied Policy Research, in: Bryman, A. and Burgess, R. G. (eds) *Analysing Qualitative Data*, London: Routledge: 173–194.

Scott, D. (2008) Creating Ghosts in the Penal Machine: Prison Officer Occupational Morality and the Techniques of Denial, in: Bennett, J., Crewe, B. and Wahidin, A. (eds) *Understanding Prison Staff*, Cullompton: Willan: 168–186.

Shefer, G. and Liebling, A. (2008) Prison Privatization: In Search of a Business-like Atmosphere?, *Criminology and Criminal Justice*, 8 (3): 261–278.

Silvestri, A. (2009) *Partners or Prisoners? Voluntary Sector Independence in the World of Commissioning and Contestability*, London: Centre for Crime and Justice Studies.

Tennant, M. (2007) *The Fabric of Welfare: Voluntary Organisations, Government and Welfare in New Zealand, 1840–2005*, Wellington: Bridget Williams.

Warr, J. (2008) Personal Reflections on Prison Staff, in: Bennett, J., Crewe, B. and Wahidin, A. (eds) *Understanding Prison Staff*, Cullompton: Willan: 17–29.

8
Women's Voluntary Organisations and the Canadian Penal 'Culture of Control'

Paula Maurutto and *Kelly Hannah-Moffat*

By the late 1980s, Canada was at the forefront of women's prison reform: it was poised to be the first country to integrate feminist principles into the development of a new prison regime for women (Hannah-Moffat and Shaw, 2000). The design of this new model was laid out in the document *Creating Choices: The Report of the Task Force on Federally Sentenced Women* (Task Force, 1990). This plan for prison redevelopment symbolised a unique turn in the history of the Correctional Service of Canada (CSC). For the first time, the government partnered with women's organisations in a collaborative effort to advance a new vision for women's punishment. This collaboration with community organisations was championed as evidence of an opening of the political process that would invite women's prison advocates and organisations to play a greater role in prison reform.

The collaborative efforts that infused the drafting of *Creating Choices* quickly dissipated in the 1990s, primarily because women's organisations were excluded from the implementation phase as the CSC moved towards a 'crime control' agenda characterised by penal conservatism and a 'carceral clawback' in resources (Garland, 2001; Hannah-Moffat, 2001; Carlen, 2002). This marked the beginning of a growing rift between the CSC and organisations advocating for women in prison. Women's community and advocacy organisations experienced diminished political influence and were effectively excluded from internal penal decision-making. Given the barriers to political advocacy, women's organisations have adapted and developed new legal strategies to continue their advocacy for women in prison.

This chapter explores the involvement of women's organisations in the Canadian criminal justice system. It draws on a range of evidence including 32 interviews with feminist prison advocates and community agencies involved in Domestic Violence Courts have, along with participant observations of prison advocacy and analysis of reports from women's organisations. The first section begins with a general overview of the early history of women's voluntary work in prison reform. Since the early 1850s, women's voluntary sector organisations (VSOs) played a fundamental role in the development of a separate system of punishment for women (Hannah-Moffat, 2001). Particular attention is paid to the development of the Canadian Association of Elizabeth Fry Societies (CAEFS), Canada's largest and most influential women's prison advocacy organisation. This is followed by an account of the collaborative partnership that developed between CAEFS and the CSC that led to the formation of the Task Force on Federally Sentenced Women and the ensuing *Creating Choices* document released in 1990. During this time period CAEFS, along with other women's organisations, played a critical role in framing correctional policy for women's penal institutions. Section three investigates the growing rift between CAEFS and the CSC as the latter embraced a neoliberal culture of control. By the 1990s, the CSC sought to reposition CAEFS, along with other women's organisations, not as national organisations representing the voice of women, but as mere interest groups that could easily be dismissed if their views were perceived as unsupportive of the CSC's vision. As political lobbying became less effective, CAEFS developed new legal tools of engagement to push for women's prison reform.

The final section moves beyond an exclusive focus on CAEFS's interrelationship with the CSC and, instead, draws on the role of women's VSOs in the development of domestic violence courts. The objective of this account is designed to highlight the need for research that examines the multiple ways in which women's organisations intersect with the neoliberal state. Since the late 1980s, two dominant frameworks have characterised the criminal justice voluntary sector. On the one hand, organisations engaged in political advocacy are depicted as having been pushed to the margins where their credibility and influence is diminished. On the other hand, organisations involved in service delivery are presumed to be co-opted by the state and forced to adjust their mandates to fit the priorities of the criminal justice market in which they now compete to deliver penal services (Neilson, 2009; Corcoran, 2011; Mills et al., 2011). Several criminologists, in particular Garland, have identified how crime control moves 'beyond the state' to engage community partners in the 'social control efforts' of 'official crime control agencies' (2001: 123–127). These characterisations, however, oversimplify a highly complex interaction. Neoliberal policies have significantly impacted on the voluntary sector; however, its influence is neither monolithic nor absolute (Tomczak, 2014). While the voluntary sector's ability to influence penal reforms has been curtailed under neoliberalism, spaces do exist where women's organisations are able to affect the legal and penal process. One area where women's VSOs have played an instrumental role in shaping decision-making is through the development of specialised courts, specifically Domestic Violence Courts (DVCs).

The final section draws on the example of women's VSOs and their impact in DVCs to highlight the importance of considering the multi-layered and diverse ways in which the voluntary sector interacts with neoliberal penal regimes. This example is not intended to provide an in-depth overview of DVCs, but rather to highlight the need for further research that explores the multifaceted ways in which women's organisations are responding to and devising new strategies to engage with the state. The example allows for a more nuanced understanding of how VSOs are seeking to modify practices, adapting and working within a neoliberal culture to advance the rights of women in conflict with the law.

Women activism and prison reform movements

The activities of the Canadian voluntary sector and the state in the field of criminal justice have long been interwoven. Canada has a rich history of VSOs involvement in the criminal justice system dating back to the 1830s, when religious organisations along with social reformers spearheaded a series of prison reforms (Maurutto, 2003). Women's reform movements in Canada, inspired by the American maternalists and the work of Elizabeth Fry in England, called for the construction of separate prisons for women. This led to the formation of Canada's first women's prison, the Ontario Andrew Mercer reformatory for women in 1874. Secular and evangelical penal philosophies were combined with maternal logics to devise a separate strategy of moral reform for women prisoners (Hannah-Moffat, 2001: 47). Representatives from local churches, the Prisoners' Aid Society, the Salvation Army, the Women's Christian Temperance Union and the Catholic Ladies Visiting Society visited the women and provided a variety of religious services, such as preaching, bible reading, prayer and counselling. Organisations such as the Salvation Army, the Prisoner's Aid Society and the Good Shepherd also assisted with women's reintegration into the community by providing them with monetary, spiritual and emotional support. The Salvation

Army, the Prisoner's Aid Society and the Good Shepherd operated homes for released women. If women were not prepared for release, they could choose to go to a home of refuge, such as a Magdalene Asylum, a Salvation Army Prison Gate Home, or a Rescue Home (Hannah-Moffat, 2001). The range of services provided by these organisations gives an example of the public–private collaboration that characterised the beginnings of the criminal justice system. Local and provincial governments at the time provided the legal framework, financial resources and bureaucratic supervision, enabling the formation and proliferation of VSOs (Maurutto, 2003).

By the 1920s, organisations involved in criminal justice were expanding as were the types of services they provided. In 1939, the first Elizabeth Fry Society in Canada was founded by Agnes Macphail in Vancouver to advocate for the fair treatment of women and girls in custody. Shortly thereafter, similar organisations were formed across Canada. In 1949, the Kingston Elizabeth Fry Society began regular visits to the Prison for Women, Canada's first federal penitentiary opened in 1934. By the 1950s, Elizabeth Fry Societies across the country had emerged as significant agents of social change that were instrumental in promoting a new image of women in conflict with the law. They worked extensively in collaboration with state correctional institutions to provide an array of programmes and services, including recreation, temporary absence supervision, release planning, parole supervision, second-stage housing, substance abuse counselling, employment training and general counselling (Hannah-Moffat, 2001).

VSOs, in particular the Elizabeth Fry Societies, were acknowledged by the state as having a particular expertise and were often consulted on policy development. These societies began developing public action committees, permanent speaker bureaus, active research programmes and newsletters outlining their positions. Independently and collaboratively, these agencies began to publish a wide variety of position papers on issues facing women in conflict with the law. The public advocacy role of individual Elizabeth Fry Societies was solidified with the formation of CAEFS, which was founded in 1969 and incorporated as a national non-profit organisation in 1978.

CAEFS emerged during the second wave of the women's movement, which at the time had gained considerable prominence in policy circles. During the 1950s and well into the 1970s, as the state was expanding welfare provisions and extending civil rights, governments often perceived their interests as aligned with and supported by women's organisations. Within this context, governments provided substantial support to women's organisations and, more generally, the non-profit sector. It was during this period that several prominent national organisations advocating for women's legal rights were established, including the National Action Committee on the Status of Women (NAC founded in 1971 as Canada's feminist activist organisation with over 700 members), the Women's Legal Education and Action Fund (LEAF formed in 1985), the Native Women's Association of Canada (NWAC incorporated in 1974) and CAEFS. Collectively, these organisations advanced women's equality and social justice issues and fought their way to become recognised lobby groups and stakeholders often consulted in policymaking (Brodie, 1995). Most were supported through substantial federal funding, and were perceived as legitimate voices representing a key sector of the electorate in political debates (Brodie, 1995; Luxton, 2001). This environment set the stage for the inclusion of women's VSOs in the Task Force on Federally Sentenced Women that produced *Creating Choices* (1990). At the time, women's organisations had the power to demand and expect representation on issues related to women, and the CSC was committed to ensuring a renewal process that respected and included representation from women's organisations advocating for women on the inside.

Creating choices: forging community–government partnerships

During the 1980s, the Canadian criminal justice system, and, in particular, the CSC, was permeated by a strong rehabilitative focus and a desire to 'do good corrections' (Jackson, 2002). Ole Ingstrup was the Commissioner of the CSC at the time. He envisioned good corrections as a commitment to the values entrenched in the Canadian Charter of Rights and Freedoms relating to respect for 'freedom, safety and human dignity' (Vantour, 1991: 22). The CSC, at least publicly, maintained a commitment to progressive organisational change that would position Canada as a leader of prison reform, and to pursuing this change by drawing on shared knowledge and the expertise of a wide spectrum of criminal justice organisations, including the expertise of VSOs working with incarcerated populations (Jackson, 2002: 2).

This commitment was enshrined in the Task Force on Federally Sentenced Women commissioned in 1989. The Task Force was designed to overhaul the treatment and conditions of confinement, particularly at the Prison for Women in Kingston, Ontario. Previous Task Forces that explored women's imprisonment had collectively called for the closure of the Prison for Women and its replacement with regional or community-based facilities. The Prison for Women, located in central Canada, was originally designed as a maximum security facility for men. The facility was critiqued for its inability to meet the needs of the women, most of whom were minimum or medium security risk, for its lack of rehabilitative and treatment programmes, for its ignorance of the cultural dislocation of Native women and, in particular, for isolating women from their families in a facility that was geographically far removed from the communities that women would return to.

The Task Force included an eclectic group of 41 individual members representing a broad spectrum of government and VSOs, which marked it 'as unique from any previous government committee in Canada or elsewhere' (Shaw, 1993: 53). The commitment to forging partnerships with women's organisations was evident in the composition of the Steering Committee, which had two co-chairs: James Phelps, the Deputy Commissioner of the CSC Correctional Programmes and Operations, and Bonnie Diamond, the Executive Director of CAEFS. Two-thirds of the task force members were women, and two of these had served federal sentences. Moreover, more than half of the members were from non-governmental organisations, including a broad spectrum of women's organisations, with five members from Aboriginal women's organisations, and the Executive Director of the National Organisation of Immigrant and Visible Minority Women (Hayman, 2006). No previous government inquiry into women's imprisonment had included such a broad spectrum of representation from women's interests or groups (Hannah-Moffat, 2001). Many of the task force members championed a feminist perspective and were committed to promoting the rights of incarcerated women.

The Task Force embodied a commitment to 'giving voice' to a range of women who had previously been excluded or silenced within criminal justice circles. The structure of the Task Force's report *Creating Choices*, published in the 1990s, included chapters devoted to various 'women's voice[s]'. Different sections were devoted to 'the wisdom of different voices', 'the voices of women who have been federally sentenced', 'the voices of Aboriginal people' and 'the voices of others who care', the latter including correctional staff members and others working with women. The sections attest to the concerted effort to include those marginalised voices traditionally excluded from government debates but most affected by its punishment regime such as Aboriginal and incarcerated women. The inclusion of these diverse women's voices was intended to ensure that the ensuing recommendations were informed by a 'women-centred' vision of punishment that recognised the fact that women's needs differ from men's. The report outlined a set of principles that were designed to initiate institutional change and be congruent with liberal feminist strategies of empowerment, helping women strive for meaningful and responsible choices, and fostering respect and dignity in a supportive environment. The central recommendations of the subsequent report refocused work with women around a network of community-based supports, specifically the creation of community release centres, halfway houses run by VSOs and Aboriginal centres (Task Force, 1990).

This commitment to radical penal reform, however, had unintended and adverse consequences to the point where *Creating Choices* soon came to be viewed as a veil for re-legitimating a renewed form of punishment. On the one hand, *Creating Choices* did result in the closure of the large Prison for Women and the opening of smaller regional facilities across the country. On the other hand, however, institutional decision-making remained rigid and insular. As Hannah-Moffat (2001: 77) observed, '[w]hile the benevolent rhetoric of empowerment and healing embodied in *Creating Choices* . . . permeated correctional discourses, the more sinister and punitive disciplinary reality of "corrections" persist[ed]'. There are a number of reasons for this paradox. First, the commitment to community involvement fostered during the drafting of *Creating Choices* in the late 1980s quickly eroded in the early 1990s as the CSC began to embody a neoliberal, centralised bureaucratic management style. As a result, VSOs such as CAEFS, which were pivotal to the drafting and formulation of *Creating Choices*, were by the early 1990s excluded from membership in the National Implementation Committee and the planning of the new regional prisons. Subsequently, few of the initiatives proposed in *Creating Choices* were ever implemented, and the document became more of a 'statement of philosophy' than a blueprint for change. Although the federal Prison for Women had closed, this did not reduce the number of imprisoned women as the opening of regional facilities had increased capacity, and consequently enabled more women to be incarcerated. Meanwhile, community supports such as halfway houses were being eroded, and conditions within the regional prisons were increasingly becoming less therapeutic and more punitive.

Women's organisations cautioned against this increasingly punitive environment, which was in stark contrast to the original recommendations and spirit embodied in *Creating Choices*. By 1992, many of the original partners, most notably CAEFS, had withdrawn support for the CSC's reforms. Pat Carlen (2002: 159) has observed that whilst reforms offer great promise, they are continually susceptible to being co-opted by punitive backlashes. It is worth noting that the women's organisations involved in *Creating Choices* were aware that their participation would serve to legitimate the CSC's punishment regime but they had hoped it could also lead to improved conditions for women living on the inside. When evidence emerged that women's conditions were deteriorating and that the CSC was backing away from its commitment to community alternatives, many women's organisations pulled their support for the reforms.

Advocating within the context of a neoliberal carceral penality

By the 1990s, CAEFS was operating within a new political context that was increasingly characterized by a neoliberal political and cultural conservatism (Vantour, 1991; Garland, 2001; Pratt, 2011). This era has been characterised by fiscal restraint, welfare state retrenchment and the downloading of services to the voluntary sector. This neoliberal trend, while sporadically introduced in the mid-1980s, had by the 1990s become an ingrained feature of the CSC's institutional practices. Within the field of criminal justice, prison governance became encapsulated in a focus on economies of efficiency, the rule of law and the risk management of offenders.

Within this climate, advocacy for women on the inside became ever more challenging. Women's organisations that challenged neoliberal policies of retrenchment were repositioned as merely self-interested, oppositional lobby groups (Yeatman, 1990). In Canada, previously publicly funded national women's organisations, notably the NAC, lost all federal government support, leading both to a reduction in their lobbying power and shrinkage of political spaces for collective action and empowerment (Brodie, 1995). Although CAEFS was able to maintain federal funding, this funding became increasingly precarious and was directed towards the provision of programmes and services rather than organisational infrastructure and advocacy, further restricting advancement of prison reforms. Moreover, once CAEFS withdrew its support from the CSC following its failure to implement the recommended reforms advanced within *Creating Choices*, it became politically positioned as an adversarial singular interest group, hostile to government policy, thereby allowing the CSC to readily dismiss its concerns. CAEFS now had to operate in a climate characterised by the decline of the women's movement, a loss of its political influence and a correctional system that increasingly became informed by a new carceral logic emphasising more punitive policies justified under the umbrella of evidence-based practices and risk management.

Marginalisation

With the expansion of services offered by non-profit organisations, the voluntary sector emerged as an area that increasingly demanded the federal government's attention. In a strategic move to enhance its relationship with the non-profit sector, the federal government launched the Voluntary Sector Initiative in 2000 (Elson, 2007). This initiative was intended to strengthen Canada's commitment to be more open, consistent and collaborative in relation to civil society and to ensure that statutory institutions such as the CSC maintained a commitment to broad consultation. Within this context, women's prison advocacy organisations such as CAEFS were brought back into a consultative process with the CSC. However, the government's commitment to effective collaboration with community stakeholders often resulted in strategically selective engagement. Although organisations including CAEFS were regularly invited to the CSC stakeholder discussions to provide input on emerging issues, they were not involved in setting the agenda or framing the problems for discussion. Despite the pretext of collaboration, their input had to fall within the parameters set by the CSC, and, as a consequence, 'consultations' rarely extended to seeking the voluntary sector's views regarding the implementation of procedures and practices within prisons.

Government engagement with the community through broad consultation forums did bring together diverse stakeholders; however, it effectively diminished the influence of CAEFS. Additionally, the government's commitment to broad consultations facilitated the involvement of a new set of stakeholders including right-wing organisations such as REAL Women, conservative think tanks, victim's rights organisations, and lawyers and academics, many of whom had little contact with, or sympathy for, women prisoners. Organisations such as CAEFS were no longer situated as the primary expert on women's needs; rather, CAEFS was repositioned as one voice among many, and increasingly perceived more as an advocate than as an objective expert on women's issues. For the CSC, consulting widely enabled it to appear both transparent and engaged with all stakeholders, while in reality it was selecting and promoting those organisations that it deemed to be most aligned with its agenda. Those advocating for women in prison were selectively incorporated or excluded in relation to the degree to which their claims coincided with the CSC priorities. Thus, the expansion of community engagement increased the range of stakeholders consulted, but also served to legitimate a correctional system that could strategically manage and select which voices to exclude and which to incorporate.

At the same time that it was perceived to be engaging in collaborative efforts, the CSC became increasingly insular and impenetrable, thereby hindering the ability of advocacy groups to access information. Access to information on the treatment and experiences of those behind bars diminished, especially on matters such as placing individuals in segregated regimes or solitary confinement, involuntary transfers and administration decisions related to the restriction of institutional liberties. Moreover, advocates were finding it ever more difficult to enter penal institutions to work with those on the inside. Despite correctional policy documents and public research being readily available on government web sites, access to information about institutional directives or protocols has been impeded through a range of new measures, including, among others, delaying responses to requests for access to information, imposing prohibitive fees on such requests and putting pressure on officials to keep sensitive information hidden.

Risk logics as exclusionary tactics

The incorporation of new carceral logics into the CSC strategic development created additional obstacles for women's advocacy groups. Beginning in the mid-1980s, both probation and correctional institutions in Canada began integrating evidence-based actuarial evaluations into every level of prison decision-making. These evidence-based risk logics restructured virtually every aspect of institutional assessment, management and planning. As we have argued elsewhere (Maurutto and Hannah-Moffat, 2006), actuarial practices prioritize risk and security. Institutional practices governed by principles of risk and security operate according to different logics than the rights-based claims often advanced by prison advocates. Advocacy by prisoner rights groups are often framed within the language of rights, typically civil or humanitarian rights. Yet, rights-based claims no longer fit within a paradigm governed by principles of risk and security. Within this context, individual rights are not simply overruled by concerns about risk. Rather, they can potentially be perceived as risks to the security of the prison and, hence, a problem to be managed by the institution which can often lead to more punitive penal outcomes. Individual civil rights are often consequently re-inscribed as a risk, specifically, an organisational and potentially security organisation risk, that the institution becomes obliged to regulate. By this means, when feminist groups attempt to advance the rights of women, their claims conflict with institutional logics and, hence, are more easily dismissed.

Legal advocacy

Neoliberalism has reshaped the political and institutional environment in which VSOs operate, making it more challenging to advance the rights of women in prison. At the same time that conditions and treatment of women in prisons are deteriorating, organisations such as CAEFS are experiencing increasing barriers to political advocacy. In response, VSOs involved in advocacy have had to adapt, innovate and develop new strategies of engagement. In a climate where political advocacy has diminished and where access to the CSC internal operations has become ever-more restrictive, CAEFS has adopted a range of legal advocacy instruments to advance prison reform. Using the legal realm to advance the rights of women in conflict with the law has enabled CAEFS to expose, at a minimum, the more punitive policies and practices adopted by the CSC.

Beginning in the 1990s, CAEFS has sought to advance the rights of women in prison through legal advocacy. In 1992, CAEFS appointed a new Executive Director, Kim Pate, a lawyer and current university Chair in law and human rights. Her legal training proved instrumental in CAEFS' pursuit of legal advocacy. CAEFS has participated in submissions to Supreme Court cases and pushed for standing on Commissions of Inquiry. For example, CAEFS played an instrumental role in the Commission of Inquiry into Certain Events at the Prison for Women in Kingston (the Arbour Commission) (1996), the System Review of Human Rights in Correctional Services for Federally Sentenced Women (2003) and inquests into deaths in custody, most notably the highly publicised case of Ashley Smith in 2007, who was incarcerated as a young offender with mental health concerns, and the Kinew James case at the Regional Psychiatric Centre in Saskatoon in 2013. During the Arbour Commission (1996), CAEFS provided a submission that revealed the layers of decision-making and institutional protocols and practices that had eroded the rights and humane treatment of women in prison. Legal advocacy strategies have also fostered increased disclosure of information and a push for progressive and proactive policies and practices.

In addition, the writ of *habeas corpus* has been increasingly used by CAEFS to challenge charges and increased time in detention, which women may acquire while in prison. In prison, it is not uncommon for women to accrue charges for breaches of prison discipline resulting in longer sentences, transfers to higher-security correctional units or facilities, and/or segregation. A writ of *habeas corpus* is a form of judicial review that is used to ensure the procedural fairness of such charges and detention. The writ places reverse onus on the institution to justify sanctions brought against individual prisoners, including extensions to sentences of imprisonment or use of segregation, as a consequence of internal disciplinary hearings convened by prison authorities. It operates as a safeguard for the rights of women against the illegal charges, unconstitutional detention and other forms of infringements on civil rights. CAEFS has successfully used the writ to challenge the use of segregation and the transfer of women to higher-security institutions (CAEFS, 2014b).

The CSC has attempted to limit the use and parameters of applications of *habeas corpus* by dismissing their legality and attempting to limit their obligation to disclose the kind of information that is often required in such cases. Supreme Court decisions in 2005 (May v. Ferndale, 2005) and, more recently in 2014 reaffirmed the right of prisoners to use *habeas corpus* to challenge the legality of increased sanctions (Mission Institution v. Khela, 2014). The decision also secured the right to demand full disclosure of CSC's institutional decision-making and treatment of individual prisoners in such applications, thereby making public the internal practices of the CSC. CAEFS along with the Canadian Civil Liberties Association and the John Howard Society acted as intervener in these Supreme Court cases. It is through such a mechanism that CAEFS and other organisations advocating for prisoners' rights have been able to obtain information on the conditions facing women on the inside. The disclosure of information through *habeas corpus* cases has also brought media and public attention to the problems of overcrowding, the extensive abuse of segregation of prisoners and the lack of training and resources among staff to address the broad needs of women, particularly those with mental health issues.

Perhaps one of the most useful strategies adopted by CAEFS has been to educate women in prison about their legal rights and how to challenge infringements of their civil liberties while in prison. Recently, CAEFS published a document entitled *Human Rights in Action: Handbook for Women Serving Federal Sentences* (CAEFS, 2014a). This handbook is distributed to imprisoned women. It includes easy-to-read practical information about laws in Canada and how they apply to women in prison, along with how prison advocates can help them to protect their rights while in prison. It also outlines the steps that are required to embark on a legal action, how the suitability of their case will be assessed, and what information individual petitioners can demand assess to. Through such mechanism, CAEFS is attempting to build a 'culture of rights' by mobilising women in prison to legally challenge infringements imposed by CSC institutions.

Neoliberal advancements have certainly altered the environment in which VSOs operate. However, VSOs involved in criminal justice are finding new spaces to advance the rights of women in prison. The review of CAEFS's experiences with the CSC illustrates that organisations are adapting to and developing new mechanisms of engagement. Far from being rendered powerless, CAEFS has adopted a range of new legal strategies to advocate for changes to the internal practices of women's prisons.

Domestic Violence Court and community engagement

The criminology literature on voluntary sector involvement within the criminal justice system has tended to adopt monolithic analyses that oversimplify and obscure the multilayered ways in which VSOs are engaging with the state (Garland, 2001; Tomczak, 2014). Much of this literature has presented a rather reductionist account that pays little, if any, attention to the micro practices adopted by VSOs to advance reforms within crime control institutions. VSOs have not simply been co-opted or rendered powerless as a result of the advancement of neoliberal policies. They have encountered barriers to traditional advocacy avenues, but they continue to search for and advance innovative strategies to push for reforms. Our analysis of CAEFS points to the legal strategies adopted by one organisation, but there are multiple and varied spaces in which women's organisations are seeking to address the conditions of women in conflict with the law.

The following part of this section provides a brief overview of women's community organisations' involvement in Domestic Violence Courts (DVCs) across Canada. The objective here is not to provide an in-depth overview of DVCs, but rather to highlight the multilayered and diverse ways in which women's organisations are interacting with neoliberal punitive regimes. Our intent is to draw attention to the need for further research to explore the complex spaces and multilayered strategies used by women's organisations as they engage with the state.

DVCs were first introduced in Canada in the 1990s and have now opened in almost all jurisdictions across the country. DVCs typically handle first appearances, remands and, in some cases, more serious trials relating to spousal abuse. The critical difference between DVCs and the regular prosecution process is the involvement of community partners. DVCs partner with a range of women's organisations and service providers within local communities (Singh, 2012). DVCs do share similarities and borrow techniques from each other; however, the particular associations and assemblages formed between a court and community organisation have significant impact on the inner workings, the configurations of the court and punishment practices (Hannah-Moffat and Maurutto, 2012). In these courts, ultimate responsibility rests with the judge or crown attorney, but women's organisations involved in DVCs provide more than simply service delivery. They are regularly consulted on policy changes, programme development and best practices. Several courts have advisory committees that provide an institutionalized mechanism for information sharing, consultation and problem solving between the court and community organisations. These advisory committees typically include a range of women's organisations and local community agencies including victims services, health services, shelters and organisations advocating for women in conflict with the law. Local Elizabeth Fry Societies have been actively engaged in many of the advisory committees across the country. Advisory committees provide the organisational infrastructure for feminist and gendered knowledge to enter and affect the operations of the court. Essentially, they provide a venue for local communities to work with courts to shape case management recommendations for bail plans, sentencing, treatment and conditions for probation.

One specific area where advisory committees have been particularly influential is in the design of partner abuse programmes. Typically, in DVCs, offenders are required to undergo a partner or spousal abuse treatment programme. If successfully completed, offenders often receive a less severe sentence or, for low-risk cases, a discharge is imposed (which in Canada results in no criminal record after 1–3 years). Through the advisory committees, women's organisations played a significant role in ensuring that programmes for men focus not simply on aggression but also on power relations in society (Singh, 2012). For women appearing before DVCs, the programmes could be fundamentally different in structure.

The structure of programmes for women in DVCs emerged as a significant issue as the number of women appearing before the courts increased as a result of dual-charge policies. Several provinces and territories have instituted dual-charge practices whereby the police, often in an effort to avoid civil liability, charge both parties if there is a dispute over who initiated the violence. As a consequence, many women are charged as a result of using force against an abuser while trying to defend themselves (Singh, 2010). Elizabeth Fry Societies, along with other women's advocacy groups, called for women's programmes that acknowledge and incorporate the histories of women's victimisation. They pushed for programmes that recognised the power relations in domestic abuse situations that often result in histories of victimisation for women. The courts have developed a capacity to understand women offenders' victimization as a consequence of engagement with women's organisations through the advisory committees. This has fostered a new sensitivity on the part of courts that complicates the use of force and that acknowledges the cycle of victimisation and power relations experienced by women appearing before them.

The impact of such micro-level programme changes might be minimized in terms of their influence on the criminal justice system. Indeed, women's organisations have experienced limited success in challenging provincial policies and practices of dual charging. However, these examples demonstrate how VSOs involved in service provision are not merely extending the regulatory net of the state, they are also engaged in more complex interactions where they are infusing the courts with feminist knowledge that is shifting how women are framed and managed within DVCs.

Conclusions

The chapter documents the partnerships between the state and the voluntary sector that shaped the criminal justice system for women. During the 1980s, women's prison advocacy was advanced primarily through political lobbying in a culture where organisations like CAEFS were, to some extent, able to partner with the government to promote prison reform. The carceral turn of the 1990s repositioned prison advocacy, and in particular CAEFS, as a single interest group in opposition to corrections. The neoliberal culture of conservatism that came to pervade the CSC forced VSOs to reconsider their strategies and establish new mechanisms for advancing the rights of incarcerated women. Advocacy groups have reconstituted themselves and have adopted new strategies for effective engagement. The multifaceted ways in which women's organisations are advancing the rights of women have often been obscured in scholarship on the voluntary sector, particularly in the field of criminal justice. The examples of CAEFS and women's advisory committees in DVCs highlight the need for more nuanced empirical studies that explore the complex and varied ways in which the voluntary sector is developing strategies for effective promotion of the rights of women in conflict with the law.

References

Brodie, J. (1995) *Politics on the Margins: Restructuring and the Canadian Women's Movement*. Halifax: Fernwood Publishing.

Canadian Association of Elizabeth Fry Societies (CAEFS) (2014a) *Human Rights in Action: Handbook for Women Serving Federal Sentences*. Ottawa: Canadian Association of Elizabeth Fry Societies.

Canadian Association of Elizabeth Fry Societies (CAEFS) (2014b) *Annual Report CAEFS*, http://www.caefs.ca/wp-content/uploads/2013/03/CAEFS-Annual-Report-2014.pdf [accessed 26/02/15].

Carlen, P. (2002) Carceral Clawback: The Case of Women's Imprisonment in Canada, *Punishment and Society*, 4 (1): 115–121.

Corcoran, M. (2011) Dilemmas of Institutionalization in the Penal Voluntary Sector, *Critical Social Policy*, 31 (1): 30–52.

Elson, P. (2007) A Short History of Voluntary Sector-Government Relations in Canada, *The Philanthropist*, 21 (1): 36–74.

Garland, D. (2001) *The Culture of Control: Crime and Social Order in a Contemporary Society*. Chicago, IL: University of Chicago Press.

Hannah-Moffat, K. (2001) *Punishment in Disguise: Penal Governance and Federal Imprisonment of Women in Canada*. Toronto: University Of Toronto Press.

Hannah-Moffat, K. and Margaret Shaw (eds) (2000) *An Ideal Prison: Critical Essays on Women's Imprisonment in Canada*. Halifax: Fernwood Publishing.

Hannah-Moffat, K. and Maurutto, P. (2012) Shifting and Targeted Forms of Penal Governance: Bail, Punishment, and Specialized Courts, *Theoretical Criminology: An International Journal*, 16 (2): 201–219.

Hayman, S. (2006) *Imprisoning Our Sisters: The new Federal Women's Prison in Canada*. Montreal: McGill-Queen's University Press.

Jackson, M. (2002) *Justice Behind the Walls: Human Rights in Canadian Prisons*. Vancouver: Douglas and McIntyre.

Luxton, M. (2001) Feminism as a Class Act: Working-Class Feminism and the Women's Movement in Canada, *Labour/Le Travail*, 48 (Fall): 63–68.

Maurutto, P. (2003) *Governing Charities: Church and State in Toronto's Catholic Archdiocese, 1850–1950*. Montreal: McGill-Queen's Press.

Maurutto, P. and Hannah-Moffat, K (2006) Assembling Risk and the Restructuring of Penal Control, *British Journal of Criminology*, 46 (3): 438–454.

May *v.* Ferndale Institution, 2005 SCC 82, [2005] 3 S.C.R. 809.

Mills, A., Meek, R. and Gojkovic, D. (2011) Exploring the Relationship between the Voluntary Sector and the State in Criminal Justice, *Voluntary Sector Review*, 2: 193–211.

Mission Institution *v.* Khela, 2014 SSC 24, [2014] 1 S.C.R. 502.

Moore, D. and Hannah-Moffat, K. (2005) The Liberal Veil: Revisiting Canadian Penality, in: Pratt, J., Brown, D., Brown, M., Hallsworth, S. and Morrison, W. (eds.) *The New Punitiveness: Trends, Theories, Perspectives*. Cullompton, Devon: Willan Publishing: 85–100.

Neilson, A. (2009) A Crisis of Identity: NACRO's Bid to Run a Prison and What it Means for the Voluntary Sector, *Howard Journal of Criminal Justice*, 48 (4): 401–410.

Pratt, J. (2011) The International Diffusion of Punitive Penality: Or, Penal Exceptionalism in the United States? Wacquant *v.* Whitman, *Australian and New Zealand Journal of Criminology*, 44 (1): 116–128.

Shaw, M. (1993) Reforming Federal Women's Imprisonment, in: Adelberg, E. and Currie, C. (eds.) *In Conflict with the Law*. Vancouver: Press Gang: 50–75.

Singh, R. (2012) When Punishment and Philanthropy Mix: VSOs and the Governance of Domestic Violence Offender, *Theoretical Criminology*, 16 (3): 269–287.

Singh, Rashmee (2010) In Between the System and the Margins: Community Organisations, Mandatory Charging and Immigrant Victims of Abuse, *Canadian Journal of Sociology*, 35 (1): 31–62.

Task Force on Federally Sentenced Women (1990) *Creating Choices: The Report of the Task Force on Federally Sentence Women*. Ottawa, ON: Correctional Service of Canada. Available from: http://www.csc-scc.gc.ca/text/prgrm/fsw/choices/choice9e-eng.shtml [accessed 20/11/14].

Tomczak, P. J. (2014) The Penal Voluntary Sector in England and Wales: Beyond Neoliberalism?, *Criminology and Criminal Justice*, 14 (4): 470–486.

Vantour, J. (1991) *Our Story: Organisational Renewal in Federal Corrections*. Ottawa: Correctional Service of Canada.

Yeatman, A. (1990) *Bureaucrats and Technocrats and Femocrats*. Sydney: Allen & Unwin.

9
Diversity: The Voluntary Sector's Vision in Criminal Justice

Loraine Gelsthorpe and *Jane Dominey*

> 'Diversity' as a concept and as a strategy for change can easily be hijacked by the imperatives of managerialism, losing its force as a means of promoting social justice, and becoming rather a means of achieving narrower organisational aims and objectives which provide the surface appearance rather than the deeper essentials of diversity. (Bhui, 2003: 196)

Since the late 1990s in particular, issues relating to equality, diversity and anti-discrimination have had increasing influence in relation to policy development and the construction of legislation (Mitchell, 2010). Diversity has certainly been a key part of the criminal justice discourse, with a significant amount of political and media attention towards issues relating to immigration and multiculturalism (Spalek and El-Hassan, 2007). Beyond this, there have been pressures from within the European Union, shaping directives of anti-discrimination and equal opportunities that go beyond race and ethnicity – including gender/sex, religion, disability, age and sexual orientation (European Commission, 2008; Equality Act, 2010). However, it has been argued that these positive policy and legislation changes as well as commitments to address diversity have suffered from a lack of commitment and loss of enthusiasm, with some agencies instead resorting to actions which equate to general 'tick box' exercises and do little more than satisfy statutory requirements (Mitchell, 2010). Some critics have also argued that there is a lack of understanding of the difference between equality and diversity, often with equality being prioritised over the more complicated issue of diversity (Corston, 2007; Mitchell, 2010). This said, there have been some 'kick starts' along the way, arising from disturbing and tragic incidents. For example, the Stephen Lawrence Inquiry (Macpherson, 1999) seems a particularly important moment in the history of criminal justice and diversity. It drew attention not only to a catalogue of police errors and omissions in relation to the murder of Stephen Lawrence, a young black teenager murdered by a group of white men in 1993, but also to 'institutionalised' complacency and incompetence, 'institutionalised racism' as it was captioned.

This chapter examines the voluntary sector's treatment of notions of 'diversity' in its focus and functions, but also goes beyond this to examine the ethos and culture of voluntary sector involvement in criminal justice. This involves looking at both accountability and legitimacy in 'dealing with diversity' in voluntary sector initiatives in criminal justice, and also the prospects for dealing with diversity in a changing landscape of criminal justice provision. Put concisely, what are the legal requirements of voluntary sector organisations (VSOs) regarding diversity? What are the expectations of VSOs? And what might be a legitimate expectation of VSOs in relation to diversity issues? Can the voluntary sector make a specific contribution in this area? Moreover, what are the implications for equality and diversity brought about by significant criminal justice policy changes such as *Transforming Rehabilitation* (*TR*) (Ministry of Justice and NOMS, 2014) and the Equality Act 2010?

Meanings and measures

What, exactly, does diversity mean? The Equality Act 2010[1] lists a number of characteristics which are taken to be the touchstone of equality: age, disability, gender reassignment, marriage and civil partnership, pregnancy and maternity, race, religion or belief, sex and sexual orientation. But this list is not exhaustive; it misses out mental health for example (unless mental ill-health is clearly defined as a disability, which is not the case in all circumstances).[2] It is also silent on the subjects of class and poverty – two facets of difference that are highly relevant in the criminal justice context. Moreover, the government also recognises and aims to attend to other ways in which society is diverse, including recognition that English may not be the primary language for some people. Further difficulties arise from the fact that while people rarely fall neatly into one single category, they are categorized as such; but we are not just men or women, black, or Asian or white, but rather situate ourselves on a number of social and cultural planes. Whilst dyslexia can be disabling within the context of education and employment, it may be less of a disadvantage to an offender sentenced to a Community Order with an unpaid work requirement, for example. One further example of the difficulty in capturing or measuring diversity is that there is often little recognition of new ethnicities or cultural pluralism within criminal justice monitoring (Modood et al., 1994; Earle and Phillips, 2013; Phillips and Webster, 2013). But all this is to suggest that issues relating to diversity revolve around legality and management; that is, 'diversity' is something that has to be *managed*. In contrast, diversity can also be conceived of as a concept which describes the richness and opportunities of human difference. As Bhui has indicated, '"Diversity" as a concept and as a strategy for change can easily be hijacked by the imperatives of managerialism, losing its force as a means of promoting social justice, and becoming rather a means of achieving narrower organisational aims and objectives which provide the surface appearance rather than the deeper essentials of diversity' (Bhui, 2003: 196).

Thinking more broadly then, human diversity, according to Sen (1992), arises from a range of factors: personal characteristics such as physical or mental health or abilities, age and gender; external factors such as family circumstances (wealth, culture, religion) and physical environment; and a person's capacity to achieve various 'functionings', which form a valued part of life and are critical to well-being, though the exercise of freedom and choices. Some would argue that it is about understanding each other and moving beyond simple tolerance to embracing and celebrating the rich dimensions of diversity contained within each individual. Sanglin-Grant (2003: 4), for example, provides a very 'inclusive' and 'celebratory' definition of diversity away from equal opportunities and managerial conceptions:

> "[D]iversity" allows for a greater sense of "towards" an embracing of the value that differences can offer and the contribution they can make to enhancing organisations and society at large. Diversity seeks to express a higher value of harmony and, at its most elevated, a peace that comes from people "feeling" valued and appreciated, no matter what their background.

Indeed, it might be suggested that recognising 'diversity' involves a set of conscious practices that include understanding and appreciating the interdependence of humanity, cultures and the natural environment; practising mutual respect for qualities and experiences that are different from our own; understanding that diversity includes not only ways of being but also ways of knowing; recognising that personal, cultural and institutionalised discrimination creates and sustains privileges for some while creating and sustaining disadvantages for others; building alliances across differences so that we can work together to eradicate all forms of discrimination.

However, it may be argued that translating these dimensions of diversity into criminal justice practice invariably leads to a focus on those diversities identified as statutory duties for criminal justice agencies prior to the Equality Act 2010 (namely race/ethnicity, gender and disability), and to a lesser extent some on those diversities incorporated after the 2010 Act's publication (age, sexual orientation, gender reassignment, religion or belief, maternity and pregnancy, marriage and civil partnership, which are the remaining protected characteristics in law but where there has been much less discussion and debate in criminal justice circles). This is also partly because we know more (there is more evidence) about the experience of Black, Asian and Minority Ethnic (BAME) people and women in the criminal justice system. There are real research gaps in the experience of and outcomes for other disadvantaged groups – much that does exist having been led by the voluntary sector (e.g. the work of *Press for Change*, legal advisers on transgender issues http://www.pfc.org. uk/index.html).

If we acknowledge that diversity is both about celebrating difference (in a broad sense) and/or ensuring that there is no discrimination (in a narrow managerial sense), then there are challenges in regard to understanding the differences between disparity, equality and difference in the context of criminal justice. In such a context discrimination is commonly taken to mean unfavourable treatment; it is frequently tied to the concept of prejudice – that is, ideas that identify particular groups or individuals as 'inferior' or 'difficult'. 'Disparity' is sometimes used interchangeably with discrimination, and yet more accurately relates to differences in outcome where it is assumed that 'fair and equal treatment' means the impartial application of existing rules and procedures, regardless of the outcome (procedural justice). However, equal treatment policies can have the effect of punishing or controlling a higher proportion of one social group than another in ways which are seemingly unjust, with the consequence that law and policy should be adjusted so as to achieve equal outcomes (substantive justice). Thus, calls for an end to disparity are not unproblematic and the quest for 'equal treatment' is rightly questioned (Hudson, 1989), since 'difference' may justify disparity in outcomes (Gelsthorpe and McIvor, 2007). The notion that women are 'equal' but require 'different treatment from men' has long been argued (Criminal Justice Joint Inspection, 2011). We can complicate the picture further by referring to 'disproportionality'; indeed, a good deal of criminological attention has been given to the issue of whether the higher proportion of BAME groups in English and Welsh prisons

(Ministry of Justice, 2013) reflects higher rates of offending or is a result of discrimination by the police and courts.

There are inherent flaws in the evidence in relation to all of this: assignment to ethnic categories which are externally imposed rather than reflecting self-identity; ethnic categories in research which have muddled race, nationality, religion and skin colour; arrest and imprisonment statistics reflecting the outcomes of decisions rather than an independent account of offending, to name but a few methodological problems. And in areas other than race and gender, the empirical evidence about disparity and discrimination is even thinner.

Key challenges

All these uncertainties and methodological issues aside, it is possible to come to the following general conclusions which indicate concerns about 'diversity and equality' in criminal justice:

- Black and minority ethnic groups are cumulatively disadvantaged and there is evidence of both direct and indirect discrimination affecting the fair treatment of Black and Minority Ethnic offenders in the criminal justice process (Phillips and Bowling, 2012; Phillips and Webster, 2013).
- The criminal justice system has been slow to acknowledge that women are different to men, and require different treatment (Prison Reform Trust, 2000; Corston, 2007; Hedderman, 2011).
- Whilst the UK's general population includes an estimated 3.6 million people who are gay, reliable estimates of the number of gay people in prison are virtually non-existent. Prison surveys have suggested that around 4 per cent of the prisoner population within England and Wales is gay, but homophobic stereotyping and prejudice are bound to lead to underreporting (Chakraborti, 2010).
- Large numbers of disabled offenders go unnoticed within the criminal justice system and there is significant confusion about the meaning of disability; Asperger's syndrome does not count as 'disability'; HIV-positive prisoners are classified as disabled; 'mental ill-health' may not count as a disability unless it is severe (Her Majesty's Inspectorate of Prisons, 2009).
- This said, it is estimated that 75 per cent of adult prisoners have a dual diagnosis of mental health problems and substance abuse (Offender Health Research Network, 2009).

A key question for this chapter then is how far VSOs have contributed to, developed or challenged knowledge and practice about diversity.

There is some evidence to suggest that VSOs have held the lantern for issues relating to 'diversity', notwithstanding possible confusion as to its meaning.

The voluntary sector and diversity: focus and functions

As intimated, it is very clear that some voluntary organisations have been at the forefront of campaigning for change in the criminal justice system. Obvious recent examples here include Southall Black Sisters in the area of domestic violence and immigration (http://www.southall-blacksisters.org.uk/) and the groups formed in response to the Stephen Lawrence and Zahid Mubarek cases (e.g. the Stephen Lawrence Trust: http://www.stephenlawrence.org.uk and the Zahid Mubarek Trust http://www.thezmt.org/). It is widely recognised by academics, if not some of the public as well, that these are generally campaigning and policy development organisations rather than service delivery ones.[3] Indeed, one of the key contributions that the voluntary sector has made in the area of diversity has been in campaigning and awareness-raising.

Alongside campaigning groups which have single or particular diversity-related issues as their focus, there are generalist campaigning groups which have included diversity-related issues in their portfolios. For instance, the Prison Reform Trust (http://www.prisonreformtrust. org.uk) is an example of a large VSO with a broad remit which has included an educational and campaigning role. It produces material highlighting equality and diversity concerns relating to unfair, discriminatory or unjust treatment in prisons in particular. The Prison Reform Trust (PRT) was founded in 1981 in London, UK, by a small group of prison reform campaigners who, notwithstanding the work of the Howard League for Penal Reform which *included* a focus on prisons, felt that there should be specific focus on traditional prison reform issues. PRT has a strong educational role and aims to provide accessible information for students, academics and interested members of the public to further its objectives of raising awareness of issues. The PRT carries out research on all aspects of prison life. Recent studies include prisoners' views on prison education, the mental health needs of women prisoners, older prisoners, prisoner councils, resettlement, deaths in custody, disability, foreign national prisoners, prisoner votes and work examining how sentencers make decisions to imprison offenders. The PRT has championed the need to consider women's needs separately from those of men. Supported by the Bromley Trust,[4] the PRT established a time-limited, high-level, independent Women's Justice Taskforce to reinforce the idea that vulnerable women in the criminal justice system should be a priority for the government, and to set out the means by which Ministers, officials and local government might build on Jean Corston's 2007 blueprint for reform in changed economic and political times (see, for example, *Reforming Women's Justice*, the final report of the Women's Taskforce, Prison Reform Trust, 2011). But there are elements of service provision too. A smaller, but nevertheless significant, part of the PRT's work involves providing direct advice and information to prisoners, their families, prison and probation staff, and the legal profession. There are also publications directed at prisoners (on Temporary Release, Sentence Planning and Imprisonment for Public Protection, for example).

Some VSOs have combined a campaigning role with a larger service delivery role. Examples here include Nacro (www.nacro.org.uk/what-we-do/). Nacro started in 1966 with focused efforts to change criminal justice policy at the national level to reflect the support and opportunities that offenders need. Indeed, its origins lie in the Central Discharged Prisoners' Aid Society founded in 1924,[5] a telling clue to its interests, but alongside national campaigning for reform there is direct service provision to young people (through pre-vocational and vocational programmes and employment preparation programmes), accommodation provision, support and well-being services and guidance, and there is a national telephone and online advisory service relating to people's resettlement upon leaving prison. And now, Nacro, in partnership with the private company Sodexo, delivers core offender management services in six English areas. One early example of research from Nacro concerns Eric Smellie's 1991 report *Black people's experience of criminal justice*, which reflected conversation between the authors and consumers of criminal justice on negative elements of their experiences (Smellie and Crow, 1991). The research report was used to raise awareness of discrimination against BAME groups in the criminal justice system.

Similarly, Women in Prison (WIP: http://www.womeninprison.org.uk), a national charity which started in 1983, has a dual function. The charity provides specialist support services for women and seeks to enable them to make informed choices in both custody and the community. WIP also campaigns for a system which responds to the specific needs of women in the criminal justice system and promotes alternatives to custody wherever possible. Established in 1987, Women in Special Hospitals (Wish) is a national, user-led charity working with women with mental health needs in prison, hospital and the community (WISH: http://www.womenatwish.org.uk). It provides independent advocacy, emotional support and practical guidance at all stages of a woman's journey through the mental health and criminal justice systems. The overall aims are to increase women's participation in the services they receive, and to campaign to get their voice heard at a policy level. It is unique in its long-term commitment to each individual, as she moves through hospitals, prison and the community. Indeed, a conspicuous strength of the voluntary sector has been its commitment to service user involvement and voice. This is often in contrast to the way the statutory services work.

The Howard League (http://www.howardleague.org/our-work/), established as a charity for penal reform in 1866, is another example. As well as directing campaigns for penal reform to politicians, policy makers and the public, the Howard League also offers a direct advisory service to those caught up in the criminal justice system. Thus, the organisation offers free legal advice to young people who are locked up, particularly when they are bullied, disciplined or assaulted in custody. Advice is also offered on access to education, training, offending behaviour work, interpreters and signers, as well as release on temporary licences or escorted absences, access to medical care, transfers from secure detention to secure hospitals and issues relating to discrimination, for example. Notable reports from the Howard League include the All-Party Parliamentary Group on women in the penal system independent inquiry on girls and the penal system (Howard League, *Women in the Penal System*, 2011). The aim of the inquiry was to achieve changes in the lives of young girls in need and to bring about a reduction in the number of girls who entered the criminal justice system. The Howard League has also drawn attention to the role of resettlement in reducing homelessness (Cooper, 2013) and to deaths on probation, which, in contrast to deaths in custody, rarely receive any attention (Gelsthorpe et al., 2012), both themes here being relevant to social exclusion and the treatment of vulnerable people within the criminal justice system. This goes beyond traditional managerialist interpretations of diversity, but is linked to the broader social justice aspirations.

A final example of a VSO contributing to understandings of diversity within the criminal justice system concerns Stonewall (http://www.stonewall.org.uk) regarding lesbian, bisexual, gay and transgender (LBGT) issues. As a result of Stonewall's work, homophobic hate crime is now better understood and taken more seriously by the police service, the courts and more broadly in policy development. The Crime Survey of England and Wales[6] now gathers data about sexual orientation–motivated hate crime. Stonewall has also offered training and consultancy to criminal justice agencies; for example, by 2009, 33 police forces were members of its Diversity Champions Programme.

Thus the voluntary sector has certainly played an important role in campaigning and awareness-raising on various aspects of diversity. It has also provided services that supplement the work of the statutory services, sometimes highlighting gaps in provision and lack of access to services for some groups.

Legal requirements and legitimate expectations of voluntary bodies in relation to diversity issues

The voluntary sector is bound by legislation in the same way as the public sector. Whether they are held to account in precisely the same way as public services remains unclear. Although we can certainly say that quality assurance is built into the process of applying for grants from both statutory authorities and grant-giving bodies, VSOs are increasingly expected to demonstrate to funders and commissioners their approach to quality assurance; indeed, the Charity Commissioners require certain conditions to be met. Moreover, quality standards may be applied. The National Council for Voluntary Organisations (NCVO) has championed research into the perceptions and use of quality standards in the voluntary and community sector. Recent research, commissioned by the BIG Lottery Fund and carried out with OPM, investigated how VSOs use standards such as PQASSO, Investors in People, ISO 9001 and specific standards for sub-sectors and areas of work (e.g. the Matrix Standard).[7] They also found out how funders and commissioners view quality standards and how they influence funding and commissioning decisions (NCVO and OPM, 2012). Thus standards in relation to non-discriminatory practices may be upheld in this way.

Large VSOs (including those that have been successful in the *TR* process) employ significant numbers of staff. They must deal with diversity both as an employer and as a service provider. What we also know is that VSOs utilise diverse volunteer workforces – which may be more representative of the community they serve (Neuberger, 2009), although there is some scepticism here too (Clinks/ARO, 2007; Gelsthorpe and Sharpe, 2007). But the point here is that increasing partnership arrangements with the state may potentially threaten these standards and change the ethos and culture of VSOs.

The voluntary turn

It is certainly clear that the government expects VSOs to play an increasing role in delivering public services. It was not just the coalition government – the desire to see the voluntary sector play a more formal role in the delivery of public services in the UK can be traced back to more than 30 years and formed part of the agenda of Conservative and Labour governments. For example, a Government Cabinet Office Green Paper (2010) on 'modernising commissioning' set out the rationale for greater VSO involvement. Given the VSOs' championing of diversity issues, this might be something to be welcomed. At the same time, there might be concern about the 'dead hand of bureaucracy' if increased involvement means more rules and regulations as to what can be delivered on the ground in the name of diversity or means a more managerial approach to diversity. We will return to this point. First, we elaborate upon what we might call the 'voluntary turn'. This involves the idea that attempts to roll back the state in an all-encompassing notion of the 'Big Society', which can look after itself more and depend on the state less, will inevitably lead to the increased involvement of the voluntary sector.

The concept of the 'Big Society' was an idea which emerged out of the Conservative Party general election manifesto in 2010, and formed part of the Conservative–Liberal Democrat Coalition Agreement and Government 2010–2015. And, indeed, David Cameron was talking about it while in opposition (see Defty, 2014). It is a notion which applies to England rather than to Wales, Scotland and Northern Ireland, where there is devolved responsibility for the domestic policies which fall within the ambit of the concept. The aim has been to give communities more powers (localism and devolution), encourage people to take an active role in their communities (volunteerism), transfer power from central to local government, support co-operatives, mutuals, charities and social enterprises, and publish government data (open/transparent government). However, the Leader of the Labour Party, Ed Miliband, described the initiative as a cynical attempt 'to dignify the government's cuts agenda, by dressing up the withdrawal of support with the language of reinvigorating civic society' (Watt, 2010). Indeed, it can be no coincidence that the comprehensive spending review White Paper published in October 2010 emphasised *both* dramatic reductions and that the government's spending priorities and departmental budgetary settlements were to be underpinned by the idea of radically reforming public services (Morgan, 2012). In a critical analysis of the concept, Rod Morgan, a former key player on the criminal justice stage through his role as HM Chief Inspector of Probation (2001–2004) and then as Chair of the Youth Justice Board (2004–2007), suggests that behind the Big Society public sector reforms lurks the 'Big Market', although there are some subtleties in terms of policing – with the introduction of directly elected Police and Crime Commissioners – designed to enhance local accountability. There is also subtlety in the related proposals for 'justice reinvestment', which involves analysing the costs of the criminal justice system and likely savings which might accrue from expanded use of new interventions – with the provision of funds to 'upstream providers so as to kick-start a process of change which should shrink the overall use of the criminal justice system' (Morgan, 2012: 475). In turn, this means using incentives to attract new providers and new partnerships between the state, commercial and third sector providers. Social impact bonds and payment by results is thus one model to incentivise new players (a topic which is taken up in other chapters in this book).

There has been much effort to engage existing VSOs in such initiatives given their prior experience of working with challenging and vulnerable groups of people within the criminal justice system. But as Maguire (2012), Gelsthorpe and Hedderman (2012) and Hedderman (2013), amongst others, have pointed out, the competitive commissioning of criminal justice services and utilisation of VSOs is unproven in terms of effectiveness. It also potentially risks significant changes to small-scale VSOs in terms of having to scale up their operations or join consortia, change their management style and distinctive client-centred culture and potentially lose their campaigning voice, leaving aside any difficulties in measuring the impact of the 'softer' side of what it is that they deliver to clients in terms of care and support (see also Hucklesby, 2012). In many ways then the 'Big Society' is being played out in some of the managerial developments relating to opening up the criminal justice system to different providers.

What then are the potential benefits and risks to diversity policy and practice of increasing voluntary sector involvement in criminal justice? Various reports suggest that VSOs have a number of strengths. For example, cost-effectiveness, diversity of provision and relative independence from the 'official' criminal justice system may lead offenders and victims to view provision as more trustworthy and approachable (NPC, 2009). Other perceived strengths include advocacy in terms of the potential to represent service users' views to the statutory sector and innovation in terms of research (NPC, 2009; Silvestri, 2009). Furthermore, engagement with the views of service users at the planning stage of provision (Martin, 2002), social cohesion and links with the community (in terms of VSOs being based in the community) (Bryans et al., 2002) and scope for public participation via volunteering may all be seen as strengths. Another point here concerns the idea that VSOs may have an innovative ethos, being less constrained by bureaucracy and more able to respond to the needs of service users (Meek et al., 2010).

At the same time 'Big Society' thinking offers traps as well as opportunities for the voluntary sector – and VSOs with a record of innovative practice in the area of diversity may be poorly placed to benefit because they are smaller, less well-funded and committed to continue campaigning. We will return to this point in our conclusion. We turn now to broad challenges in relation to VSOs dealing with diversity.

Hidden hazards and new challenges

With statutory requirements now addressing issues relating to age, religion or belief, sexual orientation and gender reassignment in place, there has been hope that these matters will hold equal ground to issues such as race, gender and disability. However, recent concerns from within the criminal justice system do not bode well, and thus there are new challenges for both the statutory and voluntary sectors.

For instance, with most prisons now incorporating a multi-faith regime, diverse religious practices in relation to Britain's multicultural communities have been embraced. However, this progression is now being threatened by a fear, shared by security services, policy makers and the media, of a growing Muslim population in prisons, since it is popularly assumed that this means increasing radicalisation (see http://www.bbc.co.uk/news/uk-32194671, 7 April 2015, for example). Spalek and El-Hassan (2007) present research findings based on their analysis of two prisons which suggests that those who convert to Islam find that it provides a moral framework from which to rebuild their lives. Indeed, they argue that Islam appears to help prisoners to cope more positively with the prison environment, reducing their propensity to aggression and violence. A report produced by HM Chief Inspector of Prisons in 2010 (HMIP, 2010) expresses concern about converts to Islam because they may be more vulnerable to extremism. However, both this report and government responses to media-inspired panic about extremism suggest that suspicion of Muslim prisoners can be counterproductive, fuelling resentment. Notwithstanding media myths and muddles in this area, it is something to which VSOs have given some attention – particularly in their planning for through-the-gate work with prisoners moving back into the community. A number of community chaplaincy schemes have also been set up (in the main independent bodies managed by charities and trusts) (Young, 2014).

Crawley and Sparks (2005) and Ginn (2012)[8] amongst others draw attention to the increasing numbers of elderly men in prisons in England and Wales. Older prisoners are now the fastest growing subgroup of prisoners in England and Wales. There are about 8000 prisoners aged 50 and over, comprising 11 per cent of the prison population, and many have multiple health and social needs; indeed, 2 in 5 of those over 50 have a disability (Prison Reform Trust, 2014b). Some of the increase in older prisoners is attributable to the overall growth of the prison population, which has doubled in the past 20 years. The increase in older prisoners, however, outstrips that of other groups. A key factor seems to be a greater inclination on the part of the authorities to secure convictions against sex offenders. Forty-two per cent of men aged over 50 in prison have convictions for sexual offences (Prison Reform Trust, 2014b). Sex offenders are given long sentences, and advances in forensic science mean that it is possible to secure convictions for 'historical' crimes. When it comes to sentencing, the age of an older offender rarely has a bearing. At the same time, it is suggested by Bartlett and Evans (2012) that imprisonment can actually reduce some of the risks associated with an unhealthy, external lifestyle. Excess alcohol, illicit drug use, poor diet and exercise, and poor medication compliance for long-term conditions all contribute to premature ageing and are common in offenders. But the essential point here is to recognise increasing concerns about elderly offenders coming to the attention of the criminal justice system, with associated vulnerabilities such as deafness (McCulloch, 2013). A recent Justice Committee report on older prisoners (Justice Committee, 2013) gives some consideration to the work of the voluntary sector – including that of the organisation RECOOP – a VSO dedicated to work with older ex-offenders and prisoners (http://www.recoop.org.uk/pages/home/index.php).

Finally, the number of foreign national prisoners imprisoned within England and Wales has increased enormously over the last few years (Prison Reform Trust, 2014b). Unlike many British minority ethnic prisoners, foreign nationals often face the added vulnerability of 'stress, anxiety, shock and confusion' (Coffey and Church, 2002: 3). Moreover, foreign national offenders simultaneously bring with them vulnerabilities which derive from outside the UK, including both psychological and physical scars (Hales and Gelsthorpe, 2012; Prison Reform Trust, 2012).

These are but a few of the new challenges emerging in relation to recognition of diversity, of course. What are the implications of these new challenges for VSOs? One difficulty concerns the never-ending trail in the pursuit of funding for new ventures. As previously indicated, some funding streams are tied to specific agendas, which makes it difficult to be responsive to new challenges and circumstances. Another challenge relates to the voluntary sector's capacity to respond to new concerns in terms of personnel and experience. These kinds of problems can be exemplified in consideration of the role of the voluntary sector in the new landscape of *TR*, to which we now turn.

Diversity and transforming rehabilitation

This final section of the chapter considers the issue of diversity in the context of the coalition government's reforms of the prison and probation services. It acknowledges that these reforms are being pushed through at a time of continuing financial pressure and draws on themes that are explored elsewhere in this collection (particularly Maguire, Dacombe and Morrow, and Clinks). In this section we explore the extent to which the *TR* reforms help or hinder the voluntary sector's ability to provide services responsive to diversity and difference.

The impact of the TR reforms is particularly significant for those VSOs whose purpose is to provide rehabilitation services for offenders. These organisations have had to decide how to position themselves in the new environment; some partnered with private companies to bid for Community Rehabilitation Companies (CRCs) and others have become part of the supply chains created by the successful prime providers. It is an inevitable consequence of the competition process that, when the successful bidders for the CRCs were announced, some VSOs found themselves with expanded responsibilities for service delivery while others lost out. In addition, the TR reforms have implications for the many VSOs, concerned with diversity and equality, which do not provide specific rehabilitation services. For example, VSOs working in areas like health and housing must now negotiate new links with CRCs to replace their previous relationships with Probation Trusts. VSOs with a campaigning mission must take account of new patterns of power and policy development.

There are two particular concerns about the extent to which CRCs will be able to develop or maintain services that meet the diverse needs of offenders: the impact of the payment-by-results mechanism and the extent to which small VSOs will be able to make a contribution to offender supervision. Including payment by results as part of the funding mechanism for CRCs has been a particularly controversial aspect of the TR reforms (Burke and Collett, 2015; Maguire, chapter three, this volume). It is particularly controversial when applied to groups of service users who deserve to be dealt with differently in response to their specific circumstances. Payment by results brings with it the possibility that providers will focus on work most likely to produce the required outcome and neglect work which is seen as complex and unprofitable. Evidence from the Work Programme (which uses payment by results to reward providers who successfully move service users into work) suggests that this 'creaming' and 'parking' effect is real and, significantly, that the payment mechanism does not adequately reflect the differences between various groups of service users. Rees et al. (2014), in a conclusion that sounds a warning for probation services, state:

> Far from delivering 'differentiated universalism', the Work Programme at present seems instead to be reinforcing, exacerbating and making systemic the negative impacts of employment disadvantages. (Rees et al., 2014: 236)

In prisons and probation, it remains to be seen whether the new environment will be conducive to the development of projects with outcomes that are not easily quantified, whose results cannot be attributed to a single provider and that respond to the needs of minority groups of offenders. Women's community centres are an example of such projects and their future under TR is not yet assured (Gelsthorpe and Hedderman, 2012).

The provision of services that are responsive to the diverse needs of offenders may well be hampered by payment by results. It will also be made more difficult if smaller VSOs are excluded from involvement because they are unwilling or unable to enter into contractual arrangements with prime providers. For example, CRCs do have links with VSOs that provide mentoring services but not necessarily with particular groups that can provide mentoring services tailored to the needs of (to give two examples) young Muslim men or transgender prisoners. Marketisation has the potential to turn partners into rivals (Minow, 2002), reducing the chance of collaborative practice that aims for equality and fairness.

The TR reforms and creation of CRCs clearly impact on the voluntary sector, but the overarching economic climate is important too. The capacity of the sector to provide services and influence the policy agenda is shaped by organisational structures but also the funding available. VSOs draw on a variety of income streams (philanthropic donation, income from commercial activity or service provision, government grant) and differ greatly in the relative importance of these different streams. However, financial austerity and cuts in government spending are felt across the sector (NCVO, 2013). Arguably, they have a particular impact on VSOs that have traditionally found it hard to secure reliable and predictable funding. For example, Mayblin and Soteri-Proctor (2011) identify restricted access to funding as a factor limiting the development of the BAME voluntary sector. Responding in an innovative way to diversity is harder in the absence of VSOs whose knowledge about equality issues is comprehensive and informed by experience.

There are, therefore, real concerns that the combination of financial austerity and the TR reforms limit the voluntary sector's scope to enhance the way that the criminal justice system deals with diversity. However, there are practical steps that, at least in part, can mitigate these concerns, for example:

- CRCs should be held to account, by the inspection and contract management processes, for their performance on diversity and equality issues. The quest for accountability should focus on whether equality and diversity are embedded in the work of the CRC or dealt with tokenistically. Questions about accountability should include a focus on the training and support that staff receive, and should include service user feedback drawn from a sufficiently diverse group.
- CRC supply chains should include VSOs with the skills and experience to work with the wide variety of service users. However, and of equal importance, CRCs should also be open to the contribution of VSOs from beyond their supply chain that can make a particular contribution to some aspect of diversity policy or practice.
- Joint work between criminal justice agencies, the voluntary sector, local authorities and the health service is arguably the best way of responding to the needs of many offenders, as demonstrated, for example, by the work of community women's centres (see *Women's Break Out*⁹ and Prison Reform Trust and Soroptimist International (2014a), for example). Such work does not lend itself well to simple payment-by-results mechanisms and deserves dedicated funding.

In *conclusion*, the voluntary sector has contributed much to extending and developing the way that the criminal justice system understands, values and responds to the diversity of human need and experience. The sector has particular strengths in campaigning and awareness-raising. It has provided a voice for many service user groups and has created and supported innovative services. Allowing the sector to retain these strengths in the context of public sector reform and continuing financial austerity must be a policy priority in the new landscape of criminal justice provision.

Notes

1 A new Equality Act came into force on 1 October 2010. The Equality Act brings together over 116 separate pieces of legislation into one single act. Combined, they make up a new act that provides a legal framework to protect the rights of individuals and advance equality of opportunity for all. Most of the provisions of the Equality Act 2010 came into effect in October 2010; however, the public sector duties did not come into place until April 2011. Other commencement dates followed, notwithstanding the coalition government's temporary suspension of the timetable for broad implementation.

2 Mental ill health might only be defined as a disability if it recognises formal clinical criteria and impacts on someone's ability to function in everyday life, whereas it is commonly recognised that mental health and ill health might be represented along a broad continuum.

3 The Stephen Lawrence Trust does deliver broad educational and training programmes to support young people who are living in disadvantaged areas in thinking about their next steps and future employment, as well as delivering bursaries for BAME students who wish to study architecture or the built environment.

4 The Bromley Trust (http://www.thebromleytrust.org.uk/index.php?/about-us/) was set up in 1989 as a grant-making trust relating to work in the areas of human rights, prison reform and the protection of the environment.

5 It was renamed the National Association of Discharged Prisoners' Aid Societies (Incorporated) in October 1960, and the National Association for the Care and Resettlement of Offenders (NACRO) in March 1966. It developed into one of the largest criminal justice–related charities in England and Wales; in the 1970s and 1980s it became involved in policy discussions with the British Government particularly with the Home Office which, at that time, had responsibility for both prisons and probation. Since 2011, its strategy has focused on extending its high-level influence at government level, with commissioners, policy makers and practitioners. In 1999 the charity became known as Nacro, the crime reduction charity.

6 The Crime Survey England and Wales (CSEW) measures the extent of crime via a household survey by asking people whether they have experienced any crime in the past year. The survey has measured crime in this way since 1982 and is seen as a valuable source of information for the government about the extent and nature of crime in England and Wales. The Crime Survey for England and Wales is the new name for the British Crime Survey.

7 PQASSO, Investors in People, ISO 9001 and specific standards for sub-sectors and areas of work (e.g. the Matrix Standard) are all measures which relate to quality standards in the voluntary and community sector. Further information can be found in NCVO (2012).

8 Though it should be taken into account that Ginn (2012) is criticised for his failure to challenge the notion that 50 means 'elderly'. See Bartlett and Evans (2012), http://www.bmj.com/content/345/bmj.e6263/rr/612599

9 Women's Breakout is a national network of community centres and services for women: http://www.womensbreakout.org.uk

References

Bartlett, A. and Evans, S. (2012) Response to Stephen Ginn's Paper on Elderly Prisoners, *British Medical Journal*. http://www.bmj.com/content/345/bmj.e6263/rr/612599

Bhui, H. S. (2003) Deconstructing Diversity, *Probation Journal*, 50 (3): 195–197.

Brodie, E. and Anstey, G. (2012) *Scoping Study – Quality Assurance in the Voluntary and Community Sector*, London: NCVO and Office of Public Management. Available from: http://www.voscur.org/news/qualitystandardsreport

Bryans, S., Martin, C. and Walker, R. (2002) The Road Ahead: Issues and Strategies for Future Joint Working, in: Bryans, S., Martin, C. and Walker, R. (eds) *Prisons and the Voluntary Sector*. Winchester: Waterside Press: 162–173.

Burke, L. and Collett, S. (2015) *Delivering Rehabilitation: The Politics, Governance and Control of Probation*. Abingdon: Routledge.

Cabinet Office (2010) *Modernising Commissioning. Increasing the Role of Charities, Social Enterprises, Mutual and Cooperatives in Public Service Delivery*. London: Cabinet Office.

Chakraborti, N. (2010) *Hate Crime: Concepts, Policy Future Directions*. Cullompton: Willan Publishing.

Clinks/ARO (2007) *Women Offenders. NOMS and VCS*. London: Clinks.

Coffey, E. and Church, E. (2002) *Health Needs Assessment of Immigration Detainees*. Liverpool, London: HM Prison Service.

Cooper, V. (2013) *NO FIXED ABODE: The Implications for Homeless People in the Criminal Justice System*. London: The Howard League for Penal Reform.

Corston, J. (2007) *The Corston Report: A Review of Women with Particular Vulnerabilities in the Criminal Justice System*. London: Home Office.

Crawley, E. and Sparks, R. (2005) Hidden Injuries? Researching the Experiences of Older Men in English Prisons, *Howard Journal*, 44 (4): 345–356.

Criminal Justice Joint Inspection (2011) *Thematic Inspection Report. Equal But Different*. An Inspection of the Use of Alternatives to Prison for Women Offenders. A Joint Inspection by HMI Probation, HMCPSI and HMI Prisons, October 2011.

Defty, A. (2014) Can You Tell What It Is Yet? Attitudes Towards 'the Big Society', *Social Policy and Society*, 13 (1): 13–24.

Earle, R. and Phillips, C. (2013) Muslim is the New Black: New Ethnicities and New Essentialisms in the Prison, *Race and Justice*, 3 (2): 114–129.

Equality Act 2010 (c.15). London: The Stationery Office.

European Commission (2008) *Continuing the Diversity Journey: Business Practices, Perspectives and Benefits*. Luxemburg: Office for Official Publications of the European Communities.

Gelsthorpe, L. and Hedderman, C. (2012) Providing for Women Offenders: The Risks of Adopting a Payment by Results Approach, *Probation Journal*, 59 (4): 374–390.

Gelsthorpe, L. and McIvor, G. (2007) Difference and Diversity in Probation, in: Gelsthorpe, L. and Morgan, R. (eds) *Handbook of Probation*. Cullompton: Willan Publishing.

Gelsthorpe, L. and Sharpe, G. (2007) *Provision for Women Offenders in the Community*. London: Fawcett Society.

Gelsthorpe, L., Padfield, N. and Phillips, J. (2012) *Deaths on Probation: An Analysis of Data Regarding People Dying under Probation Supervision*. London: Howard

League for Penal Reform. Available from: http://www.howardleague.org/deathsonprobation/

Ginn, S. (2012) Healthcare in Prisons: Elderly Prisoners, *British Medical Journal*, 345, doi: http://dx.doi.org/10.1136/bmj.e6263 (Published 15 October 2012).

Hales, L. and Gelsthorpe, L. (2012) *The Criminalization of Migrant Women*. Cambridge: Institute of Criminology.

Hedderman, C. (2011) Policy Developments in England and Wales, in: Sheehan, R., McIvor, G. and Trotter, C. (eds) *Working With Women In The Community*. Cullompton: Willan Publishing: 26–44.

Hedderman, C. (2013) Payment by Results: Hopes, Fears and Evidence, *British Journal of Community Justice*, 11 (2–3): 43–58.

Her Majesty's Inspectorate of Prisons (HMIP) (2009) *Disabled Prisoners. A Short Thematic Review of the Care and Support of Prisoners with a Disability*. London: HMIP.

Her Majesty's Inspectorate of Prisons (HMIP) (2010) *Muslim Prisoners' Experiences: A Thematic Review*. http://www.icpa.ca/tools/download/1161/HM_Chief_Inspector_of_Prisons_-_Muslim_Prisoners_-_A_thematic_review.pdf

Howard League (2011) *All Party Parliamentary Group on Women in the Penal System. Second Report on Women with Particular Vulnerabilities in the Criminal Justice System*. London: Howard League.

Hucklesby, A. (2012) *The Third Sector in Criminal Justice. Feedback from the Seminar Series*. http://www.law.leeds.ac.uk/assets/files/research/ccjs/towards/hucklesby/pdf

Hudson, B. (1989) Discrimination and Disparity: The Influence of Race on Sentencing, *New Community*, 16 (1): 23–34.

Justice Committee (2013) Fifth Report. *Older Prisoners*. http://www.parliament.uk/documents/commons-committees/Justice/Older-prisoners.pdf

Macpherson, W. (1999) *The Stephen Lawrence Inquiry. Report of an Inquiry by Sir William Macpherson of Cluny*. Presented to Parliament by the Secretary of State for the Home Department by Command of Her Majesty, February 1999. Cm 4262-I.

Maguire, M. (2012) Response 1: Big Society, the Voluntary Sector and the Marketisation of Criminal Justice, *Criminology and Criminal Justice*, 12 (5): 483–505.

Martin, C. (2002) Recent Progress in Community Based Voluntary Sector Work with the Prison Service, in: Bryans, S., Martin, C. and Walker, R. (eds) *Prisons and the Voluntary Sector*. Winchester: Waterside Press: 63–73.

Mayblin, L. and Soteri-Proctor, A. (2011) *The Black Minority Ethnic Third Sector: A Resource Paper*. Working Paper 58, Birmingham: Third Sector Research Centre.

McCulloch, D. (2013) *Not Hearing Us: An Exploration of the Experience of Deaf Prisoners in English and Welsh Prisons*. London: Howard League for Penal Reform.

Meek, R., Gojkovic, D. and Mills, A. (2010) *The Role of the Third Sector in Work with Offenders; The Perceptions of Criminal Justice and Third Sector Stakeholders*. Birmingham: Third Sector Research Centre (TSRC).

Ministry of Justice (2013) *Statistics on Race and the Criminal Justice System 2012. A Ministry of Justice Publication under Section 95 of the Criminal Justice Act 1991*. London: Ministry of Justice.

Ministry of Justice and National Offender Management Service (2014) *Transforming Rehabilitation*. https://www.gov.uk/government/policies/reducing-reoffending-and-improving-rehabilitation/supporting-pages/transforming-rehabilitation

Minow, M. (2002) *Partners not Rivals: Privatization and the Public Good*. Boston: Beacon Press.

Mitchell, M. (2010) Diversity and the Policy Agenda in Criminal Justice, in: Pycroft, A. and Gough, D. (eds) *Multi-agency Working in Criminal Justice: Control and Care in Contemporary Correction Practice*. Bristol: The Policy Press, 51–64.

Modood, T., Beishon, S. and Virdee, S. (1994) *Changing Ethnic Identities*. London: Policy Studies Institute.

Morgan, R. (2012) Crime and Justice in the 'Big Society', *Criminology and Criminal Justice*, 12 (5): 463–481.

NCVO (2013) *Counting the Cuts: The Impact of Spending Cuts on the UK Voluntary and Community Sector – 2013 Update*. Available from: http://www.ncvo.org.uk/images/documents/policy_and_research/funding/counting_the_cuts_2013.pdf [accessed 26/3/15].

NCVO and OPM (2012) *Scoping Study – Quality Assurance in the Voluntary and Community Sector*. London: NCVO and OPM.

Neuberger, B. (2009) *Volunteering Across the Criminal Justice System*. London: The Cabinet Office.

New Philanthropy Capital (NPC) (2009) *Breaking the Cycle: Charities Working with People in Prison and on Release*. London: New Philanthropy Capital.

Offender Health Research Network (2009) *A National Evaluation of Prison Mental Health In-reach Services*. Manchester: University of Manchester.

Phillips, C. and Bowling, B. (2012) Ethnicities, Racism, Crime, and Criminal Justice, in: Maguire, M., Morgan, R. and Reiner, R. (eds) *The Oxford Handbook of Criminology* (Fifth edition). Oxford: Oxford University Press: 370–397.

Phillips, C. and Webster, C. (2013) New Directions and New Generations – Old and New Racism?, in: Phillip, C. and Webster, C. (eds) *New Directions in Race, Ethnicity and Crime*. Abingdon, Oxon: Routledge: 178–186.

Prison Reform Trust (2000) *Justice for Women: The Need for Reform. The Report of the Commission on Women's Imprisonment*. London: Prison Reform Trust [Chaired by Baroness Dorothy Wedderburn].

Prison Reform Trust (2011) *Reforming Women's Justice. Final Report of the Women's Taskforce*. London: Prison Reform Trust.

Prison Reform Trust (2012) *No Way Out. A Briefing Paper on Foreign National Women in Prison in England and Wales*. London: Prison Reform Trust.

Prison Reform Trust and Soroptimist International (2014a) *Transforming Lives. Reducing Women's Imprisonment*. London: Prison Reform Trust.

Prison Reform Trust (2014b) *Bromley Briefings Prisons Factfile* (28.10.14). London: Prisons Reform Trust.

Rees, J., Whitworth, A. and Carter, E. (2014) Support for All in the UK Work Programme? Differential Payments, Same Old Problem, *Social Policy and Administration*, 48 (2): 221–239.

Sanglin-Grant, S. (2003) *Divided by the Same Language? Equal Opportunities and Diversity Translated. A Runnymede Trust Briefing Paper*. London: Runnymede.

Sen (1992) *Inequality Re-examined*. Oxford: Clarendon Press.

Silvestri, M. (2009) *Partners or Prisoners? Voluntary Sector Independence in the World of Commissioning and Contestability*. London: Centre for Crime and Justice Studies.

Smellie, E. and Crow, I. (1991) *Black People's Experiences of Criminal Justice*, London: NACRO.

Spalek, B. and El-Hassan, S. (2007) Muslim Converts in Prison, *The Howard Journal of Criminal Justice*, 46 (2): 99–114.

Watt, N. (2010) Cameron Promises Power for the 'Man and Woman on the Street', *The Guardian* (London: Guardian Newspapers). Archived from the original (19 July). http://www.theguardian.com/politics/2010/jul/19/david-cameron-big-society-cuts [accessed 3/4/15].

Young, L. (2014) *The Young Review. Improving Outcomes for Young Black and/or Muslim Men in the Criminal Justice System*. London: Clinks [Chaired by Baroness Lola Young].

10
Victims and the Voluntary Sector: A Torrid Affair

Katherine S. Williams

The emergence of victims

For many years victims in the criminal justice system were ignored, and treated merely as witnesses to help bring offenders to justice. This ensured that offenders faced 'deserved' state punishment for breaching societal criminal laws. Under classical ideologies this was seen as necessary to keep crime in check. For researchers, victims were often merely sources of information about crime and offenders. The position of victims is now markedly different. Their changed situation has grown out of various factors: the influence of the international community through various declarations at the Council of Europe (e.g. 1983, 1985, 1987), the United Nations (e.g. 1985, 1999, 2000, 2002) and the European Union (2012); political and judicial rulings which increasingly recognise the interests of victims; and political movements and the work of voluntary sector organisations (VSOs) amongst others. In every state the metamorphosis of victims has grown from rather different roots (Shekhar and Williams, 2014). What these have in common is that victims of crime have come to the fore and criminal justice systems and researchers increasingly strive to address their plight and consider and protect their interests. The way in which, and the extent to which, their interests are addressed depends heavily on how they have been brought into the limelight (Shekhar and Williams, 2014).

In the United Kingdom, and in many other nations, the ascendance and the articulation of victims' interests rely heavily on, and have been shaped by, the actions of the voluntary sector. Indeed, in England and Wales, the very way in which the concept of 'victim' is viewed by society is often largely shaped by the way in which their needs are met by VSOs. The relationship is, or should be, symbiotic. In certain respects an understanding of the voluntary sector and how it is embraced and even possibly shaped or controlled by the state and by criminal justice agencies can be more completely understood through an analysis of its work with victims. Over the past 30–40 years VSOs who used to rely entirely on charitable monies have become more reliant on state funding, or funding which is channelled through state agencies or partnerships in which these agencies have a strong voice. Successive governments have devolved some responsibility for core criminal justice provision to local authority and community levels and both governments and these local groupings have incorporated 'non-traditional' providers such as housing associations, dedicated one-stop shops and others into the provision of criminal justice services (Carter, 2003; Ministry of Justice, 2011; Cabinet Office, 2012; NOMS, 2012). This way of working has leaked into other areas including those where governments have felt they have an ethical, even if not a core, responsibility for service provision such as in meeting the needs of victims.

What is patently evident is that in the United Kingdom since 1970 there has been a rapid expansion of both VSOs serving victims and of services available to victims through VSOs and the state. This suggests that both provision for victims and VSOs has flourished, but this would be naive. Some VSOs have floundered along the way, have not survived or have not flourished and some types of victims and victim groups have been ignored. Understanding how and why this has happened is essential to a deeper and more profound comprehension of VSOs, their sustainability and resilience (Salaman, 2013) and the extent and price of survival. Survival is often spoken of as wholly positive – as delivering sustained growth to VSOs – but this may only happen if organisations change in ways which are in tune with prevailing policy demands. All VSOs alter over time. For most this is a natural growth and in line with their core aims. However, others change in some vital respects merely to fit the prevailing policy and political climate. This chapter will question whether sustainability of VSOs is sufficient, whether organisational survival at the price of some of the core aspects of the organisation (maybe even its essence) is worse than allowing the organisation to 'die' or contract.

Clearly the expansion in VSOs and the private sector working with the government has qualitatively altered relations between the VSOs, central and local government, government agencies and the private sector. It has also altered each of these sectors and the organisations working in them. Such changes are important to prevent stagnation, yet some changes may cause VSOs to jeopardise their important independent role in civil society, so reducing the power of their advocacy resulting in poorer communities and state. VSOs' independence is essential, without it they are, arguably, no longer true voluntary agencies and the relationship between civil society and the state may become unhealthy and unbalanced (Knight, 1993; Deakin and Kershaw, 1996; Smerdon, 2007, 2009; Baring Foundation, 2013). The independence of VSOs covers freedom to discover new social problems, bring them to light and give voice to the issues and those who suffer as a result; innovate (especially in terms of finding new ways of tackling social problems); provide for clients' needs; uphold values; discuss with and represent their client base, even when their interests are marginalised and unpopular; and challenge the state and others. At its core, independence means adopting values which underpin the work of VSOs, challenging when those values are undermined or ignored, and representing collective interests of those who depend on those values (advocacy).

In 2013 the Baring Foundation suggested that the voluntary sector might be in danger of losing its distinctive and independent identity. It argued that working to fulfil contracts can stifle creativity and innovation and that working with policy makers (and/or some contractors) may mute the voice of the voluntary sector. The claim is threefold. Firstly, VSOs might be seduced into apparent power sharing, believing their ideas and values are being taken into consideration whereas, in reality, they may be used and largely ignored. When Salaman (2013: 70) reports increased interactions with the government, this is reported positively, as resilience. However, depending on the independence of the voices and the relationship between policy and VSOs it may indicate either a respect for the external voice or a stifling of independence. Secondly, collaboration and contracts may harness VSOs to objectives that are not truly their own and may even threaten their values. Thirdly, independence may be lost if they are taken over by being wholly financed and possibly also controlled by others leading to their work becoming almost totally defined and confined by others (White, 2012: 204). This chapter considers the independence of some VSOs working in the victim arena. It traces the histories of a few victim organisations and consider whether sustainability impacts on their independence and enhances or diminishes their ability to deliver what their victim clients require. The chapter analyses the independence of VSOs but will leave to future consideration and analysis the wider question of the resilience of VSOs.

For many VSOs the imperative to adapt materialises through requirements to formalise their practices and structures. The state criminal justice sector has always been somewhat nervous of the supposedly less clear lines of professional codes of practice, record keeping and checks which (allegedly) exist in some VSOs. One of the conditions for receipt of government funds is a requirement to embrace more 'managerialist' standards, to start to become 'institutionalised' and 'professionalised' (Corcoran, 2011) and so better 'fit' the criminal justice standard (Crawford, 2008). The 'managerialist' approach prioritises business ethics such as record keeping and a professional workforce delivering similar services to all clients. By contrast, VSOs have traditionally been more flexible in their approaches and more likely to deal with clients' individual needs. This responsive approach has sometimes been thought of as less competent and as delivering a second-class service because, firstly, on a 'managerialist' assessment, it can be less efficient – each case takes longer – and, secondly, it might appear to deliver a less equal service in that some individuals/groups/clients may gain more than others. However, embracing a purely 'managerialist' approach may mean the individual perspective of each victim is missed. It may assume uniform victims' needs and deliver uniform support without exploring how each victim understands and experiences their victimisation and what they (individually and as a group) need to support them. Ultimately the flexible, more individualised, approach may prove more effective because the clients' real, rather than perceived, needs are addressed and, in the longer term, the flexibility and ingenuity of VSOs may be more efficient. Furthermore, the individualised and flexible approach ensures that VSOs listen to their clients and so are able to properly and fully represent them and give voice to an otherwise largely silent group or minority. Often it is only VSOs, sitting partly inside and partly outside the system, which have the capacity to offer this important advocacy service. Such VSOs have the privileged position of both knowing and understanding their clients and being trusted by state agencies and policy makers. This permits them to become 'outsiders within' (Collins, 1986; Harding, 2004: 75; Bowell, 2014) and therefore to offer real potential for positive change: this is effective advocacy. Some have suggested that VSOs are being overwhelmed by requirements to introduce managerial systems and have altered so much as to lose the essence of what they are (Teasdale et al., 2012); similar claims are made in relation to VSOs working with victims (Welsh, 2008). This too will be considered in the analysis of a few victim organisations.

This chapter offers an overview of the sometimes symbiotic and sometimes turbulent nature of the relationship between victims, VSOs and governments. To achieve this, the historical development of the sector and how it impacts on the complex interplay of suffering, power and provision are considered. This chapter provides neither a full nor a linear history. Rather it is one interpretation which presents an understanding of the interactions of some of the major players. It suggests that the manner in which VSOs working with victims flourished has shaped societies' view and understanding of victims and victimhood and this, in turn, has shaped VSOs working with victims. The historical account depicts three strands of victimhood: a broad conception of victims, whatever caused their plight; the construction of victims of crime, particularly of traditional 'street' crimes; and groups which are criminally victimised. There is also a fourth strand: the forgotten victims. Each has its own story, and each will be considered in turn.

All individual suffering needs support

The broad concept of victimisation embraces all victims. Whether their victimisation is caused by an act of 'God', crime, accident, violence or other misfortune, individuals may be adversely affected and, some argue, should be supported. Today, in academic terms, it might be linked to consideration of zemiology and the study of 'social harm' (Hillyard et al., 2004; *Crime, Law and Social Change*, 2007; Wilkinson and Pickett, 2009), or to critics it might seem that any definition or analysis of victims tied to crime accepts a particular political hierarchy where definitions and situations are decided from above (Hulsman, 1986). Through the late 1970s and early 1980s the VSO which provided help for victims of all misfortune was the Women's Royal Voluntary Service (WRVS, now simply the Royal Voluntary Service). Its approach was broad and close to a zemeological methodology in that it was dependent on individuals' conceptions of harm caused by any means.

The WRVS was the natural organisation to provide a support to a broad range of victims – during the Second World War it acted as a local community welfare service to help people through crisis and support those in need. Following the war, it added other services such as meals on wheels, support for the elderly and canteens in hospitals. In 1947, it started work with offenders by supporting the families of women sent to Holloway; providing canteens and contact areas in courts, prisons and remand centres; and providing homes for boys released on licence (WRVS, 1970). In the late 1970s it began, particularly in Hampshire, to provide services (Crisis Support Schemes) to any victim who had suffered a major crisis. The WRVS saw this as a natural extension of its community service and as providing balance because it delivered services to the courts and supported offenders and therefore also wanted to help those who had suffered as a result of criminal activities. However, it recognised that the devastation of victimisation might also arise out of other situations and, to ensure a holistic community service, offered support to all victims, whatever the cause of their victimisation. By 1984 there were 48 crisis centres (Rock, 1990: 177). Victims were referred to WRVS by the police and other emergency services which trusted WRVS due to its earlier crisis work. Yet, the service did not continue to flourish. Had it succeeded, presumably we would have a broader concept of 'victim' today, including children in households which suffer crime (Morgan and Zedner, 1992) or where domestic violence occurs (Clarke and Wydall, 2010); the relatives of offenders (Howarth and Rock, 2000); those who suffer from accidents; and even broader definitions of victimisation (Hulsman, 1986; Elias, 1991, 1993, 1994; Hillyard et al., 2004; *Crime, Law and Social Change*, 2007; Wilkinson and Pickett, 2009).

The demise of WRVS's work in this area is an interesting case study, especially in the light of the fact that support for its work was strong amongst the statutory emergency agencies and courts. Furthermore, it pursued no political agenda; nor did it come into conflict with the government. However, when it came to dispensing funding to VSOs working with victims, WRVS lost out in favour of organisations with a more focused clientele (see below). Normally the trust of the police and courts would have secured WRVS government funding. However, other forces were at work. The state had already limited its relief to victims through the focused and narrow provision of compensation (Criminal Injuries Compensation Scheme (CICS), 1964), only available to 'innocent' victims of violent crime in limited situations and for limited amounts. To have funded WRVS would have been to recognise, and possibly even embrace, the state's responsibility for a very broad range of victims and potential to broaden the definition of victim further. The government's view was that it was more relevant to support only 'victims of crime', which was more pertinent to one of its 'core' businesses governing crime. The result was a refocusing of sympathy and resources towards those who suffered as a result of criminal activity.

WRVS's work with victims withered as a result of the government not funding its work alongside other factors. It is almost impossible to prove how the absence of funding affected the direction of an organisation and impacted on its decision making, yet (as will be seen later) state funding does have significant effects on VSOs. In this case, other factors also contributed to the demise of WRVS's work with victims including fewer volunteers being available as more women entered the workforce and younger women volunteering for other organisations, particularly feminist groups. Together these factors placed WRVS under stress and resulted in activities being pruned, leaving it to continue with a narrower, 'core' focus. Both its work in criminal justice and with victims stopped as a result but the organisation survived and has flourished, recently becoming the Royal Voluntary Service (RVS). With state funding of its victims work different decisions may have been taken but withdrawal from this area probably helped it survive as a VSO and protected its independence. At the same time, it also contributed to the narrowing definition of victims encompassing only those whose victimisation arose from criminal activities. Consequently, it had a marked and long-lasting impact on conceptions of 'victims' and probably helped shape the voluntary sector that now supports them.

Unintentional though willing fuel for law and order crusades

Traditionally the term 'victim' was as closely associated with general adversity or misfortune as it was with crime. Until recently all victims, whether of adversity or crime, were largely ignored, and sometimes even blamed for their situation. However, following the suffering both experienced and witnessed in the Second World War the state began to provide for victims of adversity. They chose to tackle the five 'giant evils of society': ignorance, want, disease, squalor and idleness (Beveridge, 1942; Williams and Williams, 1987). This provision did not extend to victims of crime to whom the state remained largely blind (Mawby and Gill, 1987: 38). The earliest modern voices for victims of crime arose in the 1950s, largely from individuals working to improve the penal system in order to benefit offenders. These included Margery Fry (1951, 1959), whose idea that the state should 'do justice to the offended' helped form one of the earliest provisions for victims, a state compensation scheme to support victims of violent crime (CICS). No other support was forthcoming but the unmet needs of crime victims were becoming visible because media stories about the state compensation scheme cases such as the 'Moors Murders' (1963–1965). This 'unmet need' was something VSOs were well placed to meet and it was the beginnings of the second strand of voluntary sector provision for victims, one which focused on victimisation due to criminal activity (Jones, 1966; Van Dijk, 1997). Here crime, not victimisation, was the unifying and defining feature of 'victimhood'. The National Association of Victim Support Services will be used as a case study to examine these developments. By prioritising victims of crime, particularly victims of 'traditional' or 'street' crimes, this VSO necessarily took a political position despite it being commonly viewed as non-political (Christie, 1986; Walklate, 2007).

The work of Victim Support Services has complex and convoluted roots and is shaped by both power relations and victim interests. In 1970 there were no VSOs working with and for victims of crime as a united group. In 1969 a small group of people from the National Association for the Care and Resettlement of Offenders (NACRO) in Bristol set up a victim–offender study group. Initially this was to help make NACRO's work with offenders more palatable to communities, hopefully, rendering penal reform and reintegration of offenders more acceptable. The study group brought together victims of crime, offenders, academics and NACRO workers to discuss crime and how to tackle its effects. The victim's voice was central to its mission. Two groups arose from this early meeting. One, the National Victims Association (NVA) (not connected to the modern organisation of that name) was rather short-lived. It was openly political (Rolph, 1973; Rock, 1990) and fought for the interests of victims both to promote reform and resettlement of offenders (believing that inattention to harm caused by crime bred contempt and anger) and to deliver justice by ensuring victims' needs were met. Its core 'work' was political and involved media campaigns drawing attention to the plight of victims with the aim of trying to alter public and political opinion (Golding and Elliott, 1979; Ericson et al., 1987). The NVA campaigning helped bring crime victims out of the shadows but failed to attract anything except small, localised funding. Large funding bodies and the government refused to be associated with an organisation which challenged the consensus and the statutory sector.

The second, and lasting, group to arise out of the early NACRO meetings was the Bristol Victims Support Scheme, which later became the National Victim Support Service, often referred to simply as Victim Support (VS). Importantly VS avoided anything likely to be perceived as ideological, political or campaigning. It quickly moved away from both its origins in the victim-offender study group and mutually supportive resolutions to offending for both victims and offenders. Instead, with NACRO's help and using ideas from the probation service, they put together a professional and practical support system for victims (Rock, 1990), eventually winning them steady government funding.

The emergence of VS saw a change in discourse: victimhood no longer applied universally to people who had suffered or been harmed; rather it was reframed in terms of victims of *crime*. Soon 'victimhood' became synonymous with 'victims of crime'; those who suffered from other problems were 'victims of something else'. However, over time the narrowing of eligibility for assistance went further in two particular respects. Firstly, VS focused their attention on conventional crimes (usually victims of 'traditional' or 'street' crimes) with direct, immediate and tangible victims, those which would elicit most sympathy or empathy. Victims of white collar, organised or state crime were not normally amongst its clientele. Secondly, VS helped to engender a narrow view of the groups of victims who were 'deserving' or 'ideal' as those who are both 'innocent' and 'worthy' (Christie, 1986; Walklate, 2007). These victims tend to be vulnerable and/or 'respectable' and do not contribute to their victimisation. Therefore they elicit and are 'worthy' of sympathy and are the most likely to be supported and to drive social change (Valier, 2004). This client group helped make VS attractive to the government, facilitating its continued funding and leading to a different route to success but arguably at the expense of some potential clients and perhaps also its independence.

VS eschewed strong political campaigning. It pushed gently for greater official provision for victims from a moderate political stance. VS provided information which enabled politicians to make informed policy decisions and helped persuade the state to improve provision for victims through arrangements such as the Victims' Charters and Codes of Practice (Home Office 1990, 1996, 2005; Ministry of Justice, 2013), which started in 1990, with the up-to-date version found in Code of Practice (2013), and a Victims' Champion (2009–10) later replaced by the Commissioner for Victims and Witnesses (2011 and then 2013 onwards). All this indicates that VS has been instrumental in ensuring that victims' interests are taken seriously by the government. However, from another perspective, its highlighting of victims' plight reinforced a vengeful and punitive criminal justice agenda and led to criticism that they were aligned with government penal policy. Mawby and Gill (1987: 228) suggested that many of its volunteers had a right-wing, law and order outlook which resulted in a desire to support victims but also to see offenders severely punished. This was in direct opposition to its founding principles where, with NACRO, VS had set out to highlight the plight of victims by facilitating a positive resolution to crime for victims, offenders and communities. VS appeared to show little independence in so far as it eschewed its original mission and appeared to change its approach in order to survive. Whether or not VS supported government policy, successive administrations have certainly used its information to promote harsh sentences and law and order agendas (MacCormick and Garland, 1998; Ashworth, 2000: 86).

A broad conceptualisation of victimisation as encompassing all human suffering was lost (Flynn, 1982). VS's work was thereafter focused on *innocent* victims of *crime*. The focus grew out of NACRO's concentration on offending and also chimed with the desire of governments, police and public to support victims of crime. The narrower focus and simplicity of the core business helped to motivate volunteers and staff. It also permitted the organisation to measure its 'success', carry favour with government and draw attention to the plight of victims in the fractured and complicated environment of late modernity and in a multifaceted criminal justice system ill-equipped to meet their needs. The focused message helped VS to place a spotlight on 'innocent' victims of crime and to support such victims by alleviating their plight and therefore preparing the way for their interests to be more carefully protected in the criminal justice system. It empowered VS to champion the needs both of victims of conventional crimes (those with direct and tangible victims) and of 'innocent', 'deserving' or 'ideal' victims and through these to draw attention to the complex, traumatic and often lasting effects of much victimisation. In turn, the focused approach and public and state support have enabled VS to flourish – a 'symbiotic' relationship. However, there have been negative consequences. Firstly, it has supported a skewed and focused concept of victimisation, one centred on victims of conventional, often 'street crimes' and particularly sympathetic to 'ideal' victims. Secondly, VS delivered victim-focused services but often with little regard for, and/or investigation into, what each victim's needs were (Shapland et al., 1985: 178). They focused on practical issues (physical, counselling and advocacy), on providing a professional and uniform service and professional assessment of need rather than asking, and listening to, victims. This muted the utility of its voice; they were 'insiders' but not true critical friends.

The future of VS is uncertain. Since October 2014 a large proportion of state funding for victims' services has been channelled through the Police and Crime Commissioners (PCCs), to ensure a local focus on the commissioning. In October 2014 seven PCCs took over responsibility for referral and support of victims, the others following in 2015. At least one PCC has chosen not to commission VS, using the police instead. Whether more PCCs follow suit remains to be seen. VS's heavy reliance on government funding is now challenging its dominance in the provision of victims' services. Although unconnected, the changing funding landscape arose just as VS started to find a more challenging 'voice' and to broaden the concept of 'victim' (Victim Support, 2002, 2010, 2011a, 2011b). The situation in which VS finds itself illustrates the dangers of over-reliance on one funding source, something which some commentators suggest challenges independence (Knight, 1993; Deakin and Kershaw, 1996; Smerdon, 2007, 2009; Teasdale et al., 2012; Baring Foundation, 2013). At the time of writing, it is unclear how VS will respond and whether it will survive if it loses its government funding.

Victims: political pawns in a fractured terrain

At the same time as the voices of all victims of crime began to emerge, there was a growing awareness of both the existence and needs of groups who were particularly vulnerable. This had its roots in the feminist movement, which began with feminist political activists and later feminist criminologists (Rock, 2002: 3). It was centred on women and children who were victimised by men and offered another conception of 'victims', one which focused on particular types of victims rather than crime generally. By considering those victimised in the private sphere by perpetrators who were relatives or acquaintances and not strangers it questioned the emphasis on both conventional crimes and on 'ideal' victims. Whilst feminist groups were the first organisations to draw attention to the criminal victimisation of particular groups and to question the victim discourse, many VSOs have since been created which offer support to particular types of victims, or to victims of particular types of crime or other behaviour, such as racism, sexism, age, mental capacity and immigration.

These groups and their work are often inextricably linked to an open political questioning of the abuse of power which accompanies criminal violence and control (Guillaumin, 1978; Hanmer, 1978, 1990; Smart and Smart, 1978; Stanko, 1985; Pain, 1991; Tombs and Whyte, 2003; Green and Ward, 2004; Bovenkerk and Levi, 2007). Victimisation in this context is often articulated through a radical discourse (Smart and Smart, 1978; Stanko, 1985; Tombs and Whyte, 2003) and VSOs who plead the special interests of particular victim groups (women, children, the elderly, racial minority and workers) have been accused of 'hijacking the victim debate' by being both overly 'political' and driven by a specific 'agenda', thus undermining approaches based on the interests of *all* victims (Cressey, 1988; Fattah, 1992; Harding, 1994). This criticism is misplaced and assumes that providing services which support the status quo is both positive and apolitical. It also misses the point; support for particular groups has tended to grow out of a broad, politicised, desire to protect the whole group who were seen as oppressed (Stanko, 1985: 16). One example is the support provided to women who experience negative effects of male power and oppression. During the rise of the feminist movement in the 1960s, academic, political and practical sisterhood highlighted male power and control of every female (Stanko, 1985), claiming that male power and violence pervaded women's lives and represented a common threat. The Women's Movement began to provide practical support for women and to give voice to their plight. There were at least two strands: one which focused on male violence, particularly domestic violence, whilst the other focused on male sexual violence, particularly rape.

In the United Kingdom support for those suffering domestic violence started when the first refuge for battered women, Chiswick Family Rescue, opened in 1972. By 1975 the number of refugees had mushroomed. Most refuges were run under the umbrella of National Women's Aid Federation or Women's Aid (WA), a feminist organisation, whose refuges (until 2006) excluded men over 16 (following the Equality Act 2006 many local WA groups now offer services to men). The central WA body supported radical political and academic ideals intended to counteract patriarchal oppression, thus adding an expressive (political) agenda to the practical support. Over time the political zeal mellowed and now, rather than being an organisation countering patriarchal power, it has become one defined by its work in domestic violence and abuse. Compromise was necessary, firstly, to permit local WA service providers to access government funding to continue providing practical support for women (and now men) who have suffered from domestic violence and abuse; secondly, to counter the growing amount of central and local government money which had been ploughed into alternative refuges and gain some funding for local WA refuges and groups; and finally, to give WA a voice, to gain access to decision-making and power and to shape local and government policy and legislation relating to domestic violence and abuse.

Compromise went further than the political message. To begin with, WA operated on a largely cooperative basis as a shared sisterhood (Stanko, 1985; Dobash and Dobash, 1992). Over time this has changed to more managerial and hierarchical structures, partly as a result of receiving government funding. In some WA groups this change was extremely acrimonious because it dismantled the initial cooperative, feminist, way of working and replaced it with a managerial and business model with clear command structures and lines of reporting. The eschewing power structure was less feminist and egalitarian and more clearly focused on issues which resonated with both the government and the public. Some local groups have still refused to change and in others many of the volunteers and workers were left behind. For them it felt like a betrayal, especially in the light of the reasons that many started to work for such organisations (Gladstone, 2013). WA has survived by narrowing its mission and more clearly aligning with issues important to the criminal justice system. However, importantly, whilst its political zeal has been dampened, it is not dead. WA uses the trust the government places in it to shape policy to better reflect the 'true' issues many women feel are important. For example, WA was instrumental in the extension of official understandings of domestic violence to include abuse, broadening standards of protection and ensuring that the concept better reflected the experiences of oppressed women. In this way it acted as the 'outsider within' (Collins, 1986; Harding, 2004; Bowell, 2014).

WA's capacity to metamorphose in order to achieve core goals is an example of one of the key strengths of VSOs – adaptability (Campbell et al., 1998; Salaman, 2013). However, the change is not always positive or healthy (Foley, 1996; Hague and Malos, 1998; Welsh, 2008). For example, Welsh (2008: 242) suggests that embracing domestic violence and abuse as just another crime detracts from the wider problem of male control and fails to reduce the victimisation of women by men with whom they are intimate. She goes on to suggest that in doing so WA has gone too far, and altered too much.

The feminist movement gave rise to many other organisations, some, such as Women Against Rape and Women Against Violence Against Women, were short-lived (Rock, 1990: 178). The mid-1970s saw rape crisis centres emerge and by 1982 many were grouped together under the Rape Crisis Centre (RC) banner. Each RC centre seeks to empower women and support them, whatever choices they make about whether to report offences to the police. At the outset RC work was not about women as victims; rather it was focused on challenging male domination and patriarchy and supporting women who had been subjected to male domination and sexual violence. RC redefined clients as 'survivors', not 'victims'. RC worked to prevent female objectification, especially through or for sex. As with WA, over the years the political zeal has softened. Now, rather than being an organisation countering patriarchal power, it has become one defined by their work in sexual violence with a focus on the victimisation of those who suffer sexual violence. In turn, this has allowed RC more of a voice in policy making.

Its path to change was more painful and less complete than that of WA. It did not organise itself into a firm federation until 1996 when it first obtained a large charitable grant allowing it to train staff, support local centres and respond to government consultations. In 2001 it attracted government funding only to have it withdrawn two years later, causing the umbrella organisation to contract almost to a point of closure (Jones and Westmarland, 2004). By 2008, RC had lost 30 refuges (about half) and 60 per cent of the remainder were in financial difficulties. Its ability to continue operating is testimony to its dedication and staying power (Jones and Westmarland, 2004). Large-scale funding is again available (Rape Crisis, 2011a, 2011b, 2014) and is being used to build more refuges. Many local RC groups are financially strong, but the umbrella organisation is still struggling. Throughout all of this RC's advocacy has retained a questioning feminist ideology and takes the perspective of both female survivors (how they understand and view the system and their needs) and the system (interpreting the needs of victims and communities). RC groups have the privileged position of being 'outsiders within' (Collins, 1986; Harding, 2004; Bowell, 2014).

Both WA and RC have moved away from their radical feminist roots and become partially 'institutionalised'. Both started as movements bent on social change, to free women from male domination. Whilst still having a strong underlying philosophy, each now focuses on policy in its area of work, either sexual or domestic violence and abuse. Both also started as cooperative ventures where each voice was equal and each has now moved to a more hierarchical, business-type structure. This arose because state funding requires record keeping in line with organisational, managerial and business processes which have now become part of their structure (Freeman, 1995; Strobel, 1995; Welsh, 2008). By complying they survived, showing a capacity to adapt to new demands in order to ensure their continued existence but arguably at a high cost, particularly to their founding feminist ideals (Welsh, 2008). Funding has permitted each organisation to continue to provide comprehensive services for its respective 'victim' group. It has also permitted them to gain leverage with politicians, be included in policy discussions and to be listened to, hence allowing them to influence law-making and criminal justice practices. In this way, they contribute to a wider agenda of protection against sexual and/or domestic harm and control, bringing these issues into the public arena and seeking a supportive hearing from both the press and the public. For example, the impact of RC and other, largely feminist, groups led to the laws to protect against sexual violence remaining largely gendered (Jones, 2004: 62) and, partly due to WA, the legal definition of domestic violence has been broadened to encompass domestic abuse. Furthermore, the police often work with rape support centres in Sexual Assault Referral Centres (SARCS) designed to elicit evidence as respectfully as possible and support women (and others) who are sexually assaulted through both the criminal justice process and their victimisation (Kelly et al., 2005). These examples illustrate the importance of being heard by the government. So, whilst contemporary feminist groups continue to call the state to account and there are continued disagreements and problems in their relationship with official agencies and the state (Jones, 2004), their moderation has won them a chance to bring about real change (Collins, 1986; Harding, 2004; Bowell, 2014).

The continued existence of the groups, however, increasingly depends on their accepting Home Office or Ministry of Justice approaches to their area of work. For example, from the end of the 1980s the Home Office has taken increasing interest in, and control over, the strategy for preventing and dealing with domestic violence (Hanmer and Griffiths, 1998, 2000; Kelly, 1999). Following the Crime and Disorder Act 1998 the Home Office clearly set out their understanding of domestic violence and strongly (Phillips, 2002) and successfully (Taylor-Browne, 2001) urged local crime and disorder partnerships to include domestic violence in their crime reduction strategies and programmes. This led to a centralised conception of this type of offence and how it ought to be responded to. Furthermore, much government financial support for initiatives to tackle domestic violence was administered under this apparently localised but effectively highly centralised criminal justice system. As the government increasingly promoted its support in this area alternative funding became increasingly scarce and difficult to access. Therefore feminist groups were progressively forced either to lose funding or to embrace (and hope to alter from within) the criminal justice approach to domestic violence, gender relations and gender and crime, crime control and disorder in order to access the funding necessary for their continued existence (Welsh, 2008). In short, they muted their critique of unequal power balance in intimate relationships. However, importantly, they continue to act as the outsiders within, working to get victims' 'truths' recognised and acted on within the criminal justice system. Interestingly, in some areas, community safety partnerships have, often after listening to WA, created new approaches to dealing with domestic abuse and violence, which chime with WA's analysis of the causes of male violence (Clarke and Wydall, 2013). This suggests that a quiet defiance continues to permeate under the surface, retaining a feminist ideology which searches for a local and less confrontational outlet which is less directly 'political'. Arguably this reflects a real independence and dedication to ideals and purpose in the face of opposition as well as a strong desire to ensure that the 'truths' from their clients are taken into account in policy and practice arenas.

The championing of special-interest victim groups originated in feminist projects but has spread to many different types of organisations. A plethora of VSOs now provide various forms of assistance and support for different groups of victims, with a growing number competing to support victims of sexual and domestic violence and abuse. The support for victims has consequently fractured as VSOs compete for limited funds, finite sympathy and normative media coverage to support their work. This means, as in the past, that the government can use its financial power to encourage or suppress VSOs. For example, in 2011 a small victims' charity called the Eaves Poppy Project (set up in 2003) which pioneered specialist service for victims of sex trafficking (and labour trafficking of women) was almost destroyed when government funding was withdrawn after the charity successfully appealed 17 UK Border Agency decisions and forced others to be reassessed. The money previously provided to the Eaves Poppy Project went instead to an organisation with less experience of such cases but one less likely to challenge decisions, the Salvation Army. The Salvation Army also provided less. They offered to support victims over a period of 45 days whereas the Poppy project recognised the deep needs of these victims and spent much longer with them, a minimum of 90 days but more normally 3–8 months (Butler and Travis, 2011; Townsend, 2011). The Salvation Army was also less likely to challenge government decisions. This case illustrates the desire of the government to be seen to support victims, but at the lowest possible cost, on its own terms and with little, if any, questioning of the state agenda. Finally, and importantly both for the sector and for victims, the Poppy project continues to support some victims in ways most relevant to those victims by empowering them. How, why and at what expense they have survived, however, is difficult to discover.

Many organisations, if they survive for more than a couple of years, manage to respond to the changing financial and political circumstances and to continue, often in altered forms. These VSOs (many are small but include the larger feminist groups) have had a lasting and profound impact on official and popular conceptions of the 'victim' by highlighting previously 'invisible' social problems and eliciting compassion and empathy for a number of formerly disregarded groups (Fattah, 1994). They have drawn attention to problems and altered social attitudes, thus facilitating changes in social policy and legislation as well as delivering new solutions or support for newly recognised groups. They have contributed to legal, policy and practical changes such as rape suites and Sexual Assault Referral Centres (SARCs), permitting vulnerable witnesses to be screened or give evidence via video links (first introduced in the

Youth Justice and Criminal Evidence Act 1999 Part II and since extended
in various Acts) and have advocated and promoted a re-conceptuali-
sation of domestic violence to include domestic abuse. However, this
influence is not uniform or predictable. Some continue to claim that
government (central and local) 'bias' distorts the criminal justice system
by prioritising some victim groups over others and that this shapes the
sector (Welsh, 2008).

The lost victims

Support for victims in England and Wales has never been recognised
as a core responsibility of the state. The state makes provision for some
victim services, especially compensation for some victims and keeping
all victims informed; yet even at this level some victims fall through the
cracks and remain hidden. For example, offenders suffer greater victimisation than almost any other group and yet they are rarely recognised
(Victim Support, 2007). Others are almost invisible (for example the
homeless) or are on the margins of society (drug users or those with substance misuse problems) and find it more difficult to have any victimisation recognised, therefore missing out on support and justice (their
offenders are rarely convicted; Carrabine et al., 2004). Victims who
have convictions are less likely to be treated as true, 'ideal or 'deserving'
(Christie, 1986; Walklate, 2006, 2007). Offender-'victims' are unlikely to
be able to claim criminal injuries compensation because they are viewed
as 'contributing' to their own injuries. Incarcerated offenders often fail
to have their victimisation recognised and are not supported to cope
with the trauma of either criminal victimisation or the feeling of injustice they may experience from the criminal justice system itself (Farrell
and Townsley, 2007). When sex workers are attacked they are unlikely
to receive support or be taken seriously except by small, geographically
confined and specialised VSOs. Many VSOs are only truly motivated
when working with victims seen as 'deserving'. Even VS, which claims
to represent all victims of crime, tends to focus on 'deserving' victims.
Whilst there are some small dedicated and geographically limited VSOs
particularly focused on some of these groups, such as the award-winning
One25 in Bristol which supports sex workers to build a different life
(Cook, 2014), these remain in the minority.

As well as the victims who do not fit the popular conception of
victimhood there are certain groups whose victimisation would fall
within that mould which is also almost wholly neglected. These often
include the most vulnerable groups such as children (Women's Aid, 2004;

Boswell, 2005; Clarke and Wydall, 2010; Radford et al., 2011), the elderly (Pritchard, 2001; Clarke et al., 2013), minorities ethnic groups, particularly new immigrants (Knight and Chouhan, 2002; Amnesty International and Southall Black Sisters, 2008), those with mental health problems (Perry, 2004; Tarrant, 2004; Pettitt et al., 2013) and those with other disabilities. In many instances in all these groups their victimisation is downgraded to 'lesser' categories such as 'bullying' and is then not taken seriously (Williams, 1999). Taking children as an example, the United Kingdom ranked 21st out of 25 European member states in child well-being (Bradshaw et al., 2007). Whilst one might question the methodology and therefore the strength of these findings, they suggest that the suffering of children and young people needs to be taken more seriously. Although over the past 40 years there have been many agencies working to support women who suffer domestic violence few have been similarly focused on children and young people. VS cannot support children under 13 without parental consent and over that age will assess the young person's ability to consent (https://www.victim-support.org.uk). Yet, many young people suffer directly from domestic abuse and violence and others witness such violence or suffer indirectly (Wolak and Finkelhor, 1998). In all such cases, the child or young person can become severely scarred, mentally and/or physically (Wolfe et al., 2003; Buckley et al., 2007; Holt et al., 2008), but parents may either not recognise this or refuse to allow their children to be helped (possibly to protect themselves). Without support these children are also more likely to be violently abused later (Osofsky, 2003). Abused parents are in no position to fully support their children, yet many young people do not receive adequate support from elsewhere.

Children also suffer either directly or indirectly from other crimes and again little support is likely to reach them. The extent of the plight of victimised children was addressed in detail by Morgan and Zedner (1992) and yet more than 20 years later little has been done to address it. The extent of the problem is largely unknown. US research shows that children and young people are one of the most victimised groups being two or three times more likely than adults to suffer a conventional rape, robbery or aggravated assault (Finkelhor, 2008: 6; see also Snyder and Sickmund, 2006). Children suffer from all types of crime including assault by family members, rape, child abuse, child sexual abuse, sex offences generally both physical and virtual, bullying (on- and off-line) and property crimes. They also suffer secondary victimisation when members of their families are victimised, which can be traumatic (Morgan and Zedner, 1992). To the young person even seemingly 'trivial' offences may have devastating effects (Finkelhor and Dzuiba-Leatherman, 1994), under-mining confidence and limiting feelings of well-being and freedom, hence impacting negatively on life chances.

In the United Kingdom estimates of child victimisation are newly emerging. Children from 10 to 15 years were only included in the British Crime Survey from 2010–11. It is clear that children and young people in England and Wales suffer high levels of victimisation (Millard and Flatley, 2010; Chaplin et al., 2011; Smith et al., 2012). The 1992 British Crime Survey concluded that 12–15-year-olds suffered substantially higher victimisation than adults (Aye Maung, 1995). The Offending Crime and Justice Survey (2006) found higher rates of victimisation from personal theft and assault in the 10–15 age group than in the 16–25 age group (which is higher than for adults over 25) although some of the incidents reported by the younger group were assessed as less serious (Roe and Ashe, 2008). The young participants remembered the less serious offences from the previous year, suggesting they were as traumatic (for the child) as those which the researchers classed as 'more serious'. These findings make it clear that when providing support to young people, taking account of their subjective experience is vital to avoid trauma. It is surprising that more VSOs have not fully engaged with this group, by working with children and families to better understand their vulnerability and to address the traumatic effects of their victimisation. Even in 'obvious' crimes where children are affected, statutory agencies such as social services have only recently been taking victimisation into account in child protection work (McGee and Westcott, 1996). Furthermore, Youth Offending Services, who work with young offenders and those at risk of offending, do not systematically work with young victims. Instead, they only work with the victims of the crimes their cohort of young offenders have committed (adult and youth victims).

Comprehensive services for child victims do not exist, yet some organisations support this group. Some local Women's Aid groups work with young people who suffer either directly or indirectly from domestic violence and abuse. Childline provides a national service for all young people who ring for support and are sometimes able to refer children on to other agencies but otherwise can only provide support over the telephone. The Standing Committee for Youth Justice, the umbrella organisation which supports and coordinates VSOs working for young offenders, does not have members who specifically focus on child victims. Barnardo's has most coverage in working with young victims, with 23 specialised services dealing with child victims. However, even services provided by this large national children's charity are geographically limited. For example, the Barnardo's Against Sexual Exploitation project in Bristol provides long-term, individualised, support for young people but their coverage is local. Whilst Barnardo's provides an important, essential voice for young victims in the areas in which they work, there is no overarching 'outsider on the inside' to bring the experiences of children and young people to the attention of policy makers and practitioners. Other small, dedicated and usually geographically limited (local) VSOs also provide support. However, many children never find these groups and therefore never access support and their victimisation may permanently blight their life chances. The absence of VSOs for children is explicable because VSOs tend to rely on self-referral and, for those lacking full capacity (children, the elderly and those suffering from mental health issues) this is difficult. Furthermore, working with these groups is particularly challenging and may put the organisation into conflict with the parents or primary carers. The lack of services is also surprising because these vulnerable groups are often the 'ideal', 'perfect' and 'deserving' victims and although their other needs may be provided for through national VSOs such as the NSPCC and Barnardo's, their needs as victims are rarely met.

As recent high-profile cases involving serial child sexual exploitation make clear, the state (through the police, welfare, child protection agencies and education) has, in the past, failed to protect or support child victims. In cases such as these, the police and other responsible authorities have blamed young victims (Jay Report, 2014) and have even accused children of prostitution. Until recently, key agencies had evidently failed to assess the needs of children in households where domestic violence has occurred (Stanley and Humphreys, 2006). Many have been failed by social care, education and children's services as well as by the criminal justice system. The story is similar for other vulnerable groups (Clarke et al., 2013, the elderly; Pettitt et al., 2013, those with mental health problems). It seems that where capacity (legal, social or intellectual) is lacking or reduced, so is provision for victims. They are failed by the state and VSOs alike.

VSOs have done most for victim groups such as children, the elderly and those with impaired social, legal or mental capacity. Clearly, a lot more is necessary which would require dedicated, well-trained and well-financed groups, probably VSOs. However, before services are introduced it is necessary to understand how best to provide for each of the many victim groups who are presently hidden or forgotten by our system. If funding was made available, VSOs would be likely to be able to fill this gap.

Conclusion

Services for victims are splintered as their needs are increasingly responded to by many, very different, VSOs. However, it is a system which serves the state well – many 'deserving' victims are supported without the state taking responsibility for the plight of victims in general. The state provides funding but, on its own terms, chooses which VSOs to support and, by extension, which victims are the most 'deserving'. The state provides funding (without any obligation to continue to do so) but ensures that VSOs who are most politically challenging fail to access funding. To access state funding and remain viable, VSOs are often required to cease (or not start) to challenge government policy and decision-making. Some comply and this may be seen as evidence of their ability to adapt and survive; others refuse and still survive, choosing ideological independence by sticking to their original mission rather than pursuing growth or possibly even survival (at least survival in providing for victims). A third group take a middle ground, choosing to adjust sufficiently to win funding but retaining the essence of their ideology, again showing an independence and confidence in their purpose. Finally, some VSOs may comply to such an extent that they lose their independence, something essential to a VSO (Smerdon, 2007, 2009; Baring Foundation, 2013), and others, who initially strike a balance may in time become too dependent on government funding and therefore vulnerable to mission drift and losing their independence (Smerdon, 2007, 2009; Baring Foundation, 2013).

The voluntary sector has supported many victims of crime and has been instrumental in ensuring that the state takes victims' plight seriously and provides basic services. However, this is not without problems. One needs to consider whether the agenda that VSOs pursue is what victims want for themselves or what governments and VSOs think they 'deserve' or should want. Some VSOs have been ideologically and in practice aligned to the criminal justice system, allowing their information and research to be co-opted by the state to support their law and order campaigns (some see VS in this light MacCormick and Garland, 1998; Ashworth, 2000: 86). These VSOs often also deliver uniform, professional, programmes for victims which do not always suit all clients/victims. This has been mutually beneficial to these VSOs and the criminal justice system. Many victims benefit from this uniform or normative conception of what they want/need. Other victims may be less positively served. In all cases, the danger is that VSOs fail to research the experiences of their victims and discover the many 'truths' found in their client group. Their true voices are submerged beneath preferred official discourse – whether articulated by the state or VSOs and which may be experienced as another victimisation (Goodrum, 2007). This undermines the individuation of a victim's experience and commodifies victimhood in order to push certain agendas or certain victims – 'victims of political expediency' (Elias, 1983: 120; Mawby and Gill, 1987). In so doing, victims are constructed to serve the interests of power, hide inconvenient aspects of reality and then persuaded to act in ways which bolster that 'truth' (Hulsman, 1986; Kukla, 2000: 2–4). VSOs that resist this political and practical expediency are often determined (possibly driven) to challenge the status quo and allow their clients' voices to be heard. However, if the drive is too strong it may override the client's voice. The ideal is to represent not commodify victims' 'truths' (Harding, 2004).

If VSOs are overcontrolled by the state and/or state agencies, working too closely with government-set agendas, they abandon the victims they seek to protect. However, if VSOs ignore these pressures they may not survive. VSOs must mould to the expectations of the criminal justice system to the extent necessary to be embraced by it, allowing them to work within that system. However, they also need to retain independence and their core aims (the VSOs essence) in order to maintain a non-controlling, enabling working relationship with their clients so as to empower them and act as their advocates in ways meaningful to those individuals. Maintaining both these perceptions of reality and 'truth' allows them to become the 'outsiders within', able to look both from the outside in and the inside out (Collins, 1986; Harding, 2004; Bowell, 2014). It enables them to become advocates for the truths lived by their clients and to work within the system, to draw down finance and effect real change (Collins, 1986; Harding, 2004; Bowell, 2014). Achieving this requires retention of, and dedication to, the core aims and principles of the VSO and an understanding of which aspects are essential to its independence. VSOs that manage to both survive and retain their independence and true advocacy achieve change for their victim group which is 'real' and 'meaningful' to that group.

References

Amnesty International and Southall Black Sisters (2008) *'No Recourse' No Safety: The Government's Failure to Protect Women from Violence*. London: Amnesty International and Southall Black Sisters.

Ashworth, A. (2000) Victims' Rights, Defendants' Rights and Criminal Procedure. In: Crawford, A. and Goodey, J. (eds.) *Integrating a Victim Perspective Within Criminal Justice*. Aldershot: Ashgate: 185–206.

Aye Maung, N. (1995) *Young People, Victimisation and the Police: British Crime Survey Findings on Experiences and Attitudes of 12 to 15 Year Olds.* Home Office Research Study No. 140. London: Home Office.

Baring Foundation (2013) *Independence Under Threat: The Voluntary Sector in 2013*, Second Report from the Panel on the Independence of the Voluntary Sector. London: The Baring Foundation. http://www.baringfoundation.org.uk/IndependenceUnderThreat.pdf [accessed 16/10/14].

Beveridge, W. (1942) *Report on Social Insurance and Allied Services.* London: HMSO.

Boswell, G. (2005) Child Victims, *British Journal of Community Justice*, 3 (2): 9–23.

Bovenkerk, F. and Levi, M. (2007) *The Organized Crime Community: Essays in Honour of Alan Block.* New York: Springer.

Bowell, T. (2014) Feminist Standpoint Theory, *Internet Encyclopedia of Philosophy.* http://www.iep.utm.edu/fem-stan/ [accessed 22/09/14].

Bradshaw, J., Hoelscher, P. and Richardson, D. (2007) An Index of Child Well-being in the European Union, *Social Indicators Research*, 80 (1): 133–177.

Buckley, H., Holt, S. and Whelan, S. (2007) Listen to me! Children's Experiences of Domestic Violence, *Child Abuse Review*, 16: 296–310.

Butler, P. and Travis, A. (2011) Sex Trafficking Charity Loses out to Salvation Army Over £6m Contract, *The Guardian*, 11 April 2011. http://www.theguardian.com/society/2011/apr/11/eaves-housing-trafficking-salvation-army [accessed 15/04/11].

Cabinet Office (2012) *Open Public Services.* London: HM Government. https://www.gov.uk/government/organisations/open-public-services

Campbell, R., Baker, C. K. and Mazurek, T. (1998) Remaining Radical? Organizational Predictors of Rape Crisis Centres' Social Change Initiatives, *American Journal of Community Psychology*, 26 (3): 457–483.

Carrabine, E., Iganski, P., Lee, M., Plummer, K. and South, N. (2004) *Criminology: A Sociological Introduction.* London: Routledge.

Carter, P. (2003) *Managing Offenders, Reducing Crime: A New Approach.* London: Home Office.

Chaplin, R., Flatley, J. and Smith, K. (eds) (2011) *Crime in England and Wales 2010/11*, Home Office Statistical Bulletin 10/11. London: Home Office. https://www.gov.uk/government/uploads/system/uploads/attachment_data/file/116417/hosb1011.pdf

Christie, N. (1986) *Victims, Victimisation and Victimology.* New York: McGraw-Hill.

Clarke, A. and Wydall, S. (2010) *An Evaluation of Multi-agency Working with Children and Young People Who are Experiencing the Effects of Domestic Abuse in the Communities First Area of Penparcau and Aberystwyth West.* Research and Information Unit, Social Justice and Regeneration Department. Cardiff: Welsh Assembly Government. http://wales.gov.uk/statistics-and-research/evaluation-multi-agency-working-children-young-people-experiencing-effects-domestic-abuse/?lang=en [accessed 15/04/11].

Clarke, A. and Wydall, S. (2013) "Making Safe": A Co-ordinated Community Response to Empowering Victims and Tackling Perpetrators of Domestic Violence, *Social Policy and Society*, 12 (3): 393–406.

Clarke, A., Williams, J., Wydall, S. and Boaler, R. (2013) *An Evaluation of the 'Access to Justice' Pilot Project*, Welsh Government Social Research. Cardiff: Welsh Government. http://wales.gov.uk/docs/caecd/research/121220accesstojusticeen.pdf [accessed 20/08/14].

Ministry of Justice (2013) *Code of Practice for Victims of Crime*. London: The Stationary Office. https://www.cps.gov.uk/publications/docs/victims_code_2013.pdf

Collins, P. H. (1986) Learning from the Outsider Within: The Sociological Significance of Black Feminist Thought, *Social Problems*, 33 (6): 14–32.

Cook, I. R. (2014) Making Links Between Sex Work, Gender and Victimisation: The Politics and Pedagogies of John Schools, *Gender, Place and Culture A Journal of Feminist Geography*. http://www.tandfonline.com/doi/full/10.1080/09663 69X.2014.917277#.VA6WiTN0zcs

Corcoran, M. S. (2011) Dilemmas of Institutionalisation of the Penal Voluntary Sector in England and Wales, *Critical Social Policy*, 31 (1): 30–52.

Council of Europe (1983) *European Convention on the Compensation of Victims of Violent Crime*, European Treaties Series No. 116.

Council of Europe (1985) *The Position of the Victim in the Framework of Criminal Law and Procedure*. Committee of Ministers Recommendation No. R(85) 11.

Council of Europe (1987) *Assistance to Victims and the Prevention of Victimisation*. Committee of Ministers Recommendation No. R(87) 21.

Crawford, A. (2008) Refiguring the Community and Professional in Policing and Criminal Justice: Some Questions of Legitimacy. In: Shapland, J. (ed.) *Justice, Community and Civil Society: A Contested Terrain*. Cullompton: Willan: 125–156.

Cressey, D. R. (1988) Research Implications of Conflicting Conceptions of Victimology. In: Separovic, Z. P. (ed.) *Victimology: International Action and Study of Victims*. Zargreb: University of Zargreb: 43–54. Reprinted in 1992 in Fattah, E. A. (ed.) *Towards a Critical Victimology*. London: Macmillan: 57–73; Friedrichs, D. O. and Schwartz, M. (eds) *Crime, Law and Social Change*, (2007) 48 (1–2). Special issue: Social Harm and a Twenty-First Century Criminology.

Deakin, N. and Kershaw, J. (1996) *Meeting the Challenge of Change: Voluntary Action into the 21st Century: The Report of the Commission on the Future of the Voluntary Sector*. London: National Council for Voluntary Action.

Dobash, R. E. and Dobash, R. (1992) *Women, Violence and Social Change*. London: Routledge.

Elias, R. (1983) *Victims of the System – Crime Victims and Compensation in American Politics and Criminal Justice*. New Brunswick, NJ: Transaction Books.

Elias, R. (1991) Crime Control as Human Rights Enforcement. In: Pepinsky, H. and Quinney, R. (eds.) *Criminology as Peacemaking*. Bloomington, IN: Indiana University Press: 251–262.

Elias, R. (1993) *Victims Still*. Newbury Park, CA: Sage Publications.

Elias, R. (1994) Paradigms and Paradoxes of Victims. In: Sumner, C., Israel, M., O'Connell, M. and Sarre, R. (eds.) *International Victimology: Selected Papers from the 8th International Symposium*. Canberra: Australian Institute of Criminology, January 1996: 9–34.

Ericson, R., Baranek, P. and Chan, J. (1987) *Visualising Deviance: A Study of News Organisation*. Milton Keynes: Open University Press.

European Union (2012) *Establishing Minimum Standards on the Rights, Support and Protection of Victims of Crime* (Victims' Directive). Directive 2012/29/EU.

Farrell, G. and Townsley, M. (2007) Repeat Victimisation of Prison Inmates. In: Farrell, G., Bowers, K. J., Johnson, S. D. and Townsley, M. (eds.) *Imagination for Crime Prevention: Essays in Honour of Ken Pease*. New York: Criminal Justice Press: 265–277.

Fattah, E. A. (1992) The Need for a Critical Victimology. In: Fattah, E. A. (ed.) *Towards a Critical Victimology*. New York: Martin's Press: 14–23.

Fattah, E. A. (1994) Victimology: Some Problematic Concepts, Unjustified Criticism and Popular Misconceptions. In: Kirchoff, F., Kosovski, E. and Schneider, H. J. (eds.) *International Debates of Victimology*. München-Gladbach: WSV Publishing: 82–103.

Finkelhor, D. (2008) *Childhood Victimization: Violence, Crime, and Abuse in the Lives of Young*. Oxford: Oxford University Press.

Finkelhor, D. and Dzuiba-Leatherman, J. (1994) Victimization of Children. *American Psychologist*, 49 (3): 173–183.

Flynn, E. E. (1982) Theory Development in Victimology: An Assessment of Recent Progress and of Continuing Challenges. In: Schneider, H. J. (ed.) *The Victim in International Perspective*. Berlin: de Gruyter: 96–104.

Foley, M. (1996) Who is in Control? Changing Responses to Women in the Home. In: Hester, M., Kelly, L. and Radford, J. (eds.) *Women, Violence and Male Power*. Buckingham: Open University Press: 166–175.

Freeman, J. (1995) From Seed to Harvest: Transformations of Feminist Organizations and Scholarship. In: Ferree, M. M. and Martin, P. Y. (eds.) *Feminist Organizations: Harvest of the New Women's Movement*. Philadelphia: Temple University Press: 397–410.

Fry, M. (1951) *Arms of the Law*. London: Gollancz.

Fry, M. (1959) Justice for Victims, *Journal of Public Law*, 8: 191–194 (first printed in *The Observer* on 10 November 1957).

Gladstone, L. (2013) Learning from Rape Crisis Volunteers: Remembering the Past, Envisioning the Future. PhD Thesis, University of Toronto.

Golding, P. and Elliott, P. (1979) *Making the News*. London: Longman.

Goodrum, S. (2007) Victims' Rights, Victims' Expectations, and Law Enforcement Workers' Constraints in Cases of Murder, *Law and Social Inquiry*, 32 (3): 725–757.

Green, P. and Ward, T. (2004) *State Crime: Governments, Violence and Corruption*. London: Pluto Press.

Guillaumin, C. (1978) Pratique du pouvoir et idée de nature: le discours de la nature, *Questions féministes*, no. 3. Paris.

Hague, G. and Malos, E. (1998) *Domestic Violence: Action for Change*. Cheltenham: New Clarion Press.

Hanmer, J. (1978) Violence and the Social Control of Women. In: Littlejohn, G. and Yural-Davies, N. (eds.) *Power and the State*. London: Croom Helm: 217–238.

Hanmer, J. (1990) Men, Power and the Exploitation of Women, *Women's Studies International Forum*, 13 (5): 443–456.

Hanmer, J. and Griffiths, S. (1998) *Domestic Violence and Repeat Victimisation*. Police Research Group Briefing Note No. 01/98. London: Home Office.

Hanmer, J. and Griffiths, S. (2000) *Reducing Domestic Violence . . . What Works? Policing Domestic Violence*. Policing and Reducing Crime Briefing Note. London: Home Office.

Harding, R. (1994) Victimisation, Moral Panics, and the Distortion of Criminal Justice Policy, *Current Issues in Criminal Justice*, 6: 27–42.

Harding, S. (2004) *The Feminist Standpoint Theory Reader*. London: Routledge.

Hillyard, P., Pantazis, C., Tombs, S. and Gordon, D. (2004) *Beyond Criminology: Taking Harm Seriously*. London: Pluto Press.

Holt, S., Buckley, H. and Whelan, S. (2008) The Impact of Exposure to Domestic Violence on Children and Young People: A Review of the Literature, *Child Abuse and Neglect*, 32: 797–810.

Home Office (1990) *The Victims' Charter: Standards of Service for Victims of Crime*, London: Home Office.

Home Office (1996) *The Victims' Charter: A Statement of Service Standards for Victims of Crime*, London: Home Office.

Home Office (2005) *The Code of Practice for Victims of Crime*, London: Home Office.

Howarth, G. and Rock, P. (2000) Aftermath and the Construction of Victimisation: "The Other Victims of Crime", *Howard Journal of Criminal Justice*, 39 (1): 58.

Hulsman, L. (1986) Critical Criminology and the Concept of Crime, *Contemporary Crises*, 10: 63–80.

Jay Report (2014) *Independent Inquiry into Child Sexual Exploitation in Rotherham (1997–2013)*. http://www.rotherham.gov.uk/downloads/file/1407/independent_inquiry_cse_in_rotherham [accessed 03/03/15].

Jones, E. H. (1966) *Margery Fry: The Essential Amateur*. Oxford: Oxford University Press.

Jones, H. (2004) Opportunities and Obstacles: The Rape Crisis Federation in the UK, *The Journal of International Gender Studies*, 8: 55–71.

Jones, H. and Westmarland, N. (2004) *Remembering the Past but Looking to the Future Rape Crisis*. http://www.rapecrisis.org.uk/history.html (last accessed 2010, no longer accessible on the web).

Kelly, L. (1999) *Domestic Violence Matters: An Evaluation of a Development Project*. Home Office Research Study No. 188. London: The Stationery Office.

Kelly, L., Lovett, J. and Regan, L. (2005) *Gap or a Chasm?: Attrition in Reported Cases*. Home Office Research Study 293. London: Home Office.

Knight, B. (1993) *Voluntary Action*. Newcastle-upon Tyne: Centris.

Knight, C. and Chouhan, K. (2002) Supporting Victims of Racist Abuse and Violence. In: Williams, B. (ed.) *Reparation and Victim Focused Social Work*. Research Highlights 42. London Jessica Knightly Publishers: 105–129.

Kukla, A. (2000) *Social Constructivism and the Philosophy of Science*. London: Routledge.

MacCormick, N. and Garland, D. (1998) Sovereign States and Vengeful Victims: The Problem of the Right to Punish. In: Ashworth, A. and Wasik, M. (eds.) *The Fundamentals of Sentencing Theory*. Oxford: Oxford University Press: 11–30.

Mawby, R. I. and Gill, M. L. (1987) *Crime Victims: Needs, Services and the Voluntary Sector*. London: Tavistock.

McGee, C. and Westcott, H. L. (1996) System Abuse: Towards a Greater Understanding from the Perspectives of Children and Parents, *Child and Family Social Work*, 2 (1): 13–23.

Millard, B. and Flatley, J. (eds) (2010) *Experimental Statistics on Victimisation of Children Aged 10 to 15: Findings from the British Crime Survey for the Year Ending December 2009*. London: Home Office Statistical Bulletin 10/11. https://www.gov.uk/government/uploads/system/uploads/attachment_data/file/116413/hosb1110.pdf

Ministry of Justice (2011) *Competition Strategy for Offender Services*. London: HMGovernment.http://www.cjp.org.uk/publications/government/the-competition-strategy-for-offender-services-13-07-2011/

Morgan, J. and Zedner, L. (1992) *Child Victims: Crime, Impact and Criminal Justice.* Oxford: Clarendon Press.

NOMS (2012) *Commissioning Intentions.* London: NOMS. http://www.justice.gov. uk/about/noms/commissioning

Osofsky, J. D. (2003) Prevalence of Children's Exposure to Domestic Violence and Child Maltreatment: Implications for Prevention and Intervention, *Clinical Child and Family Psychology Review,* 6 (3): 33–49.

Pain, R. (1991) Space, Sexual Violence and Social Control: Integrating Geographical and Feminist Analyses of Women's Fear of Crime, *Progress in Human Geography,* 15 (4): 415–431.

Perry, J. (2004) Hate Crime against People with Learning Difficulties: The Role of the Crime and Disorder Act and No Secrets in Identification and Prevention, *Journal of Adult Protection,* 6 (1): 27–34.

Pettitt, B., Greenhead, S., Khalifeh, H., Drennan, V., Hart, T., Hogg, J., Borschmann, R., Mamo, E. and Moran, P. (2013) *At Risk, Yet Dismissed: The Criminal Victimisation of People with Mental Health Problems.* London: Victim Support. https://www.victimsupport.org.uk/sites/default/files/At%20risk%20full.pdf [accessed 03/03/15].

Phillips, C. (2002) From Voluntary to Statutory Status: Reflecting on the Experience of Three Partnerships Established under the Crime and Disorder Act 1998. In: Hughes, G., McLaughlin, E. and Muncie, J. (eds.) *Crime Prevention and Community Safety New Directions.* London: Sage: 163–181.

Pritchard, J. (2001) *Good Practice with Vulnerable Adults.* London: Jessica Kingsley Publishers.

Radford, L., Aitken, R., Miller, P., Ellis, J., Roberts, J. and Firkic, A. (2011) *Meeting the Needs of Children Living with Domestic Violence in London.* Refuge and NSPCC. London: Refuge. http://www.refuge.org.uk/files/onlineDVLondon1.pdf [accessed 22/09/15].

Rape Crisis (2011a) *Government Funding Announced.* Rape Crisis. http://www.rape-crisis.org.uk/news_show.php?id=51 [accessed 22/09/14].

Rape Crisis (2011b) *8th March Government Announces Funding for Four New Centres.* Rape Crisis. http://www.rapecrisis.org.uk/news_show.php?id=52 [accessed 22/09/14].

Rape Crisis (2014) *Ministry of Justice Funding for New Rape Crisis Centres.* Rape Crisis. www.rapecrisis.org.uk/news_show.php?id=85 [accessed 22/09/14].

Rock, P. (1990) *Helping Victims of Crime: The Home Office and the Rise of Victim Support in England and Wales.* Oxford: Clarendon Press.

Rock, P. (2002) On Becoming a Victim. In: Hoyle, C. and Young, R. (eds.) *New Visions of Crime Victims.* Oxford: Hart: 1–22.

Roe, S. and Ashe, J. (2008) *Young People and Crime: Findings for the 2006 Offending Crime and Justice Survey.* Home Office Statistical Bulletin 09/08. London: Home Office. http://dera.ioe.ac.uk/9140/1/hosb0908.pdf

Rolph, C. H. (1973) National Victims Association, *Police Review,* 13 April 1973.

Salaman, L. (2013) *The Resilient Sector: The State of Nonprofit America.* Washington, DC: The Brookings Institution.

Shapland, J., Willmore, J. and Duff, P. (1985) *Victims in the Criminal Justice System.* London: Gower.

Shekhar, B. and Williams, K. S. (2014) An Overview of Victim Interests in India and in England and Wales – A Reality or a Rhetoric. In: Kirchhoff, G. F. (ed.) *Establishing*

Victimology: Festschrift for Prof. Dr. Gerd Ferdinand Kirchhoff, 30th Anniversary of Dubrovnik Victimology Course. Vol. 59 of the Schriften des Fachbereiches Sozialwesen der Hochschule Niederrhein Series, Schafer, P. (series editor).

Smart, C. and Smart, B. (1978) *Women, Sexuality and Social Control.* London: Routledge & Kegan Paul.

Smerdon, M. (2007) *Sources of Strength: an Analysis of the STVS.* Speech at the launch of Sources of Strength. Independence Programme: The Baring Foundation. http://www.baringfoundation.org.uk/SOSspeechMS.pdf [accessed 10/10/14].

Smerdon, M. (2009) Introduction. In: Smerdon, M. (ed.) *The First Principle of Voluntary Action: Essays on the Independence of the Voluntary Sector in Canada, England, Germany, Northern Ireland, Scotland, United States of America and Wales.* London: The Baring Foundation. http://www.baringfoundation.org.uk/ FirstPrincipleofVA.pdf [accessed 15/10/14].

Smith, K., Osborne, S., Lau, I. and Britton, A. (2012) *Homicides, Firearm Offences and Intimate Violence 2010 to 2011: Supplementary Volume 2 to Crime in England and Wales 2010/11.* London: Home Office Statistical Bulletin 2011/12. https://www. gov.uk/government/uploads/system/uploads/attachment_data/file/116483/ hosb0212.pdf [accessed 22/09/14].

Snyder, H. and Sickmund, M. (2006) *Juvenile Offenders and Victims: 2006 National Report.* New York: Offices of Justice Programmes and of Juvenile Justice and Delinquency. http://files.eric.ed.gov/fulltext/ED495786.pdf [accessed 22/09/14].

Stanko, E. A. (1985) *Intimate Intrusions: Women's Experience of Male Violence.* London: Routledge & Kegan Paul.

Stanley, N. and Humphreys, C. (2006) Multi-agency and Multi-disciplinary Working. In: Humphreys, C. and Stanley, N. (eds.) *Domestic Violence and Child Protection: Directions for Good Practice.* London: Jessica Kingsley Publishers: 36–49.

Strobel, M. (1995) Organizational Learning in the Chicago Women's Liberation Union. In: Ferree, M. M. and Martin, P. Y. (eds.) *Feminist Organizations: Harvest of the New Women's Movement.* Philadelphia: Temple University Press: 145–164.

Tarrant, A. (2004) The Sexual Abuse of People with Learning Difficulties: The Problems and Possible Solutions, *Journal of Adult Protection*, 5 (3): 6–13.

Taylor-Browne, J. (2001) *What Works in Reducing Domestic Violence? A Comprehensive Guide for Practitioners.* London: Whiting & Birch.

Teasdale, S., Buckingham, H. and Rees, J. (2012) Is the Third Sector being Overwhelmed by the State and the Market? *Third Sectors Futures Dialogue: Big Picture 4.* Birmingham: Third Sector Research Centre.

Tombs, S. and Whyte, D. (2003) *Unmasking the Crimes of the Powerful: Scrutinizing States and Corporations.* New York: Peter Lang Publishing.

Townsend, M. (2011) Sex-Trafficked Women's Charity Poppy Project in Danger as Funding Withdrawn, *The Observer*, 17 April 2011. Available from: http://www. theguardian.com/society/2011/apr/17/prostitution-human-trafficking [accessed 03/03/15].

United Nations (1985) *Declaration on the Basic Principles of Justice for Victims of Crimes and Abuse of Power*, A/RES/40/34.

United Nations (1999) *Development and Implementation of Mediation and Restorative Justice Measures in Criminal Justice*, Resolution 1999/26.

United Nations (2000) *Basic Principles on the Use of Restorative Justice Programmes in Criminal Matters*, Resolution 2000/14.

United Nations (2002) *Basic Principles on the Use of Restorative Justice Programmes in Criminal Matters*, Resolution 2002/12.

Valier, C. (2004) *Crime and Punishment in Contemporary Culture*. London: Routledge.

van Dijk, J. J. M. (1997) *Introducing Victimology*, Presented to the Ninth International Symposium of the World Society of Victimology. Published in 1999. In: van Dijk, J. J. M., van Kaam, R. G. H. and Wemmers, J. (eds.) *Caring for Crime Victims: Selected Proceedings of the Ninth International Symposium on Victimology, Amsterdam, August 25–29, 1997:* 1–12. Monsey, NY: Criminal Justice Press. https://pure.uvt.nl/portal/files/1411974/INTRODUC.PDF

Victim Support (2002) *Criminal Neglect*. London: Victim Support.

Victim Support (2007) *Hoodie or Goodie? The Link Between Violent Victimisation and Offending in Young People*. London: Victim Support. https://www.victimsupport.org.uk/sites/default/files/Hoodie%20or%20goodie%20report.pdf [accessed 20/10/14].

Victim Support (2010) *Victims Justice? What Victims and Witnesses Really Want from Sentencing*. London: Victim Support. https://www.victimsupport.org.uk/sites/default/files/Victim%20Support%20sentencing%20report%20Dec-2010.pdf [accessed 20/10/14].

Victim Support (2011a) *Bout in the Open: What Victims Really think about Community Sentencing*. London: Victim Support. https://www.victimsupport.org.uk/sites/default/files/Out%20in%20the%20open.pdf [accessed 20/10/14].

Victim Support (2011b) *Breaking the Cycle: Effective Punishment, Rehabilitation and Sentencing of Offenders: A Response by Victim Support*. London: Victim Support. Published on the Breaking the Cycle. Available from: http://www.victimsupport.org.uk/About%20us/News/2011/03/~/media/Files/Policy%20and%20research/Breaking%20the%20cycle_VS%20response%20March%202011_FINAL [accessed 20/03/12].

Walklate, S. (2006) *Imagining the Victim of Crime*. Maidenhead: Open University Press.

Walklate, S. (ed.) (2007) *Handbook of Victims and Victimology*. Cullompton: Willan Publishing.

Welsh, K. (2008) Current Policy on Domestic Violence: A Move in the Right Direction or a Step Too Far?, *Crime Prevention and Community Safety*, 10: 226–248.

Welsh Government (2008) *All Wales Child Protection Procedures*. Cardiff: Welsh Assembly Government.

White, D. (2012) Interest Representation and Organisation in Civil Society: Ontario and Quebec Compared, *British Journal of Canadian Studies*, 25 (2): 199–230.

Wilkinson, R. G. and Pickett, K. E. (2009) *The Spirit Level: Why More Equal Societies Almost Always Do Better*. London: Penguin.

Williams, B. (1999) *Working with Victims of Crime: Politics and Practice*. London: Jessica Kingsley Publishers.

Williams, K. and Williams, J. (1987) *A Beveridge Reader*. London: Allen & Unwin.

Wolak, J. and Finkelhor, D. (1998) Children Exposed to Partner Violence. In: Jasinski, J. L. and Williams, L. M. (eds.) *Partner Violence: A Comprehensive Review of 20 Years of Research*. London: Sage: 73–112.

Wolfe, D. A., Crooks, C. V., Lee, V., McIntyre-Smith, A. and Jaffe, P. G. (2003) The Effects of Children's Exposure to Domestic Violence: A Meta-analysis and Critique, *Clinical Child and Family Psychology Review*, 6: 171–187.

Women's Aid (2004) *Women's Aid Welcomes the Domestic Violence, Crime and Domestic Violence Act but will Lobby for Greater Protection for Women and Children at Risk*. Press Release. London: Women's Aid. www.womensaid.org.uk/press_ releases [accessed 20/10/14].

Women's Royal Voluntary Service (WRVS) (1970) *Homes for Borstal Boys Report*. London: Women's Royal Voluntary Service.

Index

Printed and bound by CPI Group (UK) Ltd, Croydon, CR0 4YY